Antisocial Language Teaching

NEW PERSPECTIVES ON LANGUAGE AND EDUCATION

Founding Editor: Viv Edwards, *University of Reading, UK*

Series Editors: Phan Le Ha, *University of Hawaii at Manoa, USA* and Joel Windle, *Monash University, Australia.*

Two decades of research and development in language and literacy education have yielded a broad, multidisciplinary focus. Yet education systems face constant economic and technological change, with attendant issues of identity and power, community and culture. What are the implications for language education of new 'semiotic economies' and communications technologies? Of complex blendings of cultural and linguistic diversity in communities and institutions? Of new cultural, regional and national identities and practices? The New Perspectives on Language and Education series will feature critical and interpretive, disciplinary and multidisciplinary perspectives on teaching and learning, language and literacy in new times. New proposals, particularly for edited volumes, are expected to acknowledge and include perspectives from the Global South. Contributions from scholars from the Global South will be particularly sought out and welcomed, as well as those from marginalized communities within the Global North.

All books in this series are externally peer-reviewed.

Full details of all the books in this series and of all our other publications can be found on http://www.multilingual-matters.com, or by writing to Multilingual Matters, St Nicholas House, 31-34 High Street, Bristol, BS1 2AW, UK.

NEW PERSPECTIVES ON LANGUAGE AND EDUCATION: 110

Antisocial Language Teaching

English and the Pervasive Pathology of Whiteness

JPB Gerald

MULTILINGUAL MATTERS
Bristol • Jackson

DOI https://doi.org/10.21832/GERALD3276
Library of Congress Cataloging in Publication Data
A catalog record for this book is available from the Library of Congress.
Names: Gerald, J.P.B., author.
Title: Antisocial Language Teaching: English and the Pervasive Pathology of Whiteness/JPB Gerald.
Description: Jackson: Multilingual Matters, [2022] | Series: New Perspectives on Language and Education: 110 | Includes bibliographical references and index. | Summary: "This book examines major issues with the ideologies and institutions behind the discipline of ELT and diagnoses the industry as in dire need of treatment, with the solution being a full decentering of whiteness. A vision for a more just version of ELT is offered as an alternative to the harm caused by its present-day incarnation"—Provided by publisher.
Identifiers: LCCN 2022018071 (print) | LCCN 2022018072 (ebook) | ISBN 9781800413276 (hardback) | ISBN 9781800413269 (paperback) | ISBN 9781800413290 (epub) | ISBN 9781800413283 (pdf)
Subjects: LCSH: English language—Study and teaching. | Antisocial personality disorders. | Racism in education. | Multicultural education. | White people—Race identity.
Classification: LCC LB1576 .G437 2022 (print) | LCC LB1576 (ebook) | DDC 428.0071—dc23/eng/20220629
LC record available at https://lccn.loc.gov/2022018071
LC ebook record available at https://lccn.loc.gov/2022018072

British Library Cataloguing in Publication Data
A catalogue entry for this book is available from the British Library.

ISBN-13: 978-1-80041-327-6 (hbk)
ISBN-13: 978-1-80041-326-9 (pbk)

Multilingual Matters
UK: St Nicholas House, 31-34 High Street, Bristol, BS1 2AW, UK.
USA: Ingram, Jackson, TN, USA.

Website: www.multilingual-matters.com
Twitter: Multi_Ling_Mat
Facebook: https://www.facebook.com/multilingualmatters
Blog: www.channelviewpublications.wordpress.com

Copyright © 2022 JPB Gerald.

All rights reserved. No part of this work may be reproduced in any form or by any means without permission in writing from the publisher.

The policy of Multilingual Matters/Channel View Publications is to use papers that are natural, renewable and recyclable products, made from wood grown in sustainable forests. In the manufacturing process of our books, and to further support our policy, preference is given to printers that have FSC and PEFC Chain of Custody certification. The FSC and/or PEFC logos will appear on those books where full certification has been granted to the printer concerned.

Typeset by Deanta Global Publishing Services, Chennai, India.

Contents

Prologue — vii

Introduction — 1
   'Antisocial Thugs' — 1
   Where This Fits — 2
   Key Concepts — 4

Part 1: Disorder

The Great Pyramid Scheme — 13

Justified — 20

A Dark Projection — 27

Dis/abling Blackness — 34

Ability, Intelligence and Language — 41

Bad at English — 48

Language Teaching as an Instrument of Pathologization — 55

Part 2: Symptoms

Criterion 1 — 63

Criterion 2 — 70

Criterion 3 — 77

Criterion 4 — 84

Criterion 5 — 91

Criterion 6 — 98

Criterion 7 — 105

Part 3: Treatment…?

The Ezel Project	113
Prosocial Language Teaching	146
Conclusion	155
Pathologization Dependency	155
Heretical Whiteness	160
Acknowledgments	167
References	171
Index	179

Prologue

Who?

As of this writing, I am an education doctoral candidate, and by the time you read this book, I will have a doctorate of education (EdD) in instructional leadership, a phrase that could mean just about anything but this book is part of what I've chosen to do with my degree. More importantly, though, I am a Black and neurodivergent man who has spent his entire life immersed in white spaces, and I only recently came to understand the impact this has had on me, which is a story that will be threaded throughout the narrative of this book.

For much of my life, I refused to accept the impact of racism upon my life, chalking up my social discomfort to what I perceived as my own deficits, but once I began the inquiry required by my doctoral studies, I couldn't ignore the discomfort of my white peers whenever racism was the topic of discussion. Even my very nice, polite, liberal friends were eager to unpack *any* social issue other than one in which they might be complicit, and, a bit of an instigator at heart, I decided to keep pulling on this thread until it eventually unraveled. What I revealed to myself was the fact that, despite my childhood hopes of being accepted as part of the majoritized group, my life was always going to be different, even if it appeared superficially similar. This might seem an obvious point, but I had told myself, and been told by my schools, that I could achieve my way out of the box of racism, and, furthermore, that I should be grateful for the chance to be the Black face in these white[1] spaces. The endless papercuts I endured were more subtle than the horror stories most have heard of, and as such, it was easy for me to believe that what I experienced was something different and more innocuous. But ultimately, though I went to exclusive schools and had privileges that many Black students still don't, my education was, one might say, *extra ordinary*: *extra* in the particular clubs I was invited to join; but *ordinary* in that I was only invited inside to be subsequently isolated.

I spent the first part of my career as an English language teacher, in both South Korea and New York City, and as I came to the above realization, my own experiences in this field were thrown into sharp relief. My previously mundane research into community program attendance evolved into a deep, fundamental inquiry into the very foundation of the field itself, and I began to develop a body of work that problematized the whole of the English language teaching (ELT) industry. Accordingly, based on my identity, my experience and my research, I believe I am the person best positioned to write this book, and I hope you will agree.

What?

This is, technically, an academic book, from an academic publisher, complete with APA citations. And indeed, this book includes some of the findings from my research in Part 3. As you will see in Parts 1 and 2 of the book, however, I have specific reasons why I am not writing this book as traditional research reportage. You can choose to consider this semi-academic or non-traditionally academic, but, though I do hope educators find my work resonant enough to employ as a part of their pedagogy, I want this to be a book that can be consumed by the public, by anyone who has an interest, or a stake, in language, education, dis/ability or whiteness, which, truth be told, should be everyone, if you think about how broad those topics are.

More specifically, though, this book is a mix of conceptual arguments based on academic literature and theoretical frameworks, and a vision for the future of the ELT field based on my research findings and my own experience, with plenty of stories from my life peppered throughout the text where appropriate. If you are a doctoral student like I was when I got this book idea, you might be interested to know that, methodologically, this is a combination of autoethnography, with my reflections on my own identity and power woven throughout the text, and a bit of narrative inquiry in the interviews I conducted for Part 3.

Where and When?

I write this from unceded Munsee Lenape and Canarsie Territory, which you would know as Queens, New York. I was born and raised in this city, and for most of my life had little to no idea of its rich history prior to the arrival of settler colonialism, despite being taught to sew moccasins in second grade with the rest of my class.[2] I mention this not because I am some sort of expert in indigenous history now but because this book is ultimately about both education and language, and as I will detail in Part 2, the fact that using these names for the places we live is, itself, erasing the past many of us have profited from is relevant to the arguments I make.

I write this from the vantage point of a Black person in what we call the United States, which means that many of my sources do derive from this nation-state, but if you are a reader in a different country, please do understand that this work will be relevant to you as well. As the initial arguments of Part 1 will make clear, settler colonialism, capitalism and anti-Blackness are global issues, all tied inextricably to the whiteness that uses English teaching as an instrument of pathologization. I expect that, from, say, a British or Australian perspective, some of my writing may need to be reframed, and that is work I hope minoritized scholars in these contexts can take up after reading this book. In other words, just because I have an American passport doesn't mean that my argument doesn't apply to other places, and I plan to make that clear.

As for the *when*, I began this writing in early 2021, during a time of visceral and visible global trauma. My public scholarship grew in prominence in the summer of 2020, when, having just published an article on whiteness and language teaching, I got frustrated with white peers peppering me with questions in the wake of the murder of George Floyd and decided to start teaching classes on decentering whiteness. Most importantly, though, I wrote this book as my son grew from a baby to a toddler, and I write out of a perhaps misguided hope that addressing these intertwined issues honestly and forcefully might help protect him when he is eventually just as immersed in whiteness as I have always been.

How?

I have a particular style, for better or worse. Though there is usually a difference between written and spoken language, I don't think anything written should be difficult for me to read aloud. If I wouldn't say it, then I won't write it. I find that this makes the words much more enjoyable to read, and, although I would hope this book is both convincing and informative, if you don't enjoy the way it's written, then what good is it?

To that point, I occasionally employ language some would consider 'less formal', while I sometimes use very specific academic language if I feel the word choice is appropriate. I write however the particular point needs to be made, and despite being in full command of what I refer to as standardized English, I prefer to leave my language the room to remain unstandardized.

Why?

The system of ELT is broken. Or, truthfully, the system's working the way it's designed, it's just not designed for the benefit of very many people. It's not working for most students, it's not working for most teachers, it's not even working for most administrators, yet all of these groups often point the finger at one another, and understandably so. It's easier to tackle personified villainy. But there isn't just one bad person, or group of people, that is keeping this field stuck in its harmful patterns.

I could have chosen to write a book simply laying out the problems with ELT pedagogy, and I might have done an adequate job at this. I think such a book would have necessarily fallen short, however, because the problems with ELT aren't really limited to the teaching of the language itself. To unpack this issue, we really need to dismantle the very conceptualizations that the field both takes for granted and constantly reifies. Yes, we need to look at education, at pedagogy and language, but we also need to go farther. We need to look at history, we need to look at sociology, we need to zoom all the way out from a narrow look at ELT itself and think deeply about Blackness, about dis/ability, about capitalism and settler colonialism and the faulty structures upon which our society is built.

This book could go so far as to include almost every axis of oppression into its epistemological analysis, but I chose to focus on racialization and ability and their connections to language ideologies and education because of my own identity as a Black and neurodivergent (cishet) man with professional experience in ELT. Rest assured, there is plenty to be said about queerness, about gender identity and expression, about religion, in relation to ELT, and I pass that baton to others who identify accordingly and their ability to build upon my arguments more skillfully than I could hope to.

Nevertheless, though the aims of this book are broad in some respects, from another angle, they are actually very narrow. Yes, I am tying a lot of ideas together, but every word here serves a singular purpose, namely to take aim at the concept around which ELT is centered. Simply put, this book exists to make the case for why it is a moral imperative that ELT severs its ties to whiteness once and for all, and for the bright future that could follow if we ever manage to demolish this structure inside of which we are all trapped.

JPB Gerald, February 2021

Notes

(1) I capitalize Black and not white for reasons that will become clear throughout this book.
(2) My school sure did think this was special, though.

Introduction

'Antisocial Thugs'

> Please try to remember that what they believe, as well as what they do and cause you to endure, does not testify to your inferiority but to their inhumanity and fear.
>
> Baldwin (1963: 8)

On August 13, 2020, Fox News host Tucker Carlson delivered a signature rant on the supposed pandemic-related decline of American cities with Democratic leadership, referring to protestors as 'BLM and Antifa, crazed ideologues, grifters, criminals, antisocial thugs with no stake in society and nothing better to do than hurt people and destroy things' (Owen, 2020). He is merely hinting at it instead of saying so, but Carlson is using coded language to describe people of color, and particularly Black people, acting outside of the standardized societal boundaries to which he and others adhere. There are several dog whistles in just that short soundbite – e.g. it is easier to decry the Black people involved in Black Lives Matter if you condense it into an acronym – but I want to focus on one pertinent descriptor. When Carlson says, 'antisocial thugs with no stake in society', he and his writers are not espousing some fringe viewpoint but instead emphasizing a core tenet of his popular ideology, namely the fact that decentralized resistance and opposition to the hegemony of whiteness is anathema to what he refers to as 'society', and the common elision of Blackness and criminality as expressed via his use of the word 'thug' (Smiley & Fakunle, 2016). As odious as his ideas are to many who might be reading this work, Carlson is not speaking out of turn when compared to the epistemology and the ideology of the whiteness that retains a firm grip on the globe.

According to the fifth edition of the *Diagnostic and Statistical Manual of Mental Disorders* (aka the DSM-V), the very first criterion for antisocial personality disorder is 'failure to conform to social norms with respect to lawful behaviors as indicated by repeatedly performing acts that are grounds for arrest' (APA, 2013). By this officially codified definition, Carlson is right, and to cause property damage and perturb police officers is, in fact, antisocial behavior. Many would be quick to point out, of course, that to diagnose a large group of individuals based on short video clips is an unprofessional way to use these terms, and this is correct. Yet I would argue, in fact, that Carlson is merely amplifying a set of values upon which global social hierarchy is built, values which must be exposed, confronted and defeated if minoritized identities are ever to find safety. In short, the concept of 'society', against which antisocial and other 'disordered' behavior is measured, is merely a mask for whiteness, and considering that the epistemology responsible for these diagnostic criteria is itself an exemplar of whiteness, it is difficult to trust whiteness as an objective judge of what is and is not antisocial. Furthermore, when considering the path whiteness has chosen in order to define and protect itself and its symbolic *property* (Harris, 1993), I would argue that, if anything at all has 'no stake in society' – if that word can be redefined more broadly as equity, justice and liberation for all humans – it is whiteness itself.

Among the many groups whiteness has created and positioned in opposition to itself are those classified as Black, the dis/abled and those who do not conform to acceptable practices of languaging, particularly those who do not perform English in a way that satisfies the *white listener* or *white perceiving subject* (Flores & Rosa, 2015). These groups may seem to be separate, but all have been constructed as lesser than whiteness through a robust and centuries-old epistemology that rarely distinguishes between them. From the beginning of chattel slavery, the victims thereof were considered constitutionally dis/abled and childlike (Nielsen, 2012), and the same tropes can be found in descriptions of those who were colonized and forced to adopt their oppressors' language (Mills & Lefrancois, 2018). The gradual proliferation of English language teaching (ELT) has thus long functioned as a weapon in the arsenal of whiteness, deployed to perpetuate its global hegemony so successfully that we now barely notice the faulty foundations upon which our field was built. Language, or a supposed lack thereof, is tied very closely to harmful theories of race and ability, and all three concepts are not neutral or objective but, in fact, part of the same scheme to exploit certain people and enrich others. In an era when more of us claim to believe that Black lives matter, when we claim we want to decolonize our curricula, we as members of the ELT field cannot ignore the paths through which all of these forms of oppression intersect, and if we attempt to reform our field in incremental ways without understanding the compounded impact of these issues, we are doomed to fail at supporting the students and colleagues about whom we profess to care. Before I get into the work proper, though, I need to situate this book among the theory and some of the relevant literature that have come before it.

Where This Fits

As much as I want this work to be accessible beyond the ivory tower, it does exist in conversation with other scholarship, and if you're not interested in theory and the like, you can skip this brief chapter, but for other readers, let's ground this in what exists. For both this and my dissertation, which is far less fun to read, I am working with, within and across critical race theory (CRT), critical whiteness studies (CWS) and disability critical race studies (Dis/Crit). I will get to the latter shortly, but suffice it to say that, despite what you may read in the news, CRT is not simply any attempt to advance diversity, equity and/or inclusion (DEI) – in fact, the 'DEI' industry, such as it is, might be called into question by many CRT scholars. CRT is a framework derived from legal studies and analysis (e.g. Bell, 1980; Crenshaw, 1990), expanded into many other fields including education (Dixson, 2018) and is now a flashpoint for right-wing nonsense. In short, CRT elucidates the central role that racism plays in the structure of our society – 'our' in this case meaning the United States, but, truthfully, it applies just as well to many other contexts. Fighting the CRT backlash is not the purpose of this book, but I suspect what scares so many people is the fact that acknowledging the truth that CRT reveals would call unearned power into question, and that is, understandably, hard for the people with that power to swallow.

CWS is an outgrowth of CRT, concerned quite explicitly with analysis of whiteness and white individuals, just as this book ultimately is. You will see much of the CWS literature recur throughout the book, though I am particularly indebted to the work of Cheryl Matias (2013, 2016) and her examinations of different aspects of white emotionality, and the historical work of Ignatiev (1995) and Painter (2011), whose work you will see appear once we enter Part 1.

I suspect fewer readers are familiar with Dis/Crit, as it is known, and understandably so, as it is a relatively new addition to the literature. Dis/Crit (Annamma *et al.*, 2013), a combination of disability studies in education and CRT, is so recent in fact that it is rather shocking that scholars did not have an appropriate framework for effectively analyzing this intersection until the past decade. For those interested in pursuing this framework further, the tenets of Dis/Crit are as follows, as explained in the article cited above:

(1) Dis/Crit focuses on ways that the forces of racism and ableism circulate interdependently, often in neutralized and invisible ways, to uphold notions of normalcy.
(2) Dis/Crit values multidimensional identities and troubles singular notions of identity such as race or dis/ability or class or gender or sexuality and so on.
(3) Dis/Crit emphasizes the social constructions of race and ability and yet recognizes the material and psychological impacts of being labeled as raced or dis/abled, which sets one outside of the Western cultural norms.
(4) Dis/Crit privileges voices of marginalized populations, traditionally not acknowledged within research.

(5) Dis/Crit considers the legal and historical aspects of dis/ability and race and how both have been used separately and together to deny the rights of some citizens.
(6) Dis/Crit recognizes whiteness and ability as property and that gains for people labeled with dis/abilities have largely been made as the result of interest convergence of white, middle-class citizens.
(7) Dis/Crit requires activism and supports all forms of resistance.

Explicitly considering multiple axes of oppression and how they interact upon and within an individual is a central tenet of disability justice (Berne et al., 2018), and dis/ability cannot be divorced from the full understanding of whiteness that I hope to convey with my work, even though the two have not always been analyzed collectively.

The other aspect of my work that I need to explain is the literature from the realm of language scholars and thinkers. I will not pretend I am the first to offer a challenge to standard language ideologies, and certainly you'll find many of my forebears throughout this work. In particular, readers who are interested in the interplay between language education and power are likely familiar with the work of Motha (2014), and certainly any work that attempts to grapple with race and language explicitly is in conversation with Flores and Rosa (2015). Additionally, there are a handful of white scholars who are trying their best to break free from the ideologies handed down to them, including Ennser-Kananen (2021) and Schissel (Schissel & Kangas, 2018; Schissel et al., 2019). Perhaps the most direct forebear of this book is April Baker-Bell's (2020) *Linguistic Justice*, and if there's any particular pair of shoulders this book stands on, it's hers.

There is more innovative and radical scholarship that will be featured throughout the book, but where this work both fits and (hopefully) sets itself apart is in its efforts to bring both halves of this vast equation together. I wanted to try to start a discussion that ties race and whiteness not just to language, but also to conceptualizations of ability, and that uses the latter concept to analyze how whiteness retains its power. As such, I think what you're going to read here is unique, though it wouldn't have been possible without the work that many others have done to this point. I thank them and I thank you for allowing me into conversation.

Before I finally begin making my argument, however, there are several key concepts I need to briefly, but clearly, explain to ensure that we're on the same page.

Key Concepts

These may or may not match what you know as the dictionary definitions of some of these terms – they are more aligned with the way the theorists cited above (and below) use these words and phrases, and reject seemingly 'neutral' denotations. And a brief note here to add that all racist hate mail will be turned into future writing projects, so unless you'd like that to happen to you, don't bother.

Anyway, *racism* is the combination of racial discrimination and societal oppression. Anyone can experience the former, but only certain people can experience the combination of the two. For example, as a Black person, I could tell you I don't want to have any white friends,[1] and that would absolutely be discriminatory, but because I do not have the full power of society behind me, and because that would not materially impact the people I denied my friendship, it does not qualify. It's just kind of *mean*, and racism is a system of unequal power rather than mere interpersonal cruelty. With all this said, I have little interest in the very academic discussion about who can 'be' racist – the fact is, we can all choose to perpetuate the system or work against it. I fully do not care whether or not people who choose to support racist policies are hateful deep inside of their hearts, because all I know is that they made that choice. An important point to add here is that race is, of course, not biological fact; nothing happens to people because of their race but because of the system of racism. Hate crimes and police brutality are caused by *racism*, not *race*. So the next time you see a news report on such an incident, note how poorly and inaccurately it has been described.

Speaking of police brutality, one of the mistakes people often make regarding these issues is forgetting to center Blackness in their discussions. It will take you under a minute to google a manicured statement by a professional organization that speaks vaguely of 'racism' but is unable to include the word 'Black'. Accordingly, it is important that when we speak of harm being visited upon Black people specifically, we know that we are speaking of *anti-Blackness*. Anti-Blackness is oppression of Black people, Black bodies, Black languages and Black languaging. It is another way of saying *anti-Black racism*, one of many forms of racism, also including *anti-Asian racism* or *anti-Arab racism*, but *not* anti-white racism or reverse racism. I point this out because people often ask what it's called when one person of color harms a Black person, and that's where the utility of anti-Blackness as a term comes in. Not every country has the same conceptualizations of racism as the United States, a country founded on indigenous genocide and chattel slavery, but almost every place has some version of anti-Blackness, which you can confirm by asking any Black person who has traveled widely, myself included. I will add here also that anti-Blackness is a tried and true way for a 'liminal' group to achieve acceptance into whiteness; you can look forward to more on this topic in Part 1.

That hierarchy, of course, is the essence of what we know of as *white supremacy*. There is little need to define this phrase – it is the system by which whiteness is constructed as superior to other racial groups – but I use it here to contrast it with another term, *white nationalism*. You can be a white supremacist in your home, but as far as domestic and foreign policy is concerned, building border walls and/or leaving the European Union for no good reason are more than believing in racial superiority; they are attempts to create a white ethnostate, a country for white people. The distinction is key to keep in mind.

Back to white supremacy. My work is chiefly about *whiteness* in ELT, and in Part 2, I will discuss the impact of our field's having centered whiteness. Yet, the point I want to make here is that there is no functional difference between whiteness and white supremacy. Indeed, whiteness, as a concept, was created to justify colonialism and chattel slavery (Bonfiglio, 2002; Painter, 2011); there had to be a group exempt from these horrors, and as such, whiteness was codified. Whiteness was created to be supreme, as a protection from the oppression that others deserve because of the groups into which they have been placed.

One of the primary drivers behind the global dominance of whiteness has been *colonialism*, and in particular the *settler colonialism* visited upon the indigenous and the enslaved peoples of what was eventually named the United States. As Dunbar-Ortiz (2014: 2) explained, this system represented 'the founding of a state based on the ideology of white supremacy, the widespread practice of African slavery, and a policy of genocide and land theft'. The abject violence of the Europeans responsible for this behavior is often diluted by their classification as mere 'settlers' or 'founders', as well as by the myth, perpetuated through centuries of education, that the land was either unused or, if the indigenous warrant a mention at all, owed to those who stole it from them. Indeed, one of the most powerful tricks pulled by the system of whiteness and its supporters has been its ability to turn the reality of settler colonialism into a series of heroic folktales.

Colonialism is, of course, not at all an American invention, and one of the ways in which this book's primary argument expands beyond the borders of the nation-state where I live is the fact that I will point toward the common features of European colonialism in its avaricious adventures around the planet. The people who stole this country may have added new wrinkles to the program, but they learned from their own ancestors and their ceaseless need for expansion and exploitation. As cruel as colonialism has always been, however, in a way, that very exploitation was not a result of some sort of haphazard sadism for its own sake, but indeed was part of a system that requires an underclass from which labor can be extracted for profit.

It has become somewhat fashionable for people to criticize *capitalism*, and for good reason. You will not find a defense of the system here. It is predicated upon the belief that constant growth and profit-seeking by private owners are not just acceptable but moral, and that this competition will spur better results for all, or at least better results than if workers owned their own labor. Much of the most celebrated opposition to capitalism has come from thinkers who premised their well-reasoned theorization on the harm done to the white proletariat or commoners, though racism has always been central to the capitalist system of exploitation, and we should not make the mistake of separating the two. As Robinson (1983: 3) explained in his treatise on *racial capitalism*: 'The development, organization, and expansion of capitalist society pursued essentially racial directions, so too did social ideology'. Robinson (1983: 4) does not argue that thinkers like Marx and Engels were wrong so much as that their 'theory of revolution was insufficient in scope'. Indeed, capitalism, settler colonialism and whiteness are deeply interwoven systems, accounting not just for the people, places and products that can be turned into profit, but also the justification for precisely who those exploited people should and shouldn't be. I seek not to merely regurgitate this argument but to continue to connect these ideas to other axes of oppression, and indeed we now come to the primary concept from which I contend that the bond to whiteness must be severed.

Language ideologies descend from broadly shared societal views about languages and *languagers*[2] and shape communication and standardization in a given context (Ricento, 2013). These ideologies govern language policy and planning, for the ostensibly unbiased goals of pragmatism and economic development. In the United States, for example, though there is still technically no official language, there has long been an effort to tie American identity to English. 'A principal means of achieving Americanization was through massive education programs that sought to teach American values, ways of thinking, ways of living, and especially the national language, English' (Ricento, 2013: 4). Additionally, language ideologies create the parameters of a supposed 'standard' language, which is then viewed more highly than other languages and against which people are compared. 'Persons speaking other stigmatized ("nonstandard") varieties tend to be viewed as having deficiencies in intelligence, morality, and/or character and are often less successful in achieving upward social mobility, which generally requires proficiency in the standard "national" language' (Ricento, 2013: 5).

We can begin to see here how, when placed alongside the hierarchies imposed by whiteness through settler colonialism, capitalism and anti-Blackness, language ideologies are a powerful tool in the arsenal of stigmatization necessary to create and maintain an underclass that is categorized as not belonging to the national identity of the United States, the United Kingdom, Australia or other such countries where English has flourished. More recently, scholars have proposed the radical concept of *translanguaging* as a means of describing how minoritized languagers move fluidly among what most would classify as discrete named languages (García & Vogel, 2016). Scholarship on translanguaging represents a movement against linguistic imposition, but for our purposes, we still operate in a world where language ideologies and the standardization of English reign supreme, and this reality reifies the oppression that certain groups face, even though many are pushing back.

Another term that we need to bring into our discussion is *dis/ability*, and particularly my choice, which you may have noticed by now, to write the word with a slash in the middle of it. The definition of dis/ability has grown and shifted over the past several decades, but the way I am using (and spelling) the term denotes the fact that the concept thereof has been created, like many of the categories above, by those with an incentive to exclude and a need to categorize those they consider less useful or productive (Nielsen, 2012). Dis/ability is not just a personal attribute but the result of a series of oppressive choices made by those in power (Davis, 1995; Goodley, 2014). In other words, I would say that the slash represents a direct acknowledgment of the harm wrought by both whiteness and ability supremacy, but, like Blackness, it is a vibrant identity around which solidarity can be built. In other words, I write dis/ability as such as a reminder that if the world were designed in a way that accommodated everyone's ways of moving, feeling and thinking, then those who have been rendered dis/abled would not be given lesser status. This also ties my work to the social model of dis/ability, which 'distinguishes between the impairment (biological and functional limitation) and the disability (the social oppression that results from the category)' (Hernández-Saca *et al.*, 2019: 289). Reasonable people can disagree on that stylistic choice, but that's why I've made the decision in my scholarship.

An important set of terms I would like to center here includes some you may have noticed already, namely words such as *minoritized*, *racialized* and *standardized*. In all such instances, these words refer to a distinct categorization made by dominant groups. *Minoritized*, for example, is a more accurate way to describe the Black citizens of Detroit, Michigan or South Africa, where, in each case, they comprise the numerical majority but have long held far less power than the white numerical minority – they have been forcibly placed in the minority position. Similarly, *racialized* indicates that race is not an incontrovertible biological fact but a classification that is context dependent and has evolved over time (Omi & Winant, 2014); for example, the word 'Asian' refers to different groups in the United States and the United Kingdom. And you will see me use the word *unstandardized* here, as opposed to *non-standard*, as an attempt to provide agency to the many languagers whose communication is stigmatized and denigrated by virtue of their identities.

With these words given brief explanations, I can now preview the argument I will be making in Part 1 of this book and beyond. Figure 1 provides a visual representation of how I envision the connection between these concepts.

In short, whiteness requires people to be categorized as either *ordered* or *disordered* so that it can function effectively and to support its aims of colonialist dominance and capitalism. Accordingly, whiteness uses

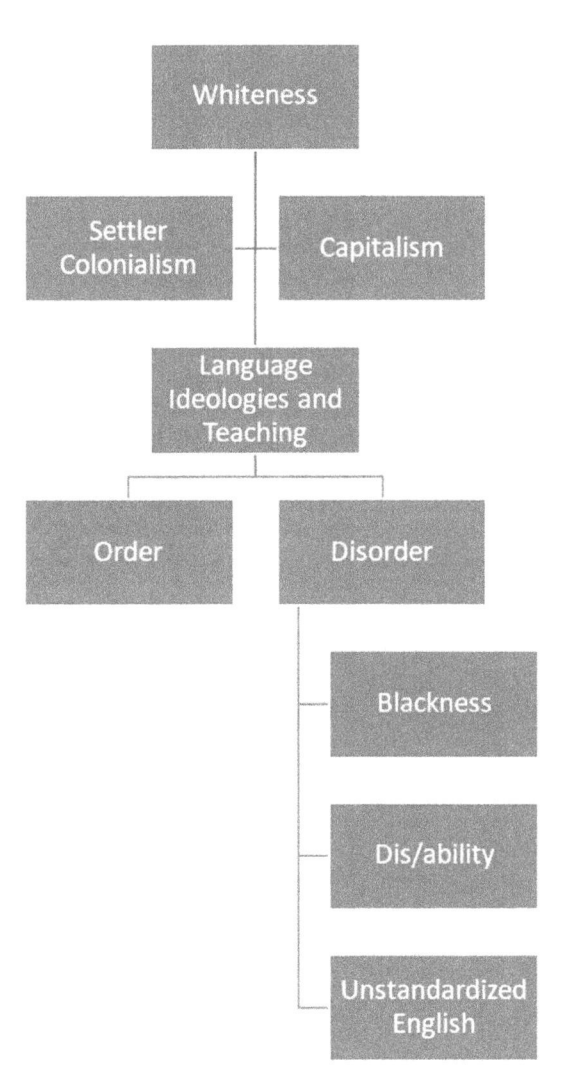

Figure 1 The central paradigm

language ideologies and language teaching to classify Blackness, dis/ability and unstandardized English as representations of pathology and disorder, and is thus able to justify its exploitation and oppression of members of these groups. Speaking of *pathology*, then, I should pause here briefly to make clear that I am referring to the social process of categorizing individuals and groups as inferior and in need of treatment, a phenomenon upon which more powerful groups depend for their continued supremacy. More on this throughout the book.

As we saw in the previous chapter, figures like Tucker Carlson haphazardly describe these people as having 'no stake in society', and this book will detail the ways in which whiteness constructs these groups as representatives of disorder fully deserving of their treatment at the hands of the powerful. In Part 1, I will start by tracking the history of whiteness and its chameleonic and self-serving definitions alongside the way it has positioned Blackness, dis/ability and unstandardized English as its opposites, making the case that language ideologies and language teaching have been employed as instruments of pathologization for members of these groups. In Part 2, I will follow this by demonstrating how the field of ELT and its adherence to whiteness has led to pervasive oppression, and how its harmful habits can be mapped neatly onto the official criteria for antisocial personality disorder, not to stigmatize the disorder but to counterpathologize whiteness and the destruction it causes. Finally, in Part 3, using my interview data and the implications thereof, I will advance an argument for how we as language educators can play a central role in the demolition of whiteness in our field and in our society. Let's go!

Notes

(1) Not true, but for the sake of argument.
(2) A term more accurate than 'language speakers'.

Part 1
Disorder

The Great Pyramid Scheme

I debated what to title this chapter, which is essentially a description of how whiteness has been defined and constructed and how that history ties into a present-day discourse that protects its interests. I considered 'Defining Whiteness', but I felt that was too narrow as, although the language used is central to the discussion, evoking a mere denotation is not broad enough to encompass the work that went into creating this system. I thought of 'The Whiteness Project' as that does convey the fact that its construction was intentional and the fact that it is ongoing, but it does not imply deceit or harm. I had to ask myself what I was really trying to say in this chapter. I thought of my own experience in school, being singled out for various academic achievements as a Black face in white spaces, and how I was positioned quite explicitly as an exception to my race. I studied French and Latin, and was groomed as a future 'captain of the universe', to the point where both the head of my school and my classmates joked about how excited the most exclusive universities would be to accept someone like me, except they weren't really joking. I was considered the acceptable Black student because I was the exceptional Negro, close enough to whiteness as a system to be non-threatening but far enough in appearance to be held at a distance while being promoted as a prize.

What was I being promised, ultimately? Prestige and prominence, sure, but at its core, I was being sold the idea of power, power over people who hadn't been given access to the schools and networks I was told I semi-deserved. There would always be people more powerful, but if I colored inside the lines, perhaps someday there would be fewer people above me and more and more people below me who I could then turn around and encourage to follow the same path that I had. Anyone who dismissed the path altogether wasn't worth considering, and those who tried but fell short were similarly undeserving. Only those who pledged fealty to the hierarchy stood any chance at ascending, and any such ascension was always at the expense of others who would thus be denied the power you have been handed.

When I thought of the best way to describe whiteness and the way it had been sold to me, despite rarely being named as such, I consulted the numerous metaphors that have been used in the literature, many of which remain accurate and resonant, many of which I will cite below. But, in my opinion, when searching for the best way to evoke the sheer confidence game at play, one that empowers a few while convincing the masses that their own power is waiting just around the corner so long as they convince everyone they know to also buy in, I could think only of the sad stories I've encountered of friends and acquaintances who were convinced to buy thousands of dollars of terrible products that they could never offload to others. These people are swindled into joining companies that promise them quick riches, only to find out that the vast majority never make a profit at all, and that the only way to make real money is to sign people up who will pass them a percentage of their own sales. There are examples around the globe, and these scams leave untold financial devastation in their wake (Keep, 2020). I've watched friends fall for these plots with empathy rather than schadenfreude, though, because I once believed in a much more prevalent scam, one that will give you precisely nothing even if you are willing to sacrifice everything and push others down in the process. Simply put, whiteness is perhaps the world's greatest example of multilevel marketing, a massive pyramid scheme, but unlike the companies stealing from put-upon individuals and families, there is no single chief executive officer (CEO) laughing all the way to the bank. At this point, whiteness feeds upon all of us, including the people who bow before it, and it creates no victors, only a desperate battle to avoid losing. But how did we get here, to a system that benefits no one, that hides its subterfuge so well that we rarely name it explicitly? We need to travel back to observe the construction of the pyramid of whiteness to understand how this world wonder retains its strength and structure to this day.

Were he alive today, we would likely codify someone like Julius Caesar as 'white', but in his lifetime, these concepts, both whiteness and what we refer to as 'race', had yet to be established in any fashion similar to how we might understand them, and certainly not in a way that was tied so distinctly to skin tone, though there was certainly plenty of identity-based oppression. In antiquity, historian Nell Painter (2011: 1) wrote: 'What mattered was where they lived; were their lands damp or dry; were they virile or prone to impotence, hard or soft; could they be seduced by the luxuries of civilized society or were they warriors through and through?'. There are the beginnings of a constructed hierarchy visible in this description, of course, but oppression based on group membership did not originate with the construction of whiteness – it simply had a different manifestation. Much later on, even after slavery was common in Europe, 'Geography, not race, ruled, and potential white slaves, like vulnerable aliens everywhere, were nearby for the taking' (Painter, 2011:

38). People with power have always exploited those without it, and it would be inaccurate to blame whiteness for what is clearly an upsettingly human tendency.

Once the Atlantic slave trade was developed, in large part to increase profitable sugar production, the locations where the crop flourished, along with the currents of the ocean, led to a reliance upon African labor, and an expansion into the islands of the Caribbean (Painter, 2011). From there, African bodies became a common European commodity, much like sugar itself, and as such they were imported once Europeans began their conquest of the New World. What we must remember, though, when telling this story of very explicit racial capitalism, is that their so-called exploration required the acquisition of occupied land to produce the profit upon which they depended. Here we see how settler colonialism and racial capitalism are impossible to separate, as, in reading even as comprehensive a history of whiteness as Painter provides, one could choose to ignore the presence of the indigenous in every settlement that the European slavers established.

As Painter makes clear, though, there were still white slaves when the first Europeans reached what we now call Virginia in 1619, and as such, we cannot quite say that what we call whiteness had yet been neatly organized. As we will see throughout Part 1 of the book, the codification of whiteness, while tied to economic exploitation, always requires, in addition, a certain type of fuzzy epistemology, a reliance upon a race scholarship that still exists to this day, even if no longer known as such. Originally, 'race science' had a fixation on delineating physical beauty, and this is one of the chief ways through which notions of whiteness were built. 'Nearly all those associated with brute labor – Africans and Tartars primarily – emerged as ugly, while the luxury slaves, those valued for sex and gendered as female – the Circassians, Georgians, and Caucasians of the Black Sea region – came to figure as epitomes of human beauty' (Painter, 2011: 43). The sorting mechanism is still associated with location, but now appearance and function – or, more accurately, angle of exploitation – are essential parts of the equation. And from here, the ugly and the Black are one, contrasted with the beautiful and the white, the latter requiring and deserving of protection from the former, who are damned to occupy the lowest rungs of humanity as their race is built and defined around them.

When I say that the pyramid of whiteness was constructed, I do not mean to imply that a handful of men made a series of quick decisions and then, from one day to the next, whiteness went from non-existent to central. No, this development was gradual and multifaceted, until it became an organizing feature of a powerful new nation-state. From the formal beginnings of the United States, whiteness was codified as a category defined by its exclusions. The first United States census in 1790 mentioned only whiteness as a racial group and categorized others by their distance from it. These definitions changed rapidly and repeatedly, however. As Painter explained:

> Census categories kept changing every ten years, as governmental needs changed and taxonomical categories shifted, including taxonomies of race. Throughout American census history, non-Europeans and part-Europeans have been counted as part of the American population, usually lumped as 'non-white,' but occasionally disaggregated into black and mulatto. (Painter, 2011: 106)

Theories of race fluctuated wildly, ascribing differences to divine intervention and climate, searching constantly for an explanation or what we might even call a diagnosis for the existence and presence of the subhumans they owned and exploited. Throughout all of it, whiteness occupied a sort of negative space, with no need for its own explanation or diagnosis, instead serving as a model against which all others would be measured. As mentioned above, whiteness meant beauty and also came to imply wealth. But perhaps above all else, whiteness meant ability and intelligence, self-justifications that excused their treatment of less powerful groups, groups often described as possessing traits more similar to apes and other such creatures.

What strikes me from Painter's exhaustive account of early American whiteness is just how exhausting these self-definitions must have been to read even at the time. Thousands upon thousands of pages were written, from those regarded as the greatest of intellectual titans,[1] and much of the argument would barely pass muster in a high school English class, despite their continued veneration. As Painter noted, the authors contradict themselves, draw upon non-existent evidence and prattle on and on about the positive traits inherent to whiteness. Even if the work were not deeply immoral and produced to assuage the moral contradiction of espousing liberty for some while denying it to others, it is poorly argued, yet these ever-shifting theories of race became the laws and ideals under which we continue to operate.

At times, people we might now classify as not being white were allowed into the club. As Roediger (2018: 41) wrote, 'the 1855 Greaser Bill in California, for example, was an antivagrant, anti-Native American, anti-Mexican law passed at a time when the landholding California ranchero elite was legally, if tenuously, accepted as white'. These conditional classifications continued in the decades that followed, and for many different racial groups. As Maghbouleh (2017: 24) wrote in her book on the racialization of Iranian Americans: 'Syrians and Armenians juxtaposed themselves against the non-whiteness of dark-skinned Muslims and Zoroastrian Persians through which they used their light skin, Zoroastrian faith, and Aryan roots from Iran to prove their whiteness, notwithstanding a millennium in India'. The examples abound, as external observers of whiteness came to readily understand the benefits of membership. Almost every immigrant group has been regarded as an invading menace in some era of white-centric history, but many have risen in status, usually by participating in the racialization of those with less power. In truth, to be white has long been synonymous with enforcing the boundaries of whiteness itself, and particularly so with stringent anti-Blackness, and in the United States and many other countries, there has been no more visible exemplar of said stringent anti-Blackness than policing.

Although it is American policing that has received most of the headlines in recent years, like our reliance upon the slave trade, it was hardly our idea originally. By the early 19th century, the British Empire had come to occupy vast swaths of territory as a result of its centuries of colonization, and the populations of these far-flung locations had long needed controlling lest they conspire to acquire their liberation. With industrialization underway, the masses back home in London required a firm hand, and a colonial officer, fresh off service oppressing the Irish, was brought back to England. Accordingly, what became modern policing is usually said to have started with the creation of the London Metropolitan Police in 1829, a time when there were thankfully no news stories about Black men being shot in the street. As Vitale (2018: 35) explained, though, 'even this noble endeavor had at its core not fighting crime, but managing disorder and protecting the propertied classes from the rabble'. This police force based its procedures on lessons learned from the oppression of impoverished people in need of control, and they maintained what they considered 'order' more effectively than previous amateur operations. These police were tasked with enforcing newly developed vagrancy laws – the sort of laws later applied to freed slaves in the United States (Tarter, 2020) – and ensuring that the lower classes remained productive[2] for work. Vitale (2018: 36) continued: 'The main functions of the new police, despite their claims of political neutrality, were to protect property, quell riots, put down strikes and other industrial actions, and produce a disciplined industrial workforce'. This policing model was quickly exported to control the rapidly growing population of what is now the Northeastern United States, and soon, the path that policing provided into whiteness became clear.

I noted above how it was in fact the Irish upon whom the creator of the London Metropolitan Police had honed his policing skills. Around the same time, those Irish who had fled British oppression to the United States were not treated all that much more favorably. It wouldn't be accurate to say they were seen quite as poorly as the enslaved, but within the pyramid, they weren't very many levels above the bottom, and as such they needed to rise in order to counter nativist sentiment. A particularly salient example of how this was accomplished can be found in the policing history of Philadelphia. Without getting too deep into the partisan political squabbles of the mid-19th century among the Whigs and the Democrats and the Know-Nothings, suffice it to say that, by the 1850s, the Irish were being used as 'Swiss guards of slave power' (Ignatiev, 1995: 162), which angered the country's nativist faction. Irish voting blocs helped elect Philadelphia's new mayor, who in turn rewarded them with powerful positions in city government, including police commissioner. As Ignatiev (1995: 163) explained, 'The Irish cop is more than a quaint symbol. His appearance on the city police marked a turning point in Philadelphia in the struggle of the Irish to gain the rights of white men. It meant that thereafter the Irish would be officially empowered (armed) to defend themselves from the nativist mobs, and at the same time to carry out their own agenda against Black people'. Italians followed a path similar to the Irish, enduring racial slurs, 'consigned to church pews set aside for black people' (Staples, 2019), before gaining power through policing. After all, police needed to do their duty, to protect and serve order, and that order meant whiteness.

There are plenty of other examples of liminal or conditional white groups using anti-Blackness and other forms of oppression to gain access to whiteness. This process was not unique to Philadelphia, and occurred contemporaneously in Boston and New York, particularly after the civil war and the great migration flooded northern cities with Black families fleeing southern states for what they perceived as greater opportunity and freedom. The process repeated itself around the country and in other white-dominated nation-states around the globe: enter the country seen as something 'other', endure mistreatment while relegated to the cellar of society, gain power through creating distance from the bottom and defend that distance by any means necessary. By the time the story reaches more recent years, the dog whistles to whiteness seem almost abstract, and rarely mention racial categorization at all, but make no mistake, this process, this desire to separate oneself from the bottom, remains central to our political discourse, and that desire remains tied inextricably to whiteness.

Recalling the sentiments that led to the original creation of the London Metropolitan Police, proponents of Brexit appealed to this same sense of panic over impending disorder in need of control. Emejulu (2016) explained accordingly: 'a key argument of the campaign was that the "working class" (who were unquestionably assumed to be white) were suffering under the burden of mass immigration, which transformed the culture of their neighbourhoods and put undue strain on public services'. In need of their votes, leaders stoked fears of threats to whiteness, and managed to succeed at the ballot box, a pattern which will certainly be familiar to American readers as well. Emejulu noted that, despite immigration being blamed for the issues at hand, 'the crisis is, in fact, the official policy of the current Conservative government: austerity measures have been the dominant policy response since the 2008 economic crisis'. The danger so rarely comes from below.

Like the 'disorder' that led to the creation of the police, those with the most power oppressed and exploited those without it, and told the people with a small sliver thereof that they needed to ensure their continued membership in whiteness by distancing themselves from the others. If we return to the concept of a pyramid scheme, the less powerful members of whiteness have been sold a useless group membership, and instead of challenging those who've sold it to them, they're being told their group membership will increase in value as long as they continue to separate themselves from the people below them. And while everyone is being told to push the next group of people farther down to solidify their own status within whiteness, a grand series of injustices has taken place, ostensibly justified by this battle for social position.

Notes

(1) Including the fondly remembered Ralph Waldo Emerson and his disgust with non-white races (Painter, 2011: 139).
(2) That is, readily exploitable.

Justified

The purpose of this chapter is not merely to list a series of atrocities committed in the name of whiteness, as that book has been written repeatedly, and indeed that is more or less the story of modern European and American history. Additionally, though terrible things may yet be mentioned, I am hesitant to traffic in the explicit trauma of the racialized, because I don't believe that shocking white readers into sympathy will ever solve these issues. No, I seek here to connect a handful of oppressive events and trends to the conceptualization of whiteness, and to the way that whiteness provides a justification for this harm that has been visited upon almost everyone, even including many white people.

Dunbar-Ortiz (2014) made an important point in describing the relative skill level of colonizers. She wrote: 'Many have noted that had North America been a wilderness, undeveloped, without roads, and uncultivated, it might still be so, for the European colonists could not have survived' (Dunbar-Ortiz, 2014: 46). American history textbooks would like to pretend that the nation-state where I reside was some untouched territory that only they could bring to glory, but the truth of the matter is that their experiment only succeeded because of what was already present when they arrived and stole it. You can see this same revisionist history at play in every country colonized by European powers: there is a broadly accepted belief that whiteness is the reason that colonized nations became worthwhile. If we think back to the connection between the trafficking of sugar and the bodies that produced it, the locations where the crop flourished only earned their places on the map when they became indispensable to whiteness, yet the exploitation of these people and the extraction of value from these lands became conflated with whiteness having conferred value upon them.

In what became the United States, Europeans brought disease alongside their ships, but smallpox didn't succeed in eliminating everyone, so they were forced to remove them directly in order to control their land (Wolfe, 2006). Generations of genocide led to the creation of a nation that claimed to be founded on liberation, and all the while, the ceaseless growth and expansion required for both capitalism and colonization were framed as the destiny of the thieves. What allowed all of this to be swallowed more easily by the public was not just a virulent interpersonal hatred of the indigenous and the enslaved,[1] but rather a growing national myth that this land was owed to those who sought it. This idea, as ever, descends from the lessons of European imperialism, which doesn't merely espouse global exploration and trade but the creation of coercive hierarchies that benefit the controlling people. Upon arrival on these shores, what must have seemed to be an unimaginably vast expanse was there for the settling, if only the people would just get out of the way.

I believe that it was theoretically possible for each venture that ended in colonization to have instead ended up with a cooperative partnership; oppression is always a choice, or a series of them. Groups from European nations could have treated leaders from other locations as equals and sought only to share in equal exchange. Capitalism didn't have to take over global commerce, and settler colonialism was not unavoidable. But I contend that, once the idea of a group meant to be excluded from exploitation was created – a group with boundaries flexible enough that many could hope to be included – the fates of the indigenous and those ultimately enslaved were sealed, and so too that of their descendants, forced to live for centuries under a system built only to allow them to survive long enough to cultivate wealth for whiteness. With these ideals in place, the oppression of Black and indigenous people could be framed as 'character building' (Fong, 2019), thereby implying that their character was deficient when compared to models set forth by the supposed virtue of whiteness, a contradiction around which much of this book is centered. Indeed, there became something to aspire to for everyone, racialized or not, as heedless competition is inherent to the values of capitalism, and the acquisition of land at the expense of others is the essence of settler colonialism. What whiteness does is help decide precisely whose land must be taken, and whose labor must be used to squeeze the financial value from said land, justifying these decisions by rendering the victims not just less worthwhile but in need of improving.

Remaining on the topic of land for a moment, the possession thereof has long had a direct connection to societal power, for a longer time than these concepts have existed. It is perhaps a separate discussion to consider whether or not one should even be able to own land, but since this is the case, we live in a world where, particularly in former colonies and capitalistic economies, land and wealth are synonymous. When I was growing up, I was told repeatedly that the very best way to secure a future for my eventual children would be to find a way to own property, and I think about that mantra frequently when I consider how whiteness and property are so closely related, as Harris (1993) made clear in her influential essay on the subject. In considering the concept of whiteness as property, I am often reminded of the signs found in many American suburbs, warning passers-by that *trespassers will be shot*. This is a very aggressive[2] message, but it's not too far off from the way that whiteness ensures its own perpetuation by erecting boundaries around its property. Though Harris's essay is mostly metaphorical, the fact that the concrete theft of land has been followed by the resolute and ongoing refusal to consistently share space with the racialized represents one of the most impactful lasting effects of the ways that whiteness justifies settler colonialism and capitalism. Indeed, one of the fiercest barriers separating whiteness from those who hope to enter its embrace is the possession of property itself, in the form of what we now, almost ironically, call 'real estate', and especially the neighborhoods, towns and villages that continue to maintain their whiteness.

The idealized version of United States homeownership includes the possession of a white picket fence, and though that particular style is now rather archaic, the fact that a stark, visible barrier is part of the image is rather apt, considering the ways that whiteness has used real estate and residence to maintain its hegemony. *Sundown towns* – so called because Black individuals and families, though allowed to pass through or be employed, were supposed to depart before dark lest they face dire consequences – were prevalent across the United States, a backlash to the migration that followed emancipation (Loewen, 2005). Though the national narrative suggests that the American South was the only dangerous place for Black lives, the discomfiting aspect of sundown towns is that they actually proliferated far from the former confederacy, with official (and unofficial) ordinances against Black residences seen in almost every state, up to and including the early 21st century. Many sundown towns arose in response to the growing racialized population of urban centers, and what Loewen classified as *sundown suburbs* can be found outside of cities as disparate as Detroit, Michigan,[3] Washington, DC[4] and, most distressingly for me given my own location, New York.[5]

Why do people move to suburbs? Is it an avowed hatred of racialized groups? Not all the time. As Loewen (2005: 119) wrote: 'First, it seemed the proper way to bring up children, and second, it both showed and secured social status'. In other words, it is what good white people, and especially good white parents, do if they can afford to. Not every white parent lives in the suburbs, surely, and not every suburb that once legally barred Black families is still a sundown town, though in most such cases, the population remains extraordinarily homogenous, as demographic shifts are slow, and the people who genuinely cherished the visible whiteness are often still present and powerful. Nevertheless, even in other contexts, the long-term effects of residential exclusion have persisted long past any explicit legal segregation (Appel & Nickerson, 2015), leading to a present day where racially mixed locales remain the exception (Williams & Emamdjomeh, 2018).

When I was growing up in Brooklyn, if I walked a few blocks in one direction, the houses became grander and larger and the residents whiter, whereas by walking in the other direction, you found yourself amidst an area populated by families who had migrated from the Caribbean. When I was eight or nine, I learned that we were considered 'minorities', and though the concept was explained to me, I remember being confused, as neither my family nor my mother's neighborhood was as white as that term implies. Over time, however, I came to understand more about the different areas of what I had assumed was a deeply mixed city. My mother's area, when she bought the house, was not the prime real estate it has since evolved into, though our home was wonderful and warm. The houses were spacious but old in a way that had yet to become attractive to the younger and whiter professionals who have since moved into the area. Our kitchen was a bizarre shade of yellow, the type that would have horrified viewers on an episode of *House Hunters*. By the time she sold the place when I was in college, however, the officially desirable areas of Brooklyn had expanded to include where we lived, and now, as I'm about the same age that my mother was when we moved there, it's a neighborhood where I couldn't even conceive of affording a house. This change in my old neighborhood can be contrasted to the area where I went to school, an exclusive locale that had never needed to be gentrified and where I was once told by residents that I didn't belong on their streets, even though I was a student there for more than a decade. I came to understand that the only reason we were considered 'minorities', or more accurately that we were *minoritized*, was because people such as my classmates and their families, many of whom lived near our school, saw people like us as not deserving of inclusion into the property to which they were entitled. Had they actually seen the house where we lived, they might have noticed that it wasn't all that different from the ones I visited on playdates and at parties, but several of them weren't allowed to venture out to our home, telling me it was 'too far into Brooklyn', even though it was maybe a 30-minute drive. On paper, we were the same in a lot of ways, what with the degrees and professions my parents had and the comfortable house where we lived, but they still erected boundaries around their space, and even when I spent time there, over the course of 15 years, I was nonetheless seen as an interloper. I spoke like them, I studied with them, I had the same educational aspirations as them, but we remained on the outside of their property. Even when we do manage to actually afford the literal property in their neighborhoods, when we are seen as relatively successful within the systems of both settler colonialism and capitalism, because of the racial category we have always been placed in, we're still seen as not deserving of membership in whiteness, and the ceaseless enforcement of this boundary has severe consequences. Many of us know how harmful the gaps in homeownership and wealth between racial groups can be for long-term stability, but to illustrate the point about the damage caused by this persistent picket fence, I think it makes sense instead to focus on the effects for the very people who have been told that the system benefits them. Indeed, if you consider the concept of *interest convergence* (Bell, 1980; Milner, 2008), which holds that there will be no progress on racial oppression if not in the interest of whites, I hope it will be clear that, though they are certainly secondary victims, the goals of my work here would benefit the white population too.

In his book *Dying of Whiteness*, Jonathan Metzl (2019) lays out a persistent trend that can be found in different areas of the United States, namely that white individuals and families have become so invested in whiteness that they are materially damaging their own prospects and literally shortening their own lives in the process. Metzl chronicles support for pro-gun legislation, refusal to extend healthcare to those in need because of the mere chance it would benefit the racialized and, perhaps most confoundingly, the way one state (Kansas) has driven their previously exemplary public school system into the ground because of who a small number of the students are. All three of his example states feature politicians warning that too much money is being spent on racialized groups and communities, dog whistles that have fueled support for policies of austerity and a decline in government funding. In the case of Kansas, although it can feel somewhat abstract to tie state education results to actual life expectancy, Metzl makes clear that the policies chosen by the state's voters have led to declines in graduation across all racial groups (though not equally), and that students who do not finish high school are likelier to have shorter life spans. It's rarely as simple as actively choosing a shorter or more difficult life out of an investment in whiteness, but frequently making decisions designed to reify the oppression of those lower in the pyramid without realizing the harm this will bring upon you as well. I say this not to absolve these people of their responsibility in making better choices but to demonstrate that, because of our society's dependence upon the centrality of whiteness, any practices that do not actively seek to support the racialized are likely to increase the harm visited upon them. In Metzl's summation of his work, he wrote:

There are mortal trade-offs white Americans make in order to defend an imagined sense of whiteness. It's a narrative about how 'whiteness' becomes a formation worth living and dying for, and how, in myriad ways and on multiple levels, white Americans bet their lives on particular sets of meanings associated with whiteness, even in the face of clear threats to mortality or common sense. (Metzl, 2019: 270)

Far be it for me to disagree with Metzl, but I would add only that this deadly adherence to whiteness is not, truly, anathema to common sense, but is in fact the most common sense of all.

Across the Atlantic, though the results are early yet, we are beginning to see the results of the United Kingdom's decision to sever itself from the European Union, which, as previously mentioned, was rooted in whiteness, much as supporters might claim otherwise. Using an analytic framework that the majoritized might prefer – the economy – the impact from Brexit is likely to be staggeringly negative, worse in some ways than the pandemic, as there is little expectation of any sort of recovery from leaving the Union (Sampson, 2020). We will need to check back in another decade to see if a sequel to Metzl's book needs to be written in a different country, but policies chosen to uphold whiteness absolutely can cause damage to the very white people who support them.

Is someone benefiting from all of this? As ever, only a very few people are materially rewarded. Even reaching back to the first colonists, many had sickly, short lives, and were controlled by those with more power, money and land – many Europeans who spent time with the indigenous abandoned their families altogether for a better lifestyle (Graeber & Wengrow, 2021). Capitalism preys upon most white people, harder though it is on the racialized. Whiteness provides justification for settler colonialism and capitalism, and to this day, leaves people striving to avoid being dragged down to the level of the people they consider below them, to the point that they will make reckless decisions as tributes to their false god. I contend that, brutal though these twin systems may have always been, they were given a ceaseless source of fuel through the way that whiteness was built, and the flames need only be lightly fanned to generate the fury that animates so much of how we are still forced to live.

It has become common, especially among academics, to acknowledge the peoples who once lived where we reside. We talk frequently about 'decolonizing' our curricula, and we make statements about our sincere commitment to the indigenous, yet we rarely take the time to grapple with exactly who and what 'happened' that removed them from their homes. Our ways of knowing and our institutions are soaked in whiteness, and until we are better able to grapple with this, we will never come close to repairing the damage of settler colonialism. Similarly, though it is gratifying to note how many people are rather fed up with capitalism – a transition that took me several years – far too many of my white peers make the mistake of moving from this valid stance to ignoring the centrality of racism and whiteness in this system of economic exploitation. Often I hear from others with nominally leftist politics that 'identity politics' is harmful, but this argument is both correct and deeply misguided. When people dismiss 'identity politics', what they tend to mean is that surface-level representation – e.g. the first Black leader of an imperialist power – does little to change the on-the-ground fortunes of the oppressed, and this is absolutely true. Yet, as soon as we accede to the argument that removing race and other markers of identity from political movements is ideal, we are playing into the idea that the unmarked identity is a neutral one, and not the reality that any identity that has the choice not to be marked is a dominant one. In other words, as soon as we stop talking about racism in our economic analysis, whiteness will regain its silent prominence; all politics is literally identity politics, the question being whether that identity is oppressed and named or dominant and unnamed. We cannot talk about the horrors of capitalism without considering racism, and we cannot fight racism without a strong conceptualization of whiteness. And, ultimately, we cannot have a full picture of whiteness without an intimate knowledge of what whiteness created for so many to fear: Blackness.

Notes

(1) Though that was surely present.
(2) And very American.
(3) For example Grosse Pointe, Michigan.
(4) For example Chevy Chase, Maryland.
(5) For example Levittown, NY and Darien, Connecticut, which has a rather astounding recent history of racism.

A Dark Projection

When I say that this chapter is about Blackness, I want to be clear that I am not speaking only of the experience of being Black. Despite the clear struggles and dangers, I can tell you that being Black is a truly remarkable and singular thing, a connection to a grand history of perseverance and defiance that I can only hope to live up to. For us, finding a path to joy and comfort is revolutionary, as these simple pleasures are what many seek to prevent us from experiencing. To be able to smile despite the fury that accompanies our every inch of progress is to spit in the face of the limits that have been placed upon us. These deeply human emotions are enraging for those who have painted us as lesser beings, and I want to focus on this when I consider not just Blackness itself but the way that whiteness has built and constricted our identity over these past few centuries. I wrote above about how our labor was sought and stolen and that through the creation of whiteness, this exploitation was justified by placing us outside of the groups deserving of protection. What I find interesting, though, is that, despite the oppression designed to hold us in our proper place, white people are truly fascinated by the shallow and superficial version of Blackness they created to comfort themselves. I consider the peculiar nature of minstrelsy to be a relevant example of the way whiteness views Blackness, both in the sense that it represents how they viewed us at the time, and that it helped cement how they continued to see us for decades after the fact.

Let's think about what minstrelsy was (and is). In its most popular format, the characters in minstrel shows were portrayed by white performers in grotesque paint and makeup, with colors that represent no actual human that has ever existed. They spoke in a bastardized form of what we might now refer to as African-American English or African-American language, though without any of the actual rules and complexity that have since been identified. The characters were often violent and unintelligent, yet almost too unintelligent not to realize that their behavior should have been embarrassing, what with their giant, frozen smiles. It is one of the earliest examples of a wholly original American art form, designed to codify whiteness and Blackness as opposites (Smithsonian

Institute, n.d.). Popular with audiences in all corners of high society, for some, these caricatures were the only version of Blackness with which they ever had direct experience.

Of course, the characters in these shows exhibited behavior that was hardly limited to Black individuals. Every ugly trait that whiteness placed onto minstrelsy was drawn not from real Black people but from a projection of their own worst impulses, a sort of Mr Hyde that Dr Jekyll wanted to make clear was no part of him. Minstrelsy was an effective way to create further distance from the people being ridiculed, and it provided cover for the real experiences that these audiences either ignored or perpetuated while they weren't watching the show. And with minstrelsy perhaps the first entrant into what has since become the dominant culture for popular entertainment worldwide, its coattails are long and persist to the present day.

Popular culture and its depiction of Blackness have only barely improved. Actual minstrel shows are long gone, but the way whiteness conceives of Blackness is much the same, particularly with respect to being violent and unintelligent, though we're sometimes allowed to have a special talent like music or sports. Even now, popular films depict white educators entering Black spaces with little more care and compassion than minstrel shows once did (Cann, 2015). The public-facing version of Blackness, as conceived by whiteness and its architects, upholds the story that has been told about us since we found ourselves on these shores. We remain portrayed as little more than a dark projection of their fears and anxieties, of the qualities and behaviors they are most ashamed of, of a way of life that not only deserves to but absolutely must be oppressed for their own lives to remain stable and orderly.

If they were accurate in their depiction of us, though, if we truly were as they conceived us to be, we could not have survived this long. If we were as worthless as they believed we were, we would have given up centuries ago, and never found our own way to joy. Taylor and Austen (2012) have argued that, harmful though minstrel shows were, and as much pain as has been caused by ongoing pop culture stereotypes, Black performers and audiences have almost always found a way to build their own autonomy within the constraints of what was given to them. So long as they played the roles they were assigned, Black performers were eventually allowed to lead minstrel shows, with some gaining fame on both sides of the Atlantic for it (Chude-Sokei, 2006), and demeaning though it might seem in retrospect, there is a subversiveness in this limited amount of control they were given.

What this demonstrates to me, though, is that they don't mind supporting us, so long as we, literally or metaphorically, slather on the grease paint and portray the version of Blackness in their minds. What this narrow conceptualization of Blackness does is provide us with a very limited number of options in which to express our own humanity, and the trick whiteness plays is that being seen as ugly, violent and unintelligent justifies all manner of mistreatment, while daring to move outside of these boundaries is also cause for severe punishment. Minstrelsy is hardly a harmless concept, but I would argue, in fact, that all of Blackness, as conceived by whiteness, is a version of a minstrel show being performed in public all day long, and that the joy we share among ourselves, without their approval, is a challenge to what whiteness believes we should be allowed to do.

I gained a fuller understanding of the ubiquity of this narrow version of Blackness when I started my career as an English teacher in Daegu, South Korea, in 2008, a dichotomous experience that mixed positions of power – standardized English, a US passport – with the Blackness that was always a part of my life. Once I met my Korean colleagues at the public high school where I had been placed, it quickly became clear to me that many of them had never actually met a Black person before, which was even more common among the students. Unlike many of my experiences in the United States, I rarely felt any anti-Black hostility in South Korea. What did happen, though, was a series of incidents that reminded me how much of their knowledge of Blackness had been built through the same popular culture that flattens us into a small number of stereotypes.

One of the most common – and most fun! – activities for a group of colleagues in South Korea is singing in *noraebangs*, which translates literally to 'song room' and is essentially private karaoke. A few months after my arrival, a faculty social was arranged for all of the teachers, which I was strongly encouraged to attend. The other teachers, most of whom spoke English confidently, sang popular Korean songs, and everyone up to and including the principal was having a great time and drinking a lot of beer and *soju*. I sang a couple of popular ballads that were well-known worldwide, but eventually, my youngest colleague, who had been assigned to help me with all of my logistical and immigration responsibilities, made a special request of me. 'Do rap', he said. 'Do rap!'. And, although I could have raised a fuss and refused, I do know the words to a lot of hip-hop songs, and I dutifully played my role, which everyone enjoyed, including the principal, who surely didn't understand a single word I said but laughed the whole time.

Later that same year, the students had a 'sports day', where everyone traveled to a park to, well, play sports. Eventually, the students decided to play basketball, and you probably know where this story is going, but they were very excited to ask me to play with them, despite the fact that they knew I was both short and not particularly coordinated. Nevertheless, the team that 'drafted' me celebrated, and I proceeded to play as poorly as I always play basketball, which actually got them viscerally angry by the end of the game. 'No good', one student said.

In no way do I intend to paint my colleagues or students as particularly ignorant. On the contrary, they were only basing their assumptions off of the limited input they had received and, especially the first year I was there, I was necessarily their ambassador for Blackness, with years of movies, music and news stories to match up to. Accordingly, though I was usually called *waegook* ('foreigner') by strangers my first year, this was not said with any kind of disdain, and indeed was lobbed at white friends all the same; it was distance from Koreanness that was being pointed out. However, after the 2008 American presidential election, I suddenly became 'Obama' to all the strangers I encountered – including on my trip to China – and despite my eventual issues with some of his policies, at the time I sure did enjoy this particular side effect of their limited experience with Blackness. In other words, the way Blackness is packaged and promoted to places where Blackness is rare absolutely has an impact on the way people around the world understand our identity, whether or not they ever encounter us in person.

I worked very hard to bond with my students during my two years in Daegu. I was only 21 at the start and had not one single bit of teaching experience, like a lot of people who had been hired by the same program.[1] I absolutely struggled through most of the first year in particular, but by my second year, I had a strong rhythm going, my students trusted me and I had come to really cherish my time with them. Though I taught more than a thousand students, I learned as much about them and from them as I could, and I shared a great deal about myself with them too. They met my family when they visited, and they knew how much I cared about my hometown of New York. When I was about to return home for good at the end of the two years, my last class was somewhat somber, but we celebrated our time together, and I hoped to prove we'd built a connection by asking them where I was from, since, when I'd first met them, they were surprised to find out I was American, and I figured they knew more by the end.

'So', I said to them, 'I'm going back home. And where am I from?'

'Africa!' they said.

Suffice it to say, it takes a lot to dislodge the influence of what pervades the popular consciousness regarding the perception and placement of Blackness. South Korea is not a country that has a large population of either Black or white people, and, like any such country, their experiences are limited to a small number of encounters that provide an opportunity to move beyond the superficial version propagated through various media. We are far removed from the actual minstrel era in time, but not in terms of the way Blackness is shoved into a corner by those who depend upon its oppression as a means of motivating others to help perpetuate the hierarchy they have developed. The difference between the 19th century and now is the speed with which these limited versions of Blackness are transmitted around the world, and the fact that the people in these same countries do have the ability to learn much more about

Blackness if they want to take the time to do the research, or if they happen to have an 'African' teacher in front of them.

DuBois (1897) famously gave us the concept of *double-consciousness*, of the Black experience requiring not only the ability to see oneself clearly but also the ability to see oneself through the eyes of the dominant group. We have to know how what we do and say will be analyzed based on how we are seen as representatives of Blackness and all the weight that that designation carries. I would add that not only must we remain constantly aware of how whiteness perceives us but also that we exist, to many, as projections of their worst fears, of a status from which they would like to remain separated, and that much of the oppression that follows is tied to this externalized self-loathing. Call me an idealist but, with a very small number of exceptions, I do believe that most people understand that cruelty is wrong, yet they find a way to justify societal stratification based on an ever-shifting set of criteria that somehow don't apply to them. By extension, if these criteria *did* in fact apply to them, then they would indeed deserve the same treatment applied to Blackness, and when reminded of their proximity to these humans whose oppression justifies their position, strong reactions ensue. It is no coincidence that many of the paroxysms of white rage that have peppered the historical record of this and other countries have occurred following examples of Black progress and comfort (Anderson, 2016); when we dare to step out of our position at the bottom of the pyramid, when we remind them that we are capable of all that they are, we come too close to whiteness not to deserve to be shoved back down to where we belong. What they see when they see us is what they've learned from how we've been constructed, and though it sometimes takes the form of not knowing what continent we're from, it often leads to much worse. This additional level of consciousness is a taxing request made of us every day, yet we can't afford to lose sight of what we represent within the conceptualization of whiteness.

As Baldwin (1955: 25–26) once told us: 'The Negro in America, gloomily referred to as that shadow which lies athwart our national life, is far more than that. He is a series of shadows, self-created, intertwining, which now we helplessly battle. One may say that the Negro in America does not really exist except in the darkness of our minds'. We represent the worst of what human society can imagine, and one can only successfully bring to mind what one is capable of in some fashion. Black *people* have existed for eons, longer than any other group, but Black*ness*, filtered though it is through the prism of what has been placed upon us, is only a small corner of what whiteness has built. We are the people who deserve our placement, who once deserved our enslavement, who to this day deserve our exploitation, and when we dare show our beauty, we are terrifying in our resemblance to the people whose shadows we are supposed to represent. They project a shadow by stepping into the light, and they can't escape what is attached to them. As Baldwin (1955: 66) wrote: 'We (Americans in general, that is) like to point to Negroes and to most of their activities with a kind of tolerant scorn; but it is ourselves we are watching, ourselves we are damning, or – condescendingly – bending to save'.

I will point out, again, that though Baldwin writes of Blackness in what we call the United States, these concepts are hardly constrained by our imaginary borders. As just one pertinent example, Gillborn (2015) completed a study in the United Kingdom in which he found that racism remained a central axis of oppression for his participants, even though other aspects of their identities had an impact on their lives. Any white-dominant country depends upon the shadow it has created in order to keep its society organized into its preferred method of hierarchy. As you will see in the sections on language teaching itself,[2] whiteness, racism and anti-Blackness are global issues, operating differently depending on one's context but hardly without harm, even in a country like South Korea where white people are rare. These projections shape perceptions around the world, especially in the age of mass media, where what one American filmmaker thinks about Blackness can be consumed uncritically by Korean high school students.

Morrison (1975) once taught us: 'The function, the very serious function of racism is distraction. It keeps you from doing your work. It keeps you explaining, over and over again, your reason for being'. To those who require an ocean of proof before believing in the omnipresence of racism and anti-Blackness, no smoking gun will ever be sufficient. No hard evidence will prove durable enough because by its very nature, the construction of Blackness as a projection of whiteness denies us the agency to exist and be believed as we actually are. We can continue to try and prove our value, but we are defined as inherently less valuable, so there is little purpose in trying to win at a game that has been built to ensure we will lose.

A few years ago, one of my professors told me that, in order to write a strong quantitative essay, I had to support every claim I made with empirical evidence. On its face, this is fine and certainly wise, but this guidance extended to claims I intended to make about the ubiquity of racism. I bring this up not to criticize my professor, who was merely guiding me toward what would be expected of me in creating standardized academic scholarship, but to point out that this practice forces anyone writing about oppression to attempt to prove harm *to those responsible for it*. As you may have noticed, there aren't a whole lot of numbers in this book, as I have come to understand that if people remain invested in the version of Blackness that has been inculcated within them, there is no number that will convince them to leave it behind. To them, Blackness will remain what it always has been when viewed through the lens of whiteness, a category of people so lacking in capability that their enslavement was natural, and whose attempts to extricate themselves from bondage were evidence of madness, a mere exemplar of what they were coming to classify as an abhorrent and distasteful status known as dis/ability.

Notes

(1) This underqualification is a problem that I will explore further in Part 2.
(2) And yes, I will get there soon! All this context matters.

Dis/abling Blackness

It is presumably somewhat obvious that there would be a connection between the conceptualizations of whiteness and Blackness, even to those previously unfamiliar with the ideas discussed in previous chapters. When it comes to dis/ability, however, the construction thereof is often divorced from the epistemology of racism, when these concepts are best described as having been built alongside one another.

From the beginnings of European colonialism, those who were colonized were often classified as mentally childlike, less capable than the benevolent men who thus deserved to occupy their land and force them into labor. Accordingly, those who acquired the customs of their oppressors were viewed as closer to fully mentally capable. As Mills and Lefrancois (2018: 511) wrote: 'A key effect of constructing colonized peoples through the metaphor of childhood is to justify governance of the "natives"... Moreover, assimilated colonized people in Africa – those who behaved less "native" and acquired the mannerisms of their colonizers – were seen as less childlike'. Framing the colonized as children allows their thoughts and emotions not to be valued, and helps create a supposedly natural social stratification. To be clear, children are not incapable, but an adult with the mental faculties of a child is certainly classified as such, and this rhetoric had the desired effect of positioning colonization and chattel slavery as akin to a parent educating their offspring. As Nielsen (2012: 42) wrote: 'the racist ideology of slavery held that Africans brought to North America were by definition disabled. Slaveholders and apologists for slavery used Africans' supposed inherent mental and physical inferiority, their supposed abnormal and abhorrent bodies, to legitimize slavery'. The architects of this system needed both the exploited labor of the enslaved and an epistemological justification to ensure the success of said system, and as such, our modern conceptualizations of race and dis/ability were shaped alongside one another, both as contrasts from idealized whiteness.

Unfortunately for slaveholders, those held in captivity were, of course, not fond of their conditions, and many sought their liberation. From our modern vantage point, this seems eminently logical, and most likely would have been viewed as such if the enslaved were seen as full humans deserving of freedom. However, if slavery were positioned as a moral good for not just the slaveholders but also the enslaved, then to seek liberation would be akin to lunacy, and accordingly, this supposed break from reality needed to be etched into the scientific literature. In the mid-19th century, physician (and enslaver) Samuel Cartwright theorized the concept of *drapetomania*, a mental disorder that caused slaves to flee captivity. This idea appeared alongside a flourishing subfield of supposed racial biology, rife with now-debunked theories of anti-Blackness (Willoughby, 2018). Cartwright is now thought of as a proponent of junk science, but in truth, he was a respected and popular medical scholar, fitting neatly in with the era's orthodoxy, even if drapetomania was his own idea. As Willoughby (2018) wrote:

> Cartwright's more medically sound theories gave him a reputation in medicine and American society that helped validate his more overtly political ideas about race. Cartwright often utilized observational evidence for his explications of race and disease. By pathologizing these observations into defining racial features, however, Cartwright fashioned a powerful new argument for proslavery advocates, underscoring the rhetorical power of scientific discourses. (Willoughby, 2018: 603)

Once drapetomania and other disorders of the racialized were uncritically inscribed into scientific literature, it proved difficult for the conceptualization of intelligence and ability to escape from its antecedents. Black people were eventually classified as both lacking intelligence and impervious to pain, with our modern form of gynecology based largely upon the work of James Marion Sims, who performed experiments on enslaved women without any form of numbing (Nielsen, 2012). It is easy to retroactively classify Sims and other such individuals as monsters, but, until fairly recently, he was seen as heroic, his brutality handwaved away (Sayej, 2018). We were seen as, somehow, both subhuman and superhuman, a problem created and perpetuated only for the benefit of whiteness, and so long as the pain visited upon us was in the service of that ideology, it was justified. Accordingly, it can be said that whiteness has always been a most powerful excuse, an oft-unspoken balm for the potential guilt that might have arisen had the true nature of this cruelty been deeply considered by the broader populace.

Among the many prurient qualities projected onto Blackness by whiteness is hypersexuality, with Black men's supposed pathological lasciviousness in particular seen as a constant threat to the stability of society, and Black women viewed as though they could not be victims of rape (Ferber, 2007), thus giving license to white men to treat both groups as they pleased. If we were fundamentally dis/abled and childlike, then our humanity need not be considered, and our trauma was thereby invalid.

With all of these inherently disordered individuals running around, action needed to be taken, lest we hasten the full degradation of the human race (i.e. whiteness). Without dwelling on the omnipresence of lynching,[1] one of the most effective methods that dominant groups devised for justifying controlling racialized populations was through the establishment of the 'science' of eugenics in the late 19th century. Though it eventually led to immigration restrictions and forced sterilizations and inspired brutal domestic and foreign policy around the world (Reilly, 2015), at its heart, eugenics can be summarized as follows: 'Eugenics is the study of the agencies under social control that may improve or impair the racial qualities of future generations either physically or mentally' (Galton, 2015: 335). That quote is from one of the discipline's progenitors, Sir Francis Galton,[2] who was inspired by his cousin Charles Darwin's groundbreaking work on evolution and natural selection. His application of these discoveries, though, was in helping to devise a way to exert, as he said, 'social control' over future generations, believing as he did that modern civilization protected weaker groups that would have otherwise been eliminated. Galton was British, but his ideas were taken up by American intellectuals, and eugenics was considered a legitimate field of study and expertise for decades.

The fierce bond between academia and what we can now see clearly as racist and ableist pseudo-science helped ensure its centrality in our understanding of oppressed groups, as seen through the apotheosis of men like Cartwright, Sims and Galton. It's easy to misremember axes of exploitation as the pursuits of some sort of supposedly uncultured public, but these men who shaped our epistemology and discourse were among the few with the power to shape how we viewed Blackness and dis/ability, and were among the reasons why the two were often seen as one and the same. Whiteness needed its intellectual titans to justify its position, and many were all too willing to answer the call.

Though, almost by definition, drapetomania had little use as a concept once slavery was abolished, Galton, like Sims, remained revered for far too long because of his contributions to various aspects of research. The list of ideas first devised or heavily promoted by Galton is extremely long, but for academics, among the most prominent are the initial versions of correlation and regression to the mean. There would most likely be no quantitative research as we know it today if it weren't for the innovations of Galton, so people are forced to ask themselves if these creations were worth the damage wrought by eugenics. For the purposes of this book, know that I aim to impress upon you that, though our past century of research might have been messier had it not been for Galton and his acolytes, the far-reaching impact of the epistemology that supported eugenics is what impacted the racialized and the dis/abled, from his native England to the United States, to the 'racial hygiene' program of the Third Reich (United States Holocaust Memorial Museum, n.d.). We can have the sort of detached methodological debates that are common in academia to consider how to deal with Galton's prominence in our research, but all the scholarly advances he made possible didn't matter to the people on the other end of those surgical tools.

Though we have moved on, to some extent, from drapetomania and eugenics, we nonetheless continue to pathologize Blackness as abnormal and abhorrent, as fundamentally disordered, and we can see this manifest in the way that Black students are treated in classrooms today. Much of the discussion regarding racism and dis/ability in the present day focuses on the common American debate around *disproportionality*, or the idea that more students of color are labeled 'dis/abled' than we should expect based on rates in the general public, and schools' attempts to comply with regulations on the topic (Voulgarides, 2018). Yoon (2019), however, offers an important critical perspective, theorizing that many of the students classified as dis/abled are, in fact, reacting to their suppression of intergenerational trauma. She wrote: 'They were additionally haunted by dominant narratives and expectations of them – that they would end up in jail, that they were unintelligent or lazy, that they were problems, or that they were dispensable' (Yoon, 2019: 428–429). From the history we have reviewed thus far, these students would not be wrong to believe they were considered dispensable, yet they are labeled 'disturbed' because of their understandable reaction to the realization of this truth.

In her book, *The Pedagogy of Pathologization*, Subini Annamma (2018) took the time to chronicle the experiences of young girls of color who have been classified as dis/abled and expound upon how these multiple marginalizations impact their education and their lives. As she wrote:

> Dis/abled students of color are often placed in classrooms focused on remedial curriculum and instruction, while emphasizing obedience through behavioral strategies. These pedagogical approaches are likely to antagonize and/or create resistant identities in girls with these lived her-stories. Moreover, this is where the moving of unwanted bodies is not only metaphorical, but also physical as students get educated further and further away from general education. (Annamma, 2018: 39)

In a way, the dis/ability label merely makes explicit what has long been implicit in the parallel construction of Blackness and dis/ability; that is, Blackness has always been viewed as less than fully able, and as such our bodies have always been, as Annamma says, unwanted, and subject to disposal. Students classified as dis/abled and, by extension, Blackness in general are placed as far from the standardized as possible, ostensibly for its benefit but ultimately to reify the stratification under which it is forced to exist.

The axes of oppression are, of course, compounded by other marginalized identities, be it queerness, targeted religions or the gender identity of the young girls who are the focus of Annamma's work. All of these groups find their exploitation more easily justified when they are categorized as Black, dis/abled or both. As Morris (2016) noted, this results in the inherent criminal status assigned to Black girls, with their every behavior seen as disruptive, and educators more interested in seeking effective methods for keeping them in line than in fostering positive relationships. This current pattern is, however, merely the present manifestation of centuries of attempts at 'correction' via educational institutions, as the inherently grotesque version of Blackness that whiteness had built rendered every such student a problem to be fixed by any means necessary.

I would not go so far as to say that no Black students are in need of professional assistance, particularly as a neurodivergent Black man who has experienced what is commonly referred to as a mood disorder, but I believe the entire discussion needs to be reframed. Indeed, if we had a 'proportionate' number of Black dis/abled students, it would not address the root causes of these students' trauma, or ensure they were supported and cared for by their institutions. Unfortunately, we will remain locked in this harmful cycle until the day when we view Blackness and dis/ability through a radically different lens.

Most of what I have written thus far in this chapter refers to the conceptualization of mental or emotional dis/ability, but the trick that whiteness pulled on the enslaved and other colonized people was that by essentially pre-dis/abling them, their brutal treatment was justified, and frequently rendered them physically impaired. Every part of slavery was capable of harming, maiming or killing these enslaved people, from the initial land journey, to the notorious 'middle passage', to the conditions of the forced labor itself. Managing to survive without something we might today recognize as a dis/ability was rare, and this decreased their value as property (Nielsen, 2012). Those who were hobbled by their experience were often more valuable dead than alive, as all of this brutality was in service of the capitalism and settler colonialism that were central to the burgeoning economy. An enslaved person who couldn't perform their forced labor was worthless.

Now, if this had been based only on that forced labor and economic exploitation, the slavers might have logically decided to treat their property with the utmost care and support, the way people treat prized racehorses or antique cars. It may seem derogatory to compare humans to animals or vehicles, but if they had actually treated the enslaved like objects, it would have been a considerable improvement. Indeed, because this system was tied to a growing conceptualization of dis/abled Blackness, they allowed them to suffer and then, with the help of men like Cartwright, categorized them as unwell when they sought liberation from bondage.

After emancipation, the formerly enslaved were no less likely to be forced into dangerous occupations; the hierarchies had hardly shifted, and Blackness remained in its previous position in the pyramid. To this day, in white-dominant countries, the racialized continue to live in more unsafe locations, with worse air quality and lower quality of life, a combination of factors that is often seen as random but is a result of the way that Blackness has always been seen as disordered and disposable (Pulido, 2016). The dis/abling of Blackness is tied directly to this degradation of the lives and communities of people of color, a much slower way to, ahem, improve the racial qualities of future generations than what Galton may have intended, but one that may well be similarly effective.

The result of Blackness and dis/ability being constructed alongside one another has been something of a self-fulfilling prophecy. Whiteness created the darkest projection of its worst impulses and then found a way to classify those projections within a category it considered disposable. They created us, in their minds, then destroyed us, in our lives, and have expended endless energy on ensuring our suffering was justified while telling us that we need to be fixed. The ableism endemic to anti-Blackness is tied to what Delpit (1995) termed a *deficit mindset*, a framework in which we are always seen as lacking despite the fact that the ways in which we have been systematically deprived are rarely if ever acknowledged or confronted directly.

There is constant discussion about the best way to help Black people, with much of the discourse surrounding a search for a silver bullet that will resolve their issues. Buzzwords are developed and propagated, and they are eagerly adopted by the well-meaning majoritized populations who want to solve this endless problem. Whether it's *grit* or *resilience* or *growth mindset* or *emotional intelligence* or even *financial literacy*, the pattern remains the same: something is deeply wrong with Black people, and the only thing they need is to be taught some skill so that they can escape the circumstances that are most likely their own fault in the first place.

In truth, the only thing that is 'wrong' with Black people is the idea of us that whiteness has created, and that idea cannot be separated from the way that dis/ability has been viewed through the lens of a society based on capitalism and settler colonialism. To the dominant group, what renders people dis/abled is their inability or unwillingness to happily produce excess value for their owners, and any resistance to these societal requirements, either due to physical limitations or behavior that can be dismissed as defiance, is evidence of disorder, a break from the structures into which we are all meant to be placed. Blackness represents a poor fit with the ideals of whiteness, dis/ability helps explain a lack of bodily value and the combination thereof results in a mix of disposability and pity that helps no one other than the majoritized people who can take public credit for engineering incremental progress.

This isn't quite enough for whiteness, though. Dis/abling Blackness has been a powerful force in the lives of generations of people, with a small number of individuals gaining in wealth and prominence from the oppression visited upon many, a perfect example of the way this pyramid operates. Yet, not everyone can successfully be classified as Black or dis/abled, and still more tactics were needed to ensure that fewer could rise to join the handful at the top, and to ensnare the masses in our ceaseless battle to escape the lowest rungs. Ultimately, we needed a more precise tool for separating the abled from the dis/abled, the intelligent from the unintelligent, the white from those who could never hope to be seen as such. Even the nicest among us still stratify people along this axis, mocking those who make meaning in ways with which we are unfamiliar, and using this as a further justification for what ends up leading to the same sort of racism and ableism in which whiteness has always trafficked. Yes, though settler colonialism, capitalism, anti-Blackness and ableism make for a potent stew, the pathologization whiteness requires would not be complete without the subject of the remainder of this work, our systems of communication and (mis)understanding, the tool we use to explain the very concepts of order and disorder upon which we so depend. Indeed, a full understanding of the hegemony of whiteness is not complete without taking a closer look at the ways in which languages, language ideologies and language teaching are used to uphold its power.

Notes

(1) I continue to try not to focus on anti-Black violence, but it's nearly impossible to tell the story of these connected conceptualizations without occasionally mentioning it.
(2) It bothers me to cite him, but I wanted to hear it from the man himself. And he's dead, so his h-index doesn't matter.

Ability, Intelligence and Language

Although I am grateful to be completing my doctorate at a public university, I have spent most of my academic life at very expensive and proudly exclusive institutions where I was both conditionally prized and pathologized as aberrant. Because of my parents' professions, I was raised as part of the professional-managerial class and told by my institutions that I was the equal of my white classmates, despite the many differences between us, including their several generations of wealth. My class position brought me both closer to and farther from my peers, close enough to have a comfortable, single-family home in Brooklyn but, as I said, not in an area that certain other parents considered safe, even though it was. Until I was an adult and a student again, I was certain that the social struggles I had experienced were entirely due to my own failings, and believed the interdependent narratives thrust upon me that racism was absent from nominally progressive schools and that not being poor meant that I was fully protected from the destruction of whiteness. Additionally, it eventually became clear to me, with professional aid, that I hadn't simply been an annoying child who spoke 'out of turn' and had trouble focusing, but that I, in fact, had an undiagnosed neurodivergence, a term I prefer to *neuroatypical*, for reasons including the fact that *typical* and *normal* are aligned with whiteness (Beneke, 2020), that *divergence* provides more agency and that the misbehavior of mine that was highlighted by my teachers was similar to that of my unpunished classmates. Consequently, I write from the vantage point of a person whose class status and categorization as a 'gifted' student allowed him a liminal view into a specific subset of whiteness – a whiteness that is polite and liberal and horrified by overt bigotry (Zamudio & Rios, 2006) – but whose experiences with both racism and ableism ensured he would always be held at a distinct remove.

I may never have been considered white, but I was most assuredly classified as 'smart' as a child, a categorization not nearly as objective as many assume and which indeed serves primarily to create social stratification. As Leonardo and Broderick (2011: 2215) wrote: 'what is smartness absent of privilege? Just as Baldwin once complained, What are whites but people who think they are whites? so, too, might we ask, What are smart people but people who think they are smart?'. For my adolescent self, there was a constant push and pull between the supposed advantages of being seen as smart, thereby drawing me away from what I now recognize as the supposed intellectual deficiencies of the racialized, and the fact that I could never actually be seen, in a literal sense, as white. In other words, I was often a *Black exhibit* (Kendi, 2017: 2215–2216), given affection when my achievements exceeded what was expected of my racial category and gawked at or ridiculed when I failed to hide the neurodivergence of which I was unaware. Leonardo and Broderick (2011) asked: 'But what is smartness in the absence of its stratifying privilege? What are smart people *sans* their advantage?'. I was in a school surrounded by white students who had themselves been told that they had the dual advantage of being white and being smart, and then there I was, matching them and even outdoing them in many ways. The moments when I struggled were pounced upon and relished. The social stratifications inherent to the conceptualizations of whiteness and smartness, as well as other axes of identity, left me in a strange, discomfiting middle ground until I began my doctoral research and finally started to piece my own story back together, eventually coming to a better understanding of how these concepts got hopelessly entangled in the first place. Though it might at first seem a stretch, to make sense of this mess that has affected me and many others up through this very day, we need to travel back to our previous discussion on eugenics.

We spoke earlier of the horrific treatment that eugenicists visited upon the people they considered detrimental to the human race, and how their ideas thereof were connected to notions of whiteness and ability. There was, however, a contrasting effort, an attempt not just to identify and arrest the development of the impure but also to elevate those who were categorized as the most valuable. As Mansfield (2015: 5) wrote:

> In addition to forwarding negative eugenics strategies, eugenicists have worked to accomplish so-called positive eugenics policies, including education privileges and tax preferences for the genetically fit. They consider intelligence to be the most valuable human quality and have worked to construct what they have referred to as an aristogenic caste system whereby natural leaders would be identified early and cultivated for their proper roles in society. (Mansfield, 2015: 5)

There is a lot packed into this statement, so I want to examine it in some detail. First, the direct connection between the construction of genetic 'fitness' and intentionally subsidized wealth is made clear, as is, by extension, the poverty in which the less fit deserve to wallow. One could argue, as some surely still believe, that the wealthy are more intelligent than the poor, yet, if we remember our earlier discussion of the traits attributed to whiteness, considering that the idea of intelligence was built around the population that already held power, land and money, and that these 'intellectuals' aimed to provide direct financial benefit to those classified as more fit, it is little wonder how those closer to the top of the pyramid have managed to hold onto their position. Additionally, they aimed to build what Mansfield is calling an 'aristogenic caste system', by which she means a social stratification that would produce idealized offspring. For a century (or more), those responsible for the way we view intelligence have been in the business of trying to build better children, and, perhaps just as importantly, convince them that their membership in a certain level of society meant that they were more deserving of all that they had. Indeed, more so than any measurable skill, the widely held and heavily propagated belief in the innate value of the powerful has allowed our hierarchy to remain in place.

Speaking of measurement, though, there are certainly a few very impactful two- or three-digit numbers that purport to assign comparative value to individuals. My experience within the 'gifted' world began before anything I can remember, but I do know that I was allowed entry into my school and the world it represented in part because of the high scores I received on an IQ test at age three, a sentence that is rather absurd when you consider it for more than a second, and one that concerns me greatly now that I have a son around that same age. In a world where your supposed intelligence quotient captured at a moment in time is allowed to become a grand determiner of fortune, it is worth considering the way that these scores are used and positioned, and how they relate to not just conceptions but official definitions of dis/ability.

In my own doctoral studies, the fact that the IQ test is 'normed' gave it outsize importance in our basic understanding of statistics. We used the fact that the mean of all test results is a nice, round 100 and the fact that the majority of the population falls within one standard deviation of this number as a foundation for conceptualizing any quantitative results we encountered from that point on. I don't blame my school for this – it's a straightforward way to grasp these concepts, and we were a bunch of educators who mostly didn't have math backgrounds. Yet, I do want to trouble the idea that IQs have been normalized as a measurement of innate ability, despite the access provided by my own score as a toddler.

Intelligence and ability are not quite the same thing, but it is certainly possible to be codified as dis/abled by receiving a particularly low score on an IQ test. The American Psychiatric Association (2017) defines 'intellectual disability' as scoring below a 70 or 75, though they caution that such a result must be 'interpreted in the context of the person's difficulties in general mental abilities', which, as ever, leaves the classification up to the discretion of completely unbiased and rarely homogenous officials. When we consider this in conjunction with the way that Blackness and other racialized groups have been dis/abled, we can see that it is easy enough for people to be tagged as disordered in perpetuity if they happen to score poorly on a given day.

Additionally, the test itself is deeply flawed, and deceitful in what it promises to measure. The IQ test pretends to measure aptitude, or a natural ability to achieve, and is widely considered to accurately reflect innate brilliance or a lack thereof. Yet, as Hudson (1995) noted, since students of color routinely outperform their expectations when given ample preparation for such exams, these measurements more accurately reflect *achievement*, or what people have been taught beforehand and how closely their knowledge matches what they are being tested on. Hudson explained accordingly:

> What individuals have learned (or 'achieved') is a reflection, not only of their capacity to learn, but of what they have been taught in formal educational settings and what they have absorbed from their life experiences in general. Consequently, score differences on what are, in fact, achievement tests are far more likely to reflect differences in the quality of schooling and life experiences – than to reflect differences in the inherited intellectual capacities – of those who took the tests. (Hudson, 1995: 4)

Am I saying that IQ tests do not have any value? Not quite. Rather that they are more applicable in answering a question other than the one for which they claim to have a response. IQ tests and other standardized exams mostly reflect distance from the ideal, and that ideal is one that has been constructed and reified constantly, with the aim of determining who should be elevated and who must be discarded. A professor of mine insisted that such exams were valuable because they were predictive of success in higher education, and, as you might expect by now, I do not care whether or not that holds true, because in truth that is further evidence of the same set of issues, that the students who score well, as I once did, are the students the test believes are the ones who should be protected, and those are the students who are likely to continue to succeed.

If, instead of trusting the result of standardized assessments created by institutions invested in their own survival, we instead view traditional education as a sorting tool for ability and dis/ability, then we need to consider the ways that we determine who is deserving of support rather than a mix of opprobrium and pity. Numeracy is certainly a significant portion of the equation, but I would make the argument that you cannot be considered both fully able and linguistically deficient at the same time, and that who is considered the latter is determined by the conceptualizations we have discussed throughout the past several sections. To be classified as lacking in language is to render one without full ability, and to be without full ability is to be a part of the group that whiteness needs as a target to justify the excesses of capitalism and settler colonialism.

What is commonly thought of as language skill is not just about 'named' languages such as English and Spanish, of course, but also about the way that people language, and the supposed appropriateness of how they communicate and who they are. Though we can continue to pretend that language exists in an impersonal form that is somehow disconnected from the people who produce and receive it, the reality is that our perception of languagers and their identities determines our perception of their language skill. Let's look at a pertinent example to illustrate this point.

A recent report from the federal US Department of Education (2015) sought to help educators and schools identify English learners with intellectual impairments. Before delving into this intersection, the report defined several key terms. The following is the entry for *English Learner*:

> An individual ages 3–21 who is enrolled or preparing to enroll in an elementary school or secondary school; who was not born in the United States or whose first language is a language other than English, who is a Native American or Alaska Native or a native resident of the outlying areas and comes from an environment where a language other than English has had a significant impact on his or her level of English language proficiency, or who is migratory, has a first language other than English, and comes from an environment where a language other than English is dominant; and whose difficulties in speaking, reading, writing, or understanding the English language may be sufficient to deny him or her the ability to meet the proficient level of achievement on state assessments, the ability to successfully achieve in classrooms where the language of instruction is English, or the opportunity to participate fully in society. (US Department of Education, 2015: 3)

To be clear, this is before the report begins to analyze the dis/ability aspect of its subject matter; this is merely an official definition of what constitutes someone classified as an English learner. Some of the criteria are to be expected – a federal education department would naturally concern itself with elementary and secondary students – and others are certainly based on constructs of standardization into which we will delve in future chapters; for example, the use of phrases such as 'environment where a language other than English is dominant' could easily stigmatize students from communities that are linguistically minoritized, regardless of the way they employ English. The final chapter of the definition is key to the argument I am advancing, however – English learners are codified as individuals with linguistic difficulties, as measured via state assessments, classroom performance and their ability to 'participate fully in society'. Ah. 'Society'.

Toward the end of the 2020–2021 school year in the United States, I held officership in a professional organization for English language teachers in New York State. At one point, we released a survey hoping to gather data on how the membership felt about the previous year of remote instruction. We also included a question about whether or not our state language proficiency exam should be administered, a question that was being debated at the time after more than a year during which traditional instruction had been interrupted. The responses were split almost down the middle, but among the people who believed the exam should have been administered, many of the respondents wrote that they believed that the students needed the test to help determine the services they should receive the following year, even if they had hardly attended class for 15 months. In other words, many of those who supported the test believed it was the best way to help their students, despite knowing it would show how much they had supposedly 'lost' during the pandemic. I found this surprising at first, but in looking at the way that English learners are defined in the above official terminology, they are only allowed to exist in conjunction with their test performance, and their identity in the eyes of their teachers is unfortunately yoked to the scores they receive. Even the teachers who, by all accounts, care about their students, often view them through that same deficit perspective, framing their education as a series of problems to resolve.

An old blog post (Cloud & Bernstein, 2005) for the Teaching English to Speakers of Other Languages (TESOL) International Association warns its readers not to conflate perceived dis/ability and a difference in languaging. 'Be careful not to mistake linguistic and cultural differences for a disability. What may appear to be a communication disorder could be a simple lack of English language proficiency or a cultural variation in communication style'. I would ask why it would even be seen as likely that the two would be confused, and I think the key is in the very end of the official definition of English learner that I quoted above; namely, the fact that English learners might not have the opportunity to 'participate fully in society'. We have already discussed how the conceptualization of dis/ability has helped push certain people farther into the margins, and we know well that the way that whiteness has built Blackness as a dark projection of its worst qualities has meant that participating fully in society is a privilege reserved for those who haven't been categorized accordingly. Indeed, the reference to the nebulous idea of 'society' calls to mind the 'antisocial thugs' rant that gives this book part of its title. Using English in a way that falls short of testing and teaching expectations should not prevent one from full participation in society, yet it does, because said society belongs only to those with certain identities, and power is denied from those who are seen as deserving of their powerlessness.

I am sure, to some of you, that it may seem like I am analyzing an offhand phrase in an unimportant report; however, from a previous job I held, I have enough experience in creating government-approved documents to know that every single word of such a text is viewed and reviewed *ad nauseum*. These documents contain nothing that hasn't been personally sanctioned by government officials, and when we view this specific diction alongside the parallel conceptualizations built as separate and subservient to whiteness, it is no mystery that any such individual would struggle to participate in society, because society exists to exploit them. Users of unstandardized English are thereby perceived as linguistically deficient, and accordingly are barred from inclusion in the category of fully able and fully deserving of protection. The issue for supposed English learners is never said to be the society itself that obstructs them but rather their own test scores, or the environment through which they are not exposed to an appropriate form of English, placing the blame upon their already stigmatized communities. Or, perhaps, it's something else about them, something wholly indivisible from language, yet something often ignored even by the language teachers who claim to care for them.

Bad at English

At yet another previous position, I was the manager of an adult education program at a nonprofit, which offered, among other things, free English classes. Our students came from many places, though I would say that most were from either Latin America or East Asia. Among the former group was one woman who told me that she had come to feel that she had hit a professional ceiling because of the way her speech was perceived; she was seen as foreign, regardless of what she said, even though she was absolutely an American, from Puerto Rico. Along similar lines, several of my Japanese students were highly educated women who were unable to work legally because of our arcane visa restrictions for spouses of 'professionals'. They came to our classes to improve their English, but it became clear to me rather quickly that, even by the constructed standards of dominant forms of American English, there was nothing 'wrong' with their writing or speaking. Sure, an 'error' here or there, but anyone who wanted to understand what they were saying could have done so without too much effort, even people who weren't language teachers like I was. I kept hearing a refrain from all of these students, that they were 'bad at English', and though I regretfully never had the wherewithal to ask them who had told them that that was true, instead of some mystical level of 'improvement' to which I was supposed to elevate them, I knew I was working against something other than grammar rules. At the time, I made the mistake of thinking I simply needed to help them improve their confidence, and since they did grow comfortable in our classroom, they did indeed begin to appear more comfortable making use of all of their linguistic gifts with me and with their classmates. My attempts fell short at supporting their experiences outside of our unique and comforting environment, though, because I didn't really understand what they were up against, and I didn't at all know why they would perhaps always be seen as deficient in their use of English. I was right to notice that the issue wasn't their ability, but believing the issue was their confidence instead is nonetheless an example of the aforementioned deficit mindset, and doesn't at all speak to the greater forces at play that were responsible for this supposed lack of fortitude. Unfortunately, like many language teachers, I hadn't consumed any of the scholarship that now informs this book, and I was still searching for a silver bullet that would 'fix' my students. I knew intuitively that there was something wrong with a system that would lead my students to have internalized the deficiencies that had been placed upon them, but I still thought of language in a detached, disembodied way, not yet able to fully consider how their identities played a central role in the fact that they believed that their English, exemplary even by our oppressive standards, was in fact bad. Only later would I come to understand the powerful ideologies at play, and indeed part of the reason I've done this work is that I can't go back and tell them where the problems really were. But I can tell you.

Any language training program, be it a master's degree (MA), a certification, a certificate in teaching English to speakers of other languages or what have you, should ensure that its graduates are intimately familiar with the concept of *raciolinguistic ideologies* (Flores & Rosa, 2015; Rosa, 2018; Rosa & Flores, 2017). My own now-extinct MA program didn't have the option since I graduated before the above work was published, but if you are reading this now and have any influence on future language teachers, you have no excuse, for anyone involved in English language teaching (ELT) who remains unfamiliar with these concepts is doing their students a grave disservice.

In short, as defined by Flores and Rosa (2015: 150): 'raciolinguistic ideologies produce racialized speaking subjects who are constructed as linguistically deviant even when engaging in linguistic practices positioned as normative or innovative when produced by privileged white subjects'. These ideologies, which are hardly monolithic but deeply powerful, position these languagers in opposition to, and below, white individuals and institutions that have made themselves responsible for evaluating and approving standardized English. Standardized English becomes associated with white bodies, a process Flores and Rosa (2015) call *raciolinguistic enregisterment*. This has a wide-ranging and long-lasting impact on the racialized languagers, with only people with certain identities being perceived as speaking with an accent,[1] to the fact that, no matter how hard they might try to mimic white-approved English, they will always be seen as lacking because of the bodies they inhabit and how those bodies are viewed. Racialized users of English will always be perceived as not quite good enough and asked to do just a little bit more, at which point they will be told that something else is wrong with their language.

Since both monolingualism and stark language boundaries have been normed in recent decades, racialized people who opt to mix unstandardized forms of English with other tools in their linguistic repertoire are seen not as gifted or creative but instead as inferior in all of the standardized languages in which they are evaluated by what Flores and Rosa (2015) refer to as the *white perceiving subject*. Hearkening back to an earlier chapter, I might argue that this denigration of unmistakable innovation is tied to the way that the racialized have been infantilized, constructed as dis/abled and lacking in intelligence to the point where all of their capabilities are necessarily dismissed. Consider the fact that a white politician such as Secretary Pete Buttigieg is internationally feted for his intelligence because of his skill with European languages (McKelvey, 2019), while many racialized people are instead viewed as almost without language because, while eminently capable of translanguaging, they don't conform to expected standardization.

This *languagelessness* (Rosa, 2016) pervades both external and internal perceptions of the racialized, with those classified as deficient in standardized English being seen as without a true language altogether. These perceptions are continuously reified by institutions, assessments and powerful cultural norms. As Rosa (2016: 166) explained: 'Through standardizing institutions, people are socialized to raciolinguistic ideologies about more and less legitimate language practices, the contexts where they can be used, and the people who use them'. Whereas familiar language ideologies might point toward what language choices are appropriate for a given circumstance, viewing these issues through the additional lens of raciolinguistic ideologies helps us understand how a person's classification will necessarily render their languaging illegitimate, even if their English perfectly matches the imposed standard. This widespread set of norms leads to the same sort of trap into which the students I mentioned above had fallen: their English would always be perceived as 'bad' because they were categorized as people who are not associated with standardized English.

These ideologies had a concrete impact on my own program and my students' progress, far beyond the nebulous nature of their own unfortunate but understandable negative self-talk. In assessing students' progress, we were obligated to rely upon a particular oral exam that was approved of by the city agency that provided us with the yearly grant that supported our program. Any such money comes with strings attached, and the biggest, thickest string was this oral exam. Part of the reason I was even hired for that job was because, at yet another prior position,[2] my employers had funded our certification in administering this exam since we needed to do so for their students. This test is widespread, popular and trusted, the data that emerges is seen as reliable and valid, and it is also completely beholden to and supportive of raciolinguistic ideologies.

The test is a series of questions, starting off basic and gradually becoming more complex, that are posed to students in one-on-one interviews, which are mandated to be conducted at a specific 90° angle. The students were supposed to answer the questions, and we were to rate their responses across three variables: how well they understood what we asked; how complex their answers were; and how well we understood their responses. I hope you can see how there might be some issues with these determinations, but the test company gave us very specific instructions, even more specific than the angle at which we were supposed to sit. For example, some of the questions only required 'yes' or 'no' as a response to be answered accurately – one of the questions was, 'Did you drive here today?'. While we were being trained, the company employees told us explicitly that a one-word answer was to be marked as the lowest score for complexity. The first several dozen times I administered the test, I followed the rules, marking the perfectly grammatical and complete sentence of 'no' as insufficiently complex, but eventually this started to bother me, and I refused to go along with their evaluation-suppressing game.

Along similar lines, because I had spent however many years teaching English learners, I was able to understand almost anything someone was attempting to convey, regardless of how imprecise it was, or what their accent might have been. This meant that I was prone to rating people very highly on whether or not I could understand them. In conversations with (white) colleagues about our students and their evaluations, I was told that students such as the ones I've mentioned throughout this chapter should be rated poorly on what one might call intelligibility. Though it didn't ultimately matter that much because I was the only one actually giving the tests and I was fed up, in retrospect, it has helped me understand that, without saying as much, we were not determining how well we ourselves understood the students, but rather how well the unnamed white perceiver would understand them, and with raciolinguistic ideologies in place, their racialization would ensure that they were always seen as linguistically deficient. Yet what was particularly insidious about this, though, was the fact that, if I hadn't started ignoring the rules, I would have continued to provide evidence for their belief that their English was bad, and it would have been codified into official government data. These were free community classes, so their class performance was unlikely to prevent them from any sort of school or employment, yet in some database somewhere, there's evidence that these students, whom any one of you would understand just fine, are indeed bad at English because they spoke in a way that the unnamed and unmentioned white public might have had to work slightly harder to process. What raciolinguistic ideologies do is place an immense burden upon the racialized to prove their viability as communicators, and indeed their value as able beings, and unless and until we confront these ways of thinking, then we'll still be telling our students that they are officially lacking. What's more, the students tended to 'improve' on the tests given at the end of the quarter, not particularly because of what they'd learned in class, but merely because they were more comfortable with the person giving them the exam (me) and tended to speak in longer, more complex sentences. In reality, the test company advised that the evaluation always be performed by a stranger, at the aforementioned awkward angle, which I am sure was justified in their data but mostly just made everyone uncomfortable and tense, and, of course, prevented people from speaking as freely as they otherwise might. In other words, everything about the exam was designed in such a way that it underlined the inherently minoritized nature of these students' English.

The connection between racial and linguistic ideologies doesn't stop at the assessment and perception of those classified as English learners, of course. Even so-called 'native' speakers of English can be harmed by raciolinguistic ideologies if they happen to be born into the wrong body. The construction of so-called 'standard' English not only excludes other named languages, but classifies different expressions of English as inferior because of the groups with which they are associated. Consider the conundrum of being seen as both Black and 'articulate', a label that has been applied to me more than once. It feels like a compliment and is surely meant as such, but the positive intentions cannot fully disguise the fact that the comment positions being Black and being articulate as attributes in opposition to one another. As Clemetson (2007) wrote: 'When whites use the word in reference to Blacks, it often carries a subtext of amazement, even bewilderment. It is similar to praising a female executive or politician by calling her "tough" or "a rational decision-maker"'. Even if it were to be taken as a compliment, it is, by extension, an insult to Black languaging, which is seen as inherently inarticulate and deficient because of the way that Blackness itself is viewed.

As some readers might remember, a pertinent example of this frequent conversation arose during the 2008 American presidential campaign, when one candidate referred to eventual victor Barack Obama as both 'articulate' and 'clean', the latter of which is enough for its own analysis. Whatever one's opinion of his policies, Obama is clearly a talented orator, yet as Henry (2008) made clear, the specific choice of 'articulate' to describe the skills of a Black man educated at exclusive institutions was reflective of a common set of beliefs. As Henry (2008: 6) explained: 'By way of contrast, Bill Clinton went to Yale but doesn't sound like it; Obama went to Harvard and it shows. Obama does not sound like Jesse Jackson, nor does he sound like Al Sharpton, yet both are also articulate. In short, for those who assume a homogeneous Black identity Obama does not sound Black and is therefore articulate'. Consider that, by earning the label of what this candidate[3] and many others consider 'articulate', the former president was, in their eyes, moving himself away from the deficiencies of Blackness they might otherwise have projected upon him and, unlike with Jackson and Sharpton, who communicate in a more traditionally 'Black' rhetorical style, they could close their eyes and feel safe and comfortable when he spoke. I don't say this to imply there's anything wrong with how Obama speaks – or else there's something wrong with how I talk too – but to point out that by (mostly) avoiding Black languaging in public, whiteness allowed him to be seen as articulate enough to be set aside from their assumptions of Blackness.[4]

When I refer to Black languaging, I am speaking of what, in the United States, is classified as African-American English or African-American language (AAL). The debates over which name is most appropriate are ongoing, though it has taken decades to even get to the point where people outside of the language studies community would even recognize Black languaging as being of equal value to standardized English. Indeed, when I type 'African-American language' into Google, I still get 'slang' as one of the top suggestions to help me in my search, and surely very few of you have read peer-reviewed academic literature written entirely in AAL, which means that, even when research is about the way that many of us communicate, it is necessarily written at a slight remove from how many of us make meaning. Black languaging is, to this day, viewed as illegitimate, inarticulate, unintelligent and lacking in capacity, yet this is not borne simply of discomfort with perceived linguistic inaccuracy; Black languaging is deficient because Blackness is deficient.

I always struggle somewhat in writing about this topic because here I am, writing in (mostly) standardized American English, thereby reifying this discrepancy between the perceived legitimacy of AAL and the language that whiteness would prefer to consume. AAL has an entire set of complex pronunciation and grammar rules and the people who use it more frequently than I do while still navigating a society tied to standardized English are capable of linguistic feats that are beyond me, despite their being seen as less intelligent by those who tie language to ability, as they have been taught to. Alim and Smitherman (2012), for one, noted that Black students can be in the habit of tapping into their rich linguistic repertoires while simultaneously being seen as 'incorrect' by their own teachers. I always spoke more or less this way when I was at school, and whatever my teachers thought of me, they never had occasion to use my language to discredit me. In other words, I was always 'articulate'. But, if I am going to be seen as articulate, what with my own exclusive institutional pedigree and far too many letters after my name, then I might as well use what I know about communicating in a way that whiteness finds comfortable to take aim at the ideologies supporting it.

These ideologies are neither inevitable nor immovable. Flores (2019) recounted how gaining a deeper understanding of translanguaging and its transgressive power helped him conceptualize these theories along with Rosa, and their work, along with that of others who have learned from them, has helped provide the field with a much clearer vision for what might be possible. Any one of us who works in language education has the capacity to develop an oppositional stance to the oppressive frameworks that are currently in place. I will return to what can be done about all of this in Part 3, but suffice it to say for now that anything that doesn't problematize the field is leaving these ideologies in place, to the benefit of whiteness and the great detriment of racialized learners and teachers.

Notes

(1) Though everyone has an accent, of course.
(2) The itinerant nature of English language teaching is not incidental, and will be examined in Part 2 of the book.
(3) Who just so happened to become president himself in 2021.
(4) Of course, the blinding rage many felt upon his election suggests that this didn't work on everyone.

Language Teaching as an Instrument of Pathologization

So what have we learned thus far?

Whiteness is a Pyramid Scheme

Ultimately, even for people told they're within its cold embrace, whiteness is a series of falsehoods, designed to convince individuals to battle each other until they reach a peak beyond the horizon, which never actually becomes attainable but nonetheless appears to loom closer so long as there are more people and groups that can be categorized as less valuable. As a system, whiteness derives its power from persuading individuals and institutions to buy into its value, such that even the people who may never be considered 'white' thirst after a proximity to its customs and privileges. Like any pyramid scheme, though, few ever see lasting benefits from pursuing its illusory promises, even as they perpetuate the oppression upon which it depends.

Whiteness has not always been a dominant ideology, and was hardly an accident, owing its existence to a gradual series of social classifications based on qualities that are difficult but not impossible to alter (e.g. beauty, intelligence, wealth). As such, the fact that a select few could hope to be seen as exceptional enough to rise toward what whiteness holds out as a reward, and many groups made their way into whiteness through an anti-Blackness that remains central to the modern era, on both sides of the Atlantic.

Whiteness Justifies Settler Colonialism and Racial Capitalism

Settler colonialism may well have been attempted without the codification of whiteness, and indeed, as I stated above, it began before whiteness was equated with citizenship in what became the United States, but it provided a moral backbone to the land grab that was perpetrated upon the indigenous, as well as the theft of bodies and labor from African nations. With those thefts justified by the relative supremacy of one particular group, whiteness ensured its continued dominance up through the present day by rendering it especially difficult for even wealthier racialized families to join whiteness in the exclusive spaces they had secured for themselves. Whiteness has been so successful in convincing white individuals of the lies they have been fed that they are willingly eschewing material benefits from education, employment and health care out of fear that others may also be aided, and as such are shortening their own lives in the process.

Whiteness Created Blackness out of its Own Darkest Impulses

Despite the beauty contained in Black lives, to whiteness, Blackness represents many of its very worst impulses. The violence, lasciviousness and laziness placed upon the backs of Blacks were based only on fear and designed to engender the same. Whiteness used early American popular culture to propagate its perception and construction of its own dark projection, and as such, for those with little direct contact with Black individuals, these images and stories are all they know. Importantly, it was hardly the poorest whites who created these ideas, but those with power and influence who sought to control those positioned to consume these ideas. Accordingly, no matter the complexity and nuance of Blackness, so long as whiteness is telling our stories, we will always be reduced to what they have always assumed that we are.

Whiteness Dis/abled Blackness to Ensure its Subjugation

From before the time the very first enslaved people were stolen, whiteness had begun to conceptualize these individuals as something other than fully human. At first, this helped justify their captivity, but, especially after they were forced to release the literal shackles, whiteness was determined to dis/able Blackness in both body and mind. In body, in the sense that, whether through exploitative labor or dangerous living conditions, Black individuals have long suffered disproportionately from illnesses and injuries; in mind, in that the most powerful of intellectuals expended much of their energy on proving that these same people were not capable of making decisions for themselves, and that they would diminish the human race accordingly. Up through the present day, when traumatized Black students are categorized as problems to be dealt with, Blackness is not seen as fully able, and the results reify the hierarchies that have long been in place.

Whiteness Uses Perceived Deficits in Ability, Intelligence and Language to Retain Power

One of the ways the dis/abling of Blackness works is by tying ability to the construction of intelligence. The most intelligent, as defined by examinations that just so happen to favor certain groups, are those who need to be protected and supported, and those who fail to meet a certain threshold can be safely discarded. The conceptualization of 'smartness' is designed to embrace a few at the expense of the many, and can only continue to exist if there are those placed lower in the pyramid that whiteness would hope we all buy into. A perceived or test-demonstrated deficit in constructed and standardized languaging is often enough evidence to safely classify someone as less valuable, and official documentation suggests that struggling to be accepted into a society built to exclude can be part of the way in which someone is categorized as lacking in English.

Whiteness Devalues Unstandardized English because it Devalues the Racialized

Finally, we circle back to understand that the way in which language deficits are used as a proxy for a lack of intelligence or ability is hardly a coincidence but in fact tied directly to the same racist ideologies we discussed in previous chapters. Despite what some may contend, language does not exist detached from the bodies that produce and perceive it, and as such, the evaluation of racialized languagers is unfortunately based around how whiteness is likely to interpret their English. These frameworks exist not just in the case of English language teaching but also in evaluating the languaging of so-called native English speakers who happen to be racialized, as the way their bodies are perceived will influence public and institutional opinions of their speech and writing. On a rare occasion, an exception will be praised for their ability, but usually in a way that calls attention to the discrepancy between how they are perceived and the way their racialization is assumed to limit their language skills.

Language education[1] is deeply tied to whiteness for the reasons listed above and discussed throughout the previous chapters. I know for a fact that many of us in the field are kind individuals who believe that what we do is inherently a social good, and it took me several years to accept that I might be contributing to harm when I was helping my students pass their tests and making them smile. The first article I wrote during my doctoral studies centered on what I called the *altruistic shield* (Gerald, 2020a) or the tendency for individuals in professions perceived as prosocial (such as ours) to hide behind our field's reputation rather than confronting our potential complicity. But in truth, our field, at least as currently constructed, is an instrument of societal pathologization. By classifying racialized students as linguistically deficient, even if in the process of providing them with what we consider to be help, we are aiding in their categorization as external to well-ordered society, and positioning ourselves, and our language, as the pathway in. These many centuries of whiteness may not seem relevant to how we plan a grammar lesson, but as soon as we begin to conceive of our students as having produced the 'wrong' result despite our being able to understand their meaning, we are helping to push them lower on the pyramid on which we have a slightly higher position. When we help them 'reduce' their accents, we are telling them that the white listener's opinion is all that matters. When we travel overseas and accept jobs offered to us because of the passport we hold, we are agreeing that our language itself is a credential, and that we are thus deserving of relative power over them. The way our field works now, no matter how warm and welcoming we might be, we are offering little more than a series of hoops our students have to jump through just so that they can be considered closer to the ideal, while rarely acknowledging that our entire system has been constructed to ensure they will never reach that same peak we ourselves are chasing. In a way, we are sort of in battle with our students, needing them to need us as a field, and keeping them positioned as deficient so that we might be able to step in and fix the problems we have invented. I will review all of the above points in more detail in the ensuing chapters, but, for now, suffice it to say that as long as English language teaching is tied this tightly to whiteness, it will remain callous, corrupt and cruel; in other words, to bring us all the way back to the Introduction, an English language teaching field that is based on whiteness and the many ideologies that descend from it will always remain antisocial. Indeed, if you want a one-sentence thesis statement for this entire book, here you go: the centering of whiteness in English language teaching renders the industry callous, corrupt and cruel; or, antisocial.

And so, *Antisocial Language Teaching*. Part 2 of this book will use the seven American Psychological Association (APA) criteria for the diagnosis of antisocial personality disorder as a rhetorical device to elucidate seven significant issues in English language teaching. Each of the seven chapters will center on a different issue (or conjunction of issues), taking the psychological jargon as a jumping off point for an examination of some aspect of the field that is both harmful and tied to one of the facets of whiteness outlined in Part 1. Again, I am well aware that 'diagnosing' an entire field doesn't really fit the way that an actual psychologist would treat a patient, but I also want to be clear that classifying people as 'disordered' has never been a fair or just process, considering the society that devised the rules such people were said to be breaking.

You might ask, why 'antisocial' and not, say, 'borderline' or another disorder? Aside from the fact that it was the word in the Tucker Carlson quote, the fact that, as an epithet, it has become a sort of shorthand for uncaring and socially disruptive made it applicable for the exercise in which I am engaging. As I said above, this field is callous, corrupt and cruel, and to me, that is the essence of what is implied by labeling someone antisocial, whether officially or as part of a cable news rant. My goal is to demonstrate both that the field is harmful – and, indeed, disordered – because of its ties to whiteness, and also that the actual criteria for antisocial personality disorder are, in fact, so broad that, having read through Part 1, you should be able to see how a person's identity might lead to an unjust diagnosis.

Now, you also might be saying that I am here asking for justice for, say, serial killers and the like, and, no, not particularly, though I am certainly skeptical of the value of prisons. Heinous acts are precisely that, but a classification of disorder made by a disordered society should not be accepted at face value. So, if anyone with an antisocial personality disorder diagnosis is reading this, understand that I aim not to further stigmatize any diagnosis but to use the text of the APA to counterpathologize the system that has decided who does and doesn't belong. Ideally, this rhetorical strategy will also offer a slight challenge to the medical model of dis/ability by demonstrating how said criteria are incredibly subjective, in ways that could easily be used for harm.

Whether it's something as potentially severe as antisocial personality disorder, or something as common as racialization, we cannot continue to allow whiteness to decide who and what represents order. And so, as we move into Part 2 of the book, I hope you will come to understand how the centrality of whiteness in English language teaching allows for so much ongoing harm, and how, by the APA's very standards, the field is in dire need of intensive treatment.

Note

(1) Which, in my view, includes not just English language teaching but also linguistics and literacy, though the remainder of this book is chiefly centered on the first of these.

Part 2
Symptoms

Criterion 1

> Failure to conform to social norms concerning lawful behaviors,
> such as performing acts that are grounds for arrest

I was 21 the first time I stood in front of a classroom. I had all of one week of training during which I'd basically been taught how to build a rudimentary lesson plan and then practiced teaching a handful of French vocabulary words to my classmates. I'd only bothered to take the training because I had been told that the certificate would guarantee me an extra $200 per month, which means it paid for itself pretty quickly. The point is, though, that I didn't even have to take this bare-bones training to be hired overseas. I'm sure I answered questions about why I wanted the job at some point in the application process, but truth be told, all I needed to be entrusted with the education of several hundred children was a college degree, the right passport and the 'right' English. By this point in my life, I'd interviewed for several jobs, and was always nervous when the time came. For this trip across the planet, though, all three of my interviews were but a few minutes long and, in retrospect, this makes sense, as they were really just checking to see if I sounded 'right', which, along with the prestige implied by my degree and the 'nativeness' conferred by my passport, meant I was credentialed enough to teach the language.

I don't want to belabor the point too much, as every novice teacher does have to start somewhere, but this wasn't even the same as a Teach for America graduate in over their head in a city they've never visited before (Garcia, 2019). I hadn't studied education in college, I had never seriously considered teaching and I frankly didn't start out with much interest in it; I was just an unemployed young adult who didn't want to stay on his dad's couch any longer than he had to. The story of how I became a teacher is not particularly inspirational, even if I did luck into what I feel is a genuine skill at supporting learners in the classroom. The fact that I would eventually become a good English teacher was not something the Korean government could have predicted when they hired me and, even during the week of orientation, when we were offered professional development sessions every day, the only genuinely beneficial lesson was the one in which we learned the Korean alphabet, which I mostly used to order drinks. That orientation hotel was essentially a bacchanal full of, as they called us, 'guest English teachers' from English-speaking and white-dominant countries around the world, reveling in our new experience and in the unearned fortune of being treated like we deserved what we had been given. Again, some of us turned out to be skilled educators, but we were hardly incentivized to grow and learn. For a lot of people there, at least during my time, it was a constant social revolving door, with new people arriving regularly, a birthday or a holiday seemingly every weekend and endless, empty revelry. What we were celebrating, what we had accomplished, I do not know, but as much as we were, of course, adults free to make our own poor decisions, and as much as several of the people I met are still bouncing around Asia on the strength of their nativeness and the skills it supposedly confers, it shouldn't be surprising that many of us had gone clear across the world in search of a party, because it's exactly what was promised to us.

Ruecker and Ives (2015) analyzed a selection of online advertisements for English as a foreign language (EFL) jobs, and described the landscape as follows:

> Criteria for the ideal ELT candidate are often implied through imagery rather than stated explicitly. The images of teachers on the homepage suggest that the ideal teacher is a young, white, enthusiastic native speaker of English coming from a predominantly White country where English is the official language. ELT professionals from countries other than those listed, and those for whom English is not a native language, are not addressed. The overall message is clear. There are plenty of opportunities in this industry for young, typically inexperienced, recent college graduates from Western nations interested in short-term adventure. Nonnative-English-speaking teachers from countries outside of the approved list, regardless of qualifications, need not apply. (Ruecker & Ives, 2015: 2)

I doubt anyone reading these pages is surprised by these findings, but I included that passage to make clear that, whatever issues I may have with the undeserved social status we were handed in South Korea, this was hardly an accident or a coincidence. There were exceptions to some of the above attributes – a few of us weren't white and not all of us were young – but on the whole, the description in the article above held true for my experience, and though things may have shifted slightly since my own time in Asia, or since this study was conducted, the conceptualization of a guest English teacher is still a white person with the right accent, look and passport.

Some of the recruiters, perhaps aware of how it might seem to prefer certain types of people, refuse to accept blame for their exclusion, explaining that the schools they work with are in fact responsible for these requirements (Ruecker & Ives, 2015). But this avoidance of guilt is truly besides the point, because ultimately it doesn't matter who created the requirements when they're all operating within the same structure that holds nativeness as the appropriate way to model (and teach) English, thereby invalidating any form of languaging that people outside of this category might do. Our identity was our primary credential, and the closer we were to the ideal, the more qualified we became.

Victor Ray (2019), whose work is central to my dissertation, wrote about *racialized organizations*, which, among other behaviors, credentialize whiteness and justify the unequal distribution of resources. Though the EFL world is vast, it is nonetheless fairly insular, and I think it's fair to say it's a deeply racialized *industry*, where whiteness is indeed a central credential. As we discussed throughout Part 1 of the book, whiteness is hardly a static concept that is contained entirely within the color of one's skin, so when I say the EFL industry has credentialized whiteness, I mean that the closer one can get to what whiteness represents, the easier one's entry will be into the field, a field you never really have to leave if you don't want to, as my former acquaintances demonstrate. I don't want to say that everyone I met in South Korea was some unmotivated court jester, just that they had no real reason *not* to be if they weren't interested in changing.

Though I myself chose to work for the Korean public school system back in 2008, many of the people working overseas are employed by private institutions, places whose ability to profit from the experience they offer is central to the stability of their schools, like any other capitalistic enterprise. Accordingly, though my own public school wasn't entirely exempt from such behavior, guest English teachers are a marketing tool, less so for their acumen and more for what they represent. There is little evidence that supposed native speakers are actually better at teaching the language, to be clear. As just one example, in a study of Korean EFL teachers and students' writing, Schenck (2020) found that those classified as native speakers improved creativity whereas non-native speakers were likelier to improve accuracy. Now, there are a whole lot of words in there that I might trouble the definition of (e.g. *creativity, accuracy* and, as you'll see in a moment, *native speakers*), but the point is, if there is any tangible difference contained entirely within these teachers' languaging, it is a measure of style of preference and not objective quality. There are times when what we might call accuracy is more important, and times when creativity is more central to a writing task, and of course there are other aspects to languaging. However, what so-called native speakers offer that others cannot is that they fit the image of what an English teacher is supposed to be, supposed to sound like and, most of the time, supposed to look like. These expectations play out in the experiences of racialized teachers and lead to what Ramjattan (2019) refers to as *inequality regimes* in their workplaces. The ELT field is thus rife with what are now well known as *microaggressions*, or everyday, interpersonal oppression based on group membership (Sue, 2010). The stories I shared in Part 1 about being asked to perform rap at faculty parties or being assumed to be talented at basketball would qualify as examples from my own experience as a guest English teacher, and these occasionally amusing but ultimately dispiriting moments may seem small, but they were reminders of what I now understand as my unbridgeable distance from the assumptions that surround the identity of the native speaker. Similarly, though it turned out that I found a way to connect with my students, it actually took me until my second year before I could say I was any sort of a good teacher, and my development had nothing at all to do with my native status but instead with the realization I had that my students were under an astronomical amount of academic pressure and that I could help them practice the language while having the freedom to relax for an hour a week. In other words, though I most assuredly did not know what I was doing as far as teaching standardized American English, I found my footing in the classroom because I wanted to support my students as people.

Although my experience is singular, it was hardly unique. Charles (2019) interviewed several Black teachers of English in South Korea, and their experiences were not dissimilar from mine, all the way down to one noting that her students were convinced she was from Africa.[1] Another of her participants coached one student through fears of being shot by Black people in Chicago, where he was set to study; in counseling this student, she was serving as a 'cultural ambassador' (Charles, 2019: 11). I myself had moments where I deliberately called upon my identity to support particular students, and I remember speaking honestly with a very eager boy who had independently done research on the American civil rights movement and come across the story of Emmett Till, which had left him deeply confused. As I said in the chapter on the conceptualization of Blackness, there can be a joy in our being positioned as something *not quite native*, despite the roles we are sometimes forced to play.

The binary of native and non-native is no different from any of the other categorizations we've discussed thus far in this book, concepts like ability and intelligence and whiteness, goals for those excluded to try and attain with little success, all leading to profit for a small number of people. Ultimately, whiteness extends its global reach into places where white people are rare, and the impact is felt by all, even if indirectly so. Even if nativeness could be proven to tangibly exist, it would still be a harmful hierarchy imposed upon both those classified out of it, those within it and those, like myself, tentatively embraced by its conceptualization. I put forth to you that, especially in the context of EFL instruction, teaching would be much richer and more compelling were we to fully dispense with nativeness as a goal and as a credential, and that, even if we don't mention the whiteness implied by its definition, whiteness will benefit as long as we hold onto nativeness as a means of stratification and value.

The *Diagnostic and Statistical Manual of Mental Disorders* (DSM) criterion that gives this chapter its title reads: 'Failure to conform to social norms concerning lawful behaviors, such as performing acts that are grounds for arrest'. By most standardized definitions of criminality, little written here thus far would seem to align. Though in the next chapter we will speak of economic exploitation and other forms of oppression, the adherence to native speakerism, indeed the belief in nativeness altogether, is not literally against any law. Based on what I've written in Part 1, you might expect that my objection would be to the use of 'social norms', but no, because, although I wish this wasn't the case, it is surely a social norm to hire teachers based on their alignment with the ideal of nativeness.

What I want to do here, and throughout Part 2, is return to the idea that whiteness was constructed as a means of subjugation, and a means of classifying various groups as disordered. It doesn't exist in any tangible sense, yet it is as valuable a credential for teaching English overseas as a particular passport,[2] and in some senses is more powerful than actually having studied education (Ruecker & Ives, 2015). I will be the first to admit that not everyone who has studied education is destined to become an exemplary educator, especially given the whiteness of teacher education itself (Matias, 2013), but to have actually received some basic training before stepping in front of students whose futures partially depend on you is unequivocally a positive. Furthermore, convincing people that not only do they not need to be trained, but also that their very identity entitles them to a career is, as mentioned above, a disincentive to ever bother developing into the type of educator that students deserve; some of us manage to find our way, but it's pure happenstance when it occurs.

Perhaps one of the most embarrassing things that happened during my time in South Korea was not an example of a microaggression, but quite the opposite. For some odd reason, part of my contract required me to meet with the other English teachers on a weekly basis and help them with their English. As I would learn several years later with my adult students, they, of course, thought their English was bad, but, by any possible standardized measurement, were confident speakers of the language, with just the occasional idiom or vocabulary word that confused them. Being that I had never actually studied linguistics or grammar beyond middle school and a very bad undergraduate lecture course, I had nothing to offer these experienced educators beyond my nativeness, and it quickly became apparent that they were having their time wasted. In a sense, I had been positioned not just as a guest English teacher but as an English expert by virtue of my proximity to the native ideal.

These concepts are easily internalized. I knew I was out of my depth when it came to advising these more experienced teachers, but I was hardly immune to the common guest teacher pastime of making fun of the occasional errors you'd see on signage around the country. I reflect on this now, and it's sad that it's seen as so relatively lucrative to market in English despite a lack of confidence in the language, but at the time, we all just laughed because it helped to justify our presence. If the adults couldn't even get their signs right, we told ourselves, then we really did need to help the kids. Even if we didn't actually know how to teach, we believed that Korean English was lacking, and therefore that the students would benefit from listening to us. For the most part, I really believed in the value of my nativeness, to the great detriment of my students.

Ultimately, when a system prioritizes whiteness in determining who is allowed to enter a profession, that system is taking great pains to create inherent value where there is none, and in the process expending effort on convincing the supposed beneficiaries of their deserved success. We needed to believe we were valuable based only on accidents of birth, and that our students' languaging was therefore less valuable than ours. We needed to believe that we brought something to the classroom, that we didn't need any credentials other than who we were. And if it just so happened that we stumbled into the ability to be effective educators, so be it, because the reward for that development was purely emotional; there wasn't exactly a financial bonus for becoming a good teacher.

When I think of this first criterion, then, and the idea that the ELT field might be committing a transgression that would be unlawful, or *grounds for arrest*, I think about how, in a different context, lying about your credentials is indeed a criminal act – they usually call it 'fraud'. Are we, the EFL teachers ourselves, the ones lying? Not at first, no, but even though I was only 21 at the start, I was enough of an adult to figure out how little I knew of what I was doing, happily accepting the money and the chance to travel. The EFL universe and the broader forces that created and maintain it, then, are promoting fraudulent, counterfeit goods, but they're shiny, and we take what we're offered, even though we should know better.

The fraud isn't the teaching job itself, but the belief that we are credentialed because of our identity – the fraud is the nativeness. Think about it this way: You couldn't get a job as a pilot without a license, even if they told you that you were qualified because you'd been on a transatlantic flight before. That might sound like a silly example, but we are no more qualified to teach English by virtue of our nativeness than a frequent flier is qualified to enter the cockpit, yet they entrust us with classrooms full of students anyway. With all of this said, though, and despite our complicity in this grifting, an industry that continues to subsist on the idea of nativeness is not going to be one that treats the people within it very well, and the next symptom of the antisocial nature of language teaching concerns the industry's labor conditions, from which nativeness is hardly a perfect shield.

Notes

(1) (sigh)
(2) Borders are imaginary, too, and should not determine value, but you can indeed hold a passport in your hand.

Criterion 2

> *Deceitfulness, repeated lying, use of aliases,*
> *or conning others for pleasure or personal profit*

In his study of the experiences of racialized instructors, Ramjattan (2015: 694) made the following observation: 'In ELT, race and language are also components in the aesthetic labour of teachers: to look good is to be white, while to sound right entails speaking an inner circle variety of English'. The result of this cold calculation is something akin to what Sung (2011) found at a British language school. As he wrote, 'I recall a complaint made by a parent to the clerk in 2009 that her child was being taught by a teacher of Indian descent. The teacher, who was born and raised in the UK, was a native speaker of English, yet was perceived to be someone who speaks "with an accent" because of her appearance' (Sung, 2011: 27). Now, we have already considered the harmful nature of nativeness, and the example above is further evidence of said harm, but let's think about why sounding and looking 'right' is so important to the administrators of these institutions. Yes, racism and raciolinguistic ideologies are factors in this calculation, and it's clear how harmful these hierarchies are for the racialized, but I want to extend these issues a bit further into the realm of economic exploitation. If we think back to the previous chapter, in a significant portion of the English language teaching (ELT) field, teachers are credentialed for the work primarily because of their identity. Accordingly, you end up with fully qualified racialized teachers being seen as less valuable, while at the same time, the credentials of their white counterparts are based on ideology rather than skill. This is a very long way of saying that, although it might well be easier for white language teachers to get their foot in the door, because so much of the field is based on proximity to nativeness, few such teachers are genuinely seen as experts in their pedagogy, and as such, they are just as ripe for exploitation. The field is more difficult for the racialized, but the conditions and career stability for even white 'native' teachers are far from secure, and this precarity is absolutely by design, despite what the field would prefer us to believe.

Writing about instructors in Canada, Breshears (2019) explained the situation as follows:

> Low wages, a high reliance on part-time employment, uncertainty about ongoing work, threats of funding cuts, lack of adequate benefits, lack of administrative support, and excessive unpaid work were just a few of the employment concerns voiced in the studies. These conditions converged in the daily lives of teachers to create more or less bearable working situations. (Breshears, 2019: 31)

As much as I am critical of my fellow teachers in South Korea, I did have good friends suddenly fired just before the end of their contract (thus requiring them to vacate the country), a practice so common we referred to it as being '*hagwan*'ed'.[1] Other friends would have paychecks skipped or forgotten, and there was little to no recourse for these conditions, because we didn't have a professional leg to stand on.

Upon returning to New York, I found myself in situations similar to the ones described by Breshears, taking positions with no health insurance[2] and not enough income to cover my expenses, alongside several tasks for which we were unpaid. And, of course, if we chose to pursue some other form of employment upon our return to our home nations, our time as a 'guest English teacher' was rarely seen as beneficial to our professional expertise, because it was well known how few qualifications were necessary for such jobs. Many of us become mired in a cycle of precarity, which leaves the possibility of returning to the English as a foreign language (EFL) world a constant unbroken beacon.

What we have here is a situation where the nature of racial capitalism assures that the racialized suffer more than others, struggling to be seen as equal despite our expertise, but, because we are nonetheless in a capitalist system that places a higher financial value on nativeness than it does on skill, even the people supposedly prized by the hierarchy are just as disposable, striving toward the elusive possibility of becoming one of the handful of people making an extravagant living off of ELT; that is, one of the people toward the top of the pyramid. If your greatest value is your whiteness, or how well you can approximate conceptualizations thereof, then you can easily be replaced by someone else who can convey that identity, regardless of their ability to actually teach a class.

As Walsh (2019: 461) explained: 'Precarity affects the whole profession, not just a minority within it'. When some of us are professionally insecure, and indeed when that is a norm within the field, then it bodes poorly for all of us in ELT, because even if we happen to be among the few who need not look over our shoulders, it renders us unable to feel free to explore different possibilities, or to challenge the powers within the field, for fear that we have our livelihoods imperiled. Indeed, precarity is one of the ways that the field holds its hierarchies in place, because it prevents us from amassing the power to push against what we consider to be injustice. No matter how many years we've been teaching, if we don't feel confident in our ability to cover our expenses from month to month, we will understandably do whatever it takes to be able to breathe. Ultimately, what ELT precarity does is diminish our potential, a process more commonly referred to as *deskilling*, which has become so prevalent in our field that there are efforts to work against it and its deleterious impact on our work (Pennington *et al*., 2013).

It is important to note, before delving in further, that deskilling is hardly limited to ELT, or even to education in general. ELT, like almost everything else, is an industry, and by this I mean it operates under the traditional assembly-line management structures that arose with the proliferation of factory work. As much as we educators would like to think our work is special, it has nonetheless been subsumed into the global system of capitalism,[3] thereby rendering its participants either producers or consumers (or some combination thereof). Despite the beauty that can occasionally be found in the classroom, we exist to serve the market, and our supposed skills are relevant only insofar as it allows us to generate excess value (i.e. profit).

If you remember the section in Part 1 on the work of Nelson Flores and Jonathan Rosa, and additionally the concept of *translanguaging* that I've referenced a few times, you should also note that there has been quite the backlash to the way they and others (e.g. García & Vogel, 2016; Kubota, 2015) have challenged the orthodoxy of language studies and language teaching. I will not pay particular attention to individual scholars who should know better, but while the criticisms of raciolinguistics, translanguaging and anti-racism in language teaching are certainly tied to the familiar indignation that follows when racialized thinkers provide valuable innovation, there is also the very distinct reality that this critical work, with which I can only hope to someday be included, would genuinely disrupt the profit center of the field. In capitalist terms, pushing against the racial and linguistic binaries and hierarchies would, as they say, disrupt the market, and those in power don't actually like when the market on which they depend is unsettled. Unfortunately, the backlash to these challenging concepts finds its way into the academic literature alongside the work of these innovative scholars, and to a new educator or an outsider, it might seem like a fair fight or an anodyne debate, when in reality, there's a side pushing for changes that would provide additional support for the oppressed, and a group of people that are either clinging to the traditional power structure beyond which they are incapable of imagining or, perhaps worse, desperately trying to retain their own prominence in a world that has evolved more quickly than they can bear.

When I say that ELT writ large is antisocial, I am mostly speaking of a series of systemic issues, but let it not be forgotten that there are individuals upholding this system, and that, although a white senior scholar attempting to discredit new racialized voices might appear to be engaging in an interpersonal squabble, this is precisely the way that power persists, because others see this and might be discouraged by the message this behavior sends. I say to you that if you are ever unsettled by a new idea that troubles your understanding of your work, the issue isn't your discomfort, but whether or not you attempt to apply pressure to halt this evolution and soothe your discomfort accordingly. The moderate[4] amount of backlash I have personally received as one of a few language education writers focusing on whiteness has actually emboldened me thus far, yet this has only been possible because there are enough of us who want to see a new field that I have felt more support than dismissal in my endeavors. The point here is that the people who resist new ways of thinking and knowing might well believe that their intransigence is only about the specific way they believe that language should be taught and learned, but by upholding the hierarchies of this system, they contribute to the ceaseless search for profit that allows the field to prioritize certain identities and use whiteness and a proximity to nativeness as credentials more valuable than any possible skills a teacher might have.

Accordingly, if a person's identity could possibly detract from profit, then no matter their dexterity in the classroom, they're a risk that might not be worth taking, unless something else might outweigh such a demerit, an odd balancing act I eventually realized I had experienced when my school in South Korea outright told me that my Ivy League degree had convinced them I, what with my Blackness and all, was worth employing. When a certain identity is the ideal, it can be correlated with profit (or loss), but by participating in this hierarchy, even if we match or approximate that ideal identity, we allow ourselves to be led around by the pursuit of profit, and there is little incentive for our workplaces to treat us with dignity. As Block and Gray (2015) explained:

> We need to deal with education as a superstructural phenomenon which is inextricably linked to the economic base of society and understand that profound changes in the former are difficult without profound changes in the latter. The economic base is at this point in history constituted by the model of capitalism (call it neoliberalism, call it 'late') in which we and everything we do are currently enmeshed. (Block & Gray, 2015: 12)

The fact that the field is marketed as either a party or a noble sacrifice with white savior undertones (Straubhaar, 2015) instead of a profession in which one can develop skills and live comfortably is hardly an accident, and contributes to the treatment that workers face. Indeed, despite my frustration with the way that some ELT instructors approach their discipline, the fact remains that the vast majority of us are workers rather than owners, and we do not functionally control our labor. We are given the illusion of control in that we can choose a country in which we might want to teach, and a rare minority of us generate enough income to set our own hours, but the ELT profession is comprised, largely, of an exploited labor force, even those of us who embody or approximate whiteness. Indeed, the fact that the approximation of whiteness is prized for career advancement is hardly unrelated to the constant state of precarity in which many of us find ourselves. This ubiquitous pyramid scheme serves only to create divisions among workers, who might otherwise build collective power to ensure that all of us would be treated fairly. Because some of us were handed our jobs without any real qualification, this faction of ELT instructors must defend this part of the industry lest they be exposed as fraudulent and illegitimate themselves. A fairer field would make jobs scarcer for people whose only credential is said proximity to whiteness, and this would make it more difficult to retain relative power over those who are meant to remain lower in the broader hierarchy. Again, this is not to say that anyone accepting an ELT job is actively holding back their racialized colleagues, but instead that the field depends upon there only being intermittent and disparate efforts to counteract this deskilling. A field that was a true meritocracy – and by this I mean one based upon ability to connect with students, not the way the word is usually conceptualized – would leave many of our current practitioners out in the cold, and being that many are already treated poorly but have few other options, the status quo must thus be defended at all costs.

When I think of this second *Diagnostic and Statistical Manual of Mental Disorders* (DSM) criterion – *Deceitfulness, repeated lying, use of aliases, or conning others for pleasure or personal profit* – I think, first, that this symptom is so vague that it could be applied to anyone who tells a lie, and considering the way that whiteness has constructed other groups in opposition to it, members of said other groups are, as we have discussed, often considered not to be trustworthy by the very nature of their group membership. In other words, whether it's Blackness, dis/ability or the usage of unstandardized English, this criterion can easily be mapped onto someone who represents one of the many facets of 'disorder'. Additionally, the fact that the American Psychiatric Association (APA) classifies this behavior as pathological when the deceit is in service of either 'pleasure or personal profit' means that anyone who commits what is considered a crime and attempts to hide their behavior could have this checkbox ticked off. I won't do this every single time, but it's worth pausing to consider how easily someone in difficult circumstances could be ensnared by a criterion as broadly worded as this one is.

When it comes to the past and present of ELT, though, the dishonesty is the trick played on these prized native speakers. In a way, racialized ELT instructors are better positioned not to be deceived by the field because, for the most part, we tend to be aware of the difficulties of racism that might lead to mistreatment and exploitation. For the people that the schools, companies and countries claim to want, then, ending up in a precarious vocation that is nonetheless hard to relinquish because of how uncomplicated it often feels is essentially a trap. At least for me, having years of English teaching on my CV did less than nothing to help me find a job as soon as I left South Korea, although it would have made it easy to find a series of different countries in which to work. Even for white friends of mine, the few who have been able to take their experience overseas and build it into something substantial were those who would have done so regardless. In a way, it can be a sort of professional black hole, one that's difficult to fully escape but that will do little for your prospects once you try to leave. When I think of the deceitfulness involved in this field, then, it's primarily the fact that the experience they promise you will sustain you, that because you are nominally a guest, you will be protected from the exploitation and labor strife you might have felt in your home country. The owners profit off of their instructors' identities, and the industry colludes to render said instructors relatively powerless to enact lasting change.

The diagnostic criterion also includes *use of aliases*, which I think is actually rather apt for the work that many such instructors do. We're told our role is 'English language teacher', but, as we have discussed, we often still leave our students with the belief that they struggle with the language. What we are really doing, especially when we travel to teach, is serving as ambassadors for whiteness, even if we ourselves are not white, and unless we take a distinctly critical stance to the work. Rendered powerless cogs in an inexhaustible machine, we serve the interests of those whose aim is to reify the binaries between the ordered and the disordered, and we ensure our students know that through the language we are fortunate enough to use in a way that is pleasing to the ears of white listeners, we possess a form of capital that they would do well to strive to access. They cannot, however, actually find their way inside of whiteness if they are classified as not deserving of a position within it, but they can in fact do whatever is within their power to place themselves above those who have less command of English, and it is our job to ensure that they find their way to a higher station in the hierarchy. Simply put, the deceit is the roles they tell us we will have, and the parts we are made to believe we are playing. Indeed, the people I know who have worked directly for the US Department of State are among the few I know who are well aware of their actual role; the rest of us would do well to stop believing in our relative nobility.

With all of this said, however, I wouldn't be writing this book if I didn't feel there was an opening to reshape the field into something more humanistic, and away from its current cruelty. Indeed, like the settlers once upon a time, the field of language teaching is not nearly as competent as it would like to believe, and has left itself vulnerable for entirely self-inflicted reasons. Its rigidity and ideologies have come at a cost, and the evolution in which I hope to take part is only possible because of how poorly the field has planned for the actual world it inhabits.

Notes

(1) *Hagwans* are Korean private educational institutions, and many guest English teachers are employed at English-teaching hagwans.
(2) America!
(3) Although it could be argued it has never not been a capitalist enterprise.
(4) See the Conclusion for an example of some racist hate mail.

Criterion 3

Impulsivity or failure to plan

Let's talk about acronyms for a second.

Throughout this book, I've been using 'ELT', standing, of course, for *English language teaching*. I use it because, despite my views on language boundaries and the definition of what counts as English, I think it's the most recognizable descriptor for the industry and all it entails. In the previous two chapters, I focused a bit on the specific subfield of *English as a foreign language* (EFL) or teaching the language in a country where it is not the standardized form of communication.[1] As with any of these many acronyms, the EFL faction of the ELT industry has its own foibles and flaws, but they're all tied to the general language ideologies of the broader field.

My own master's degree is in TESOL, an acronym for *teaching English to speakers of other languages*. For however many decades, the most common acronym when describing the teaching of English to people we would pathologize as non-native was ESL or *English as a second language*; however, even before getting into the way this phrase has the potential to subjugate people, it was (and remains) factually inaccurate for many, as English might well be anywhere from their first language (if their accent and/or identity is denigrated) to their third or fourth. Nevertheless, even as I write this, promotional materials for the school I currently attend for my doctorate refer to 'the ESL classroom' (Hunter College School of Education, n.d.) and it's still easier to convey my professional background to the unfamiliar by using this older acronym.

There are efforts to move away from these acronyms, and these efforts largely consist of other acronyms. My very first week of graduate study, way back in 2010, I had to memorize and differentiate between EAP (*English for academic purposes*), ESP (*English for specific purposes*, which is, ironically, a vague name), the aforementioned EFL and ESL, ELF (*English as a lingua franca*) and others. All of this was coupled with Kachru's (1997) influential article on 'world Englishes' and the *inner*, *outer* and *expanding circles* of English. I suspect you will be familiar but, briefly, the inner circle countries are, as referenced in the discussion about online recruitment, the places from which the EFL industry recruits applicants (e.g. the United States, the United Kingdom, Canada and Australia); the outer circle is, for lack of a better word, former colonial subjects (e.g. India and Singapore); and the expanding circle is everywhere else where English has gained a foothold. The class I was taking, which was in fact called 'English in the world', was making a legitimate effort to help us understand the vastness of the language, but, paired as it was with the list of acronyms, the circle framework, in retrospect, elided the power differentials and the history of how the more powerful countries centered themselves linguistically. Again, I don't really blame my program – at the time seen as one of the best around – but the broader field that would prioritize this implicitly hierarchical categorization as foundational to the teaching of the language.

There are even more acronyms to contend with, of course. In the United States, for example, one way that we have attempted to distance ourselves from the stigma of ESL is to refer to said students as ELLs, or *English language learners*. As you might notice, 'ELL' can be pronounced like the letter 'L', and that is indeed how many teachers I've met refer to said students, helping ensure that this is a label that is hard to shake, because it's just so darn catchy. Additionally, because of the label's relationship to testing, escaping the ELL label can take years, if it happens at all (Kim & Garcia, 2014).

There are plenty of other acronyms,[2] but the final one I will highlight is the decision to start referring to these students as MLLs or *multilingual learners*, which is intended to respect the linguistic repertoire the students already possess, a noble goal indeed. In my own doctoral program, the class where I was first exposed to the work of Flores and Rosa, as well as to the concept of translanguaging, had 'multilingual learners' in the title, so I do think that, in theory, this is a better acronym. Unfortunately though, this acronym, like all of them, has several issues. First, though it's intended to refer to the acquisition of English, a learner who is technically multilingual could still be a 'native' speaker of English; consequently, as high-minded an acronym as MLL might be, it still places these students in opposition to what Flores and Rosa (2015: 151) refer to as *monoglossic language ideologies*. Similarly, if this label is only applied to particular students who have been screened into certain language classes, then it does nothing to challenge the assumptions and implications generated by far too many of these acronyms. And therein lies the problem: whatever three-letter label you create, if it's just a new version of the same classification practices without a direct challenge to those who hold the power, then you're just reshuffling the cards in the deck. In other words, it really doesn't matter what you call people if you treat them the same way you've always treated them, and there's little evidence that our language ideologies have shifted substantially. Policymakers and academics are volleying acronyms back and forth across a rhetorical tennis court while the harm continues unabated, and though the field seems to be aware that something is wrong, as evidenced by its panicked embrace of new three-letter labels every few years, the fundamental status quo remains in place. Along similar lines, Kumaravavidelu (2016) has chronicled how the struggle to generate respect and equal treatment for 'non-native' teachers has now lasted more than three decades, yet their relative station has only changed in the slightest, which I would submit is due to the obstruction by those who are invested in the status quo. The only thing the field seems to notice is optics, so if it looks a little better to refer to your students as multilingual learners while you subjugate them, then you can change the letters on the promotional materials instead of the primary principles of the practice.

This constant surface relabeling without an evolution of core values is, in fact, evidence of the third criterion, *impulsivity or a failure to plan*. The various tendrils of whiteness that permeate the field are hardly unplanned or impulsive, but what this acronym battle represents, to me, is a feint toward the fact that, although the practice of ELT needs to change, the field is fully unwilling to engage in the work necessary to upend the paradigms in place. This makes sense, as the system is invested in its own perpetuation, and many of the actors within it are most comfortable with the hierarchies as they currently exist. But what ELT as a broader entity isn't actually prepared for is the mass of people within it who are hungry for a field that serves different goals. Indeed, what ELT isn't prepared for is *us*.

I assume if you are reading this that, even if you weren't aware of some of the history I shared in Part 1, you have some sort of connection to language education, be it as an academic, a classroom teacher, a materials writer, a student or some other role. Either that, or you have an interest in whiteness, or you're my friend or relative. I bring this up to say, I don't tend to write to attempt to convert those who are diametrically opposed to my work, to do what Kendi (2019) refers to as *moral suasion*. I do hope to provide some specific information to those who are either confused or curious, but I mostly preach to the choir and, to be clear, that is by design. When I started speaking out about whiteness and language teaching in early 2019, I expected to receive a powerful, intense backlash. I do experience occasional condescension and dismissiveness, as well as the sort of defensiveness common to any racial discussion with a white audience (Matias & DiAngelo, 2013). Mostly, though, I have been met with either strong support from those who choose to attend my talks and read my articles, or notable indifference from those who don't find the topic compelling. All of this has left me rather dismayed that the whiteness and language teaching discourse is still rather fresh, because clearly there are many who have valuable insights on the intersection who have yet to be heard. However, this experience has convinced me that, instead of what I assumed I might have to do and expending copious energy on debating opponents, the best way to work against the sort of mindset that would consider acronym generation to be a revolutionary practice is to build with those who align with you against the hierarchies in place.

ELT is prepared for any single person who takes issue with one aspect of it. The field will occasionally give an inch (e.g. professional organizations diversifying leadership) but the fundamental practice remains the same. Even with, say, a special theme, conferences and their attendees largely resemble one another, and journal output is mostly unevolved. English textbooks far outside of the 'inner circle' nonetheless place a higher value on the countries and customs within it (Lee, 2009). And, as mentioned earlier, the conversation about the value of supposedly non-native speakers has barely managed to push the field forward at all. ELT is ready for our piecemeal challenges to its power structure; if it weren't, it wouldn't have managed to achieve its foothold on the world stage through its usage of the insidious practices and conceptualizations that were built to create a pathologized population to which it could market itself.

ELT is, however, fully unprepared for a collective challenge to its foundations. Every small, visible adjustment will only satisfy those who feel the field is inherently virtuous and only in need of small reforms. Earlier, I referred to this tendency as the *altruistic shield*, but what this defensive stance hides is the core belief that we are already on the right path. Ultimately, if no discomfort is felt by the small number of people in ELT for whom the current system not only feels comfortable because of its familiarity but for whom the hierarchies in place are genuinely beneficial – that is, the people at the top of the pyramid – then what we are asking for and receiving is far too small. And, maybe I'm dreaming, but I think we are reaching a point where there are enough of us to make those big statements, to pose those heavy questions, to reach up for the highest shelf if we have any hope of salvaging the humanity of the field that many of us, myself included, have deep and abiding affection for. That last sentence may seem surprising to you, but I do love language and language teaching. If I felt only disdain for the practice, I would leave it to its own devices and wish my friends and former students the best, but the fact is, we have the opportunity to catch ELT off guard and build a new and better paradigm in place of the one that is intent on stratification and oppression.

I want to zero in on a specific example to demonstrate the field's lack of preparedness for the fundamental changes that are necessary. After the public murder of George Floyd, every industry was forced by the public outrage to engage in some sort of introspection, and every such industry was caught flat-footed and unable to respond with agility. For all of the issues inherent to ELT, it was hardly the only field unprepared for the demand to acknowledge the value of Black lives, so it would be unfair to single out our field for being surprised by the recent uprising. What almost every large organization decided to do was issue a statement affirming their commitment to the cause, a cause that very few of them were able to name explicitly. Elsewhere, a colleague and I analyzed the statements put forth by several professional organizations associated with language education (Bryan & Gerald, 2020), and we mostly found the statements lacking, with few willing or able to use the word 'Black' in referring to the specific acts that had inspired the uprising. The only statement that we found particularly productive was one made by a small Brooklyn chocolate company named Raaka, which had not only pledged to donate a specific percentage of their proceeds to various causes, but later followed up their pledge with visual evidence of their receipts for having followed through. While Raaka was putting their money where their mouth was, quite literally, the professional language organizations were praising themselves for the work they had, supposedly, already done on racism, with the distinct implication that there was little else they should promise to do. One of the organizations whose statement we analyzed was the TESOL International Association, a US based but nominally global organization that commands great respect within our field, and which many of my colleagues refer to as 'Big TESOL'. They are the equivalent (though on a larger scale) of the UK's International Association of Teachers of English as a Foreign Language (IATEFL) or Japan's Association for Language Teaching (JALT), and their words have impact, for better or worse. Let's look at an example of when this impact was decidedly 'worse'.

Big TESOL issued a boilerplate statement like everyone else and, again, since almost every large organization seemed to struggle with this basic task, it would be unfair to single them out accordingly. However, they can absolutely be pilloried for what they did in the aftermath. As many of you are probably aware by now, there were a large number of 'special issues' of journals initiated after the events of 2020, both because of the pandemic and because of the demand for racial justice. Indeed, considering my second journal article was released to the public just a week after Floyd's murder (Gerald, 2020b), I suspect that part of the reason my prominence increased was because the field needed to be able to have discussions that had been elusive to that point; that is, I think my work is strong, but I did end up riding a wave of opportune timing. I mention all this to say that if Big TESOL had merely commissioned one or several special issues for their journals, it might have seemed a weak response, but it would have been standard for this type of organization, and there wouldn't be much to say. But that's not all TESOL did.

About a month into the uprising, TESOL members (and social media followers) were alerted to a very special publication released by the organization. I'll let the organization's 2020 president explain. 'I am pleased to introduce this joint *TESOL Quarterly–TESOL Journal* publication on a very critical and timely topic – Race, Identity, and English Language Teaching. This special issue is the first-ever collaborative endeavor of our *TQ* and *TJ* editors' (Short, 2020). It certainly sounds momentous, especially considering the quick speed with which the publication was created, far faster than almost anything in academia. That is, until you get to the following sentence, and you learn precisely what is included in the publication. 'They have curated articles on the topic that have been published in our journals within the past 5 years in order to support TESOL's statement against racial injustice and inequality'. Ah.

The announcement goes on to praise the inherent value of ELT as pertaining to 'social justice', and the overall implication is that the articles selected are proof of how much work Big TESOL has already done to work against racism (though they never use the word 'racism' at all). To be clear, plenty of the selected articles are compelling work, including the Ruecker and Ives (2015) article on white native speaker online recruitment that I've cited several times in these pages. Indeed, no matter what one might think of organizations such as Big TESOL, there is always some compelling scholarship being produced and disseminated through its tentacles, and I certainly wouldn't want to lose the work of the authors who publish in its journals. Nevertheless, combing through its own archives to find a handful of 'race and identity' articles and then republishing them under a paywall serves only to flatter the portion of the membership that believes in the inherent value of their work. I wasn't in the room when these decisions were made,[3] but I imagine that there was a strong desire to 'get ahead' of any possible criticism they might receive, though they eventually entrusted a (Black) colleague of mine to help them create a diversity, equity and inclusion (DEI) committee, which is, you know, trying.

Ultimately, though, this slapdash recycled publication that, again, wasn't even accessible to the public is little more than an argument in favor of the status quo that led to the uprising in the first place. Big TESOL is hardly some obscure organization with little influence in the field; they are among the globe's titans, and their influence should not be underestimated. Had they taken an honest look at the hierarchies in which they were and are invested, they might have found a way to make substantive changes, but instead they patted themselves on the back. When I say ELT isn't ready, is impulsive and has failed to plan for us, this is precisely what I mean.

Before I move on, I do want to be clear that although the placement of this chapter that is essentially an attempt at encouragement in the midst of a section on ELT's foibles might seem off, you will soon see that these first few symptoms are mostly about various forms of deceit or deception, whereas the next several are a bit darker. Whatever one might say about the conceptualization of antisocial personality disorder, the fact remains that it is occasionally used as shorthand for unrest because of its proximity to violence. And so, we do need to discuss some of the ways in which ELT isn't just dishonest but is downright dangerous to the people in its path.

Notes

(1) One might use *official language*, but considering English isn't the official language in the United States, well, that wouldn't work.
(2) Including 'English as a new language', which to me is just as stigmatizing as 'ESL'.
(3) And they're not going to let me in after this…

Criterion 4

Irritability and aggressiveness, often with physical fights or assaults

When most people think of 'violence', they think of physical, tactile danger, and for good reason, as that is surely the primary connotation of the word. We often separate those classified as criminals into the buckets of 'violent' and 'non-violent', often reserving any meager systemic reforms for the latter group, the implication being that the former group has, in a sense, forfeited their right to remain included in our society. In Part 1, we discussed how certain groups are inherently categorized as more violent, and whose placement is reified by the pathologization attached to various aspects of their identities. *White-collar crime*, by contrast, is implied to be non-violent, even if various forms of financial malfeasance and corporate greed have absolutely imperiled the lives of many, not to mention the ongoing global environmental disaster that will come for all of us before too long. I say all this to say that most of us have a very clear understanding of what constitutes violence, and it is a very tangible concept, something that can and does cause us bodily harm and place us in danger. If we take this final point, the potential for danger, and extend it further, however, we might see two related things. First, we might consider how the ideologies embedded in whiteness can be psychologically damaging, even when they don't actually lead to death or injury, and second, that reifying these hierarchies does, in fact, lead to physical danger after all. In this chapter, then, I want us to consider the violence of whiteness, and how it is expressed, and supported, through the industry and the practice of English language teaching (ELT). We need to be clear in our understanding of the fact that the field, as currently constructed, is not merely exploitative and deceitful, as described in the previous chapters, but actively dangerous, not just in the metaphorical sense, but in the traditional fist-to-face version of violence with which we are most familiar and, frankly, comfortable. To illustrate these points, we are best served by returning to the subject of colonialism and its relationship to language.

As Fanon (1952) once taught us:

> Every colonized people – in other words, every people in whose soul an inferiority complex has been created by the death and burial of its local cultural originality – finds itself face to face with the language of the civilizing nation; that is, with the culture of the mother country. The colonized is elevated above his jungle status in proportion to his adoption of the mother country's cultural standards. (Fanon, 1952: 18)

He wrote of (and in) French, but the lessons are precisely the same for all colonial powers imposed upon an unwilling populace. The forced teaching of a language was hardly incidental to full occupation of a colony and, as we've mentioned, the hierarchies generated by relative valuation of skill with the imposed language remain harmful to this day; Fanon catalogues the perceived ranking of Black societies as demonstrated by the languaging and accents sought by their inhabitants. Like French, English has certainly been used to wield many different types of power, and the industry would not exist in its current form if there weren't an ongoing global pressure to achieve the status of 'English user'.

Some might argue, upon hearing this, that many millions of English students around the world are choosing to learn the language of their own accord, especially if they happen to be adults, and as such, to say that the industry is an extension of colonization is to deny them their full agency. If my point is that we shouldn't impose our hierarchies upon others, then am I not engaging in precisely the same behavior? To be clear, I am by no means, in this chapter or throughout the book, saying that no one should teach or study English – the language exists and, for all its issues, is worth learning like any other language. That's the key, though, that English should be treated like *any other language*, not positioned as an aspiration above most others, or classified as a neutral lingua franca. What's violent about ELT is not so much English itself, but all of the assumptions and ideologies swirling around it (and within it), how we go about teaching it and the conceptualizations the field seeks to uphold.

This discourse is, like the battles around native speakers, not particularly new in the field. Phillipson (1992) brought us the concept of *linguistic imperialism*, which is essentially what I have been describing above, the imposition of one more powerful language upon others. Canagarajah (1999) built upon this argument to advocate for how this practice can be fought against by those in the industry and, later, Phillipson (2008) returned to argue that his original idea was inextricable from the US and the UK's efforts at global economic and ideological dominance. As he wrote:

> There is a strong measure of wishful thinking in the projection of those who claim that English is 'the world's lingua franca,' since maximally

one-third of humanity have any competence in the language at all. Likewise, the notion that English is the language of science is contradicted by the fact that many other languages are used in higher education and research. But such discourse serves both to constitute and confirm English dominance and American empire, and the interlocking structures and ideologies that underpin 'global' English and corporate interests. Investing in the *linguistic capital* (Bourdieu & Wacquant, 1992) of English is a project that transcends national borders, with the product and processes privileging users of the language in the current world 'order'. (Phillipson, 2008: 4)

As we have seen many times thus far, the structures in place upon which we are dependent are a means of creating a dividing line between order and disorder, and, as Phillipson calls it, the *project* of ensuring that English retains its power is an important factor in the pathologization necessary to create a category out of which one can only hope to emerge by becoming a user of English.

What we might classify as 'traditional' violence requires language to retain its power. As Coates and Wade (2007: 511) explained: 'political power is linked to the management of information and the power of rhetoric. The ability of any group to advance its interests hinges in part on the group's ability to publicize its perspectives as more truthful or reasonable than others'. When power is thus concentrated within certain forms of languaging, those who are seen as capable of producing said language are not only allowed access to rights they will otherwise be denied, but would otherwise be told they are deserving of their oppression. It is not only fair that imperial languages be imposed upon a populace, for said languages have access to rhetoric and publicity on their own behalf, but any individual exercising the agency not to adopt said language is destined to be seen as farther from the social order. Fanon (1952) provided a pertinent example of this phenomenon:

> To speak a language is to take on a world, a culture. The Antilles Negro who wants to be white will be the whiter as he gains greater mastery of the cultural tool that language is. Rather more than a year ago in Lyon, I remember, in a lecture I had drawn a parallel between Negro and European poetry, and a French acquaintance told me enthusiastically, 'At bottom you are a white man.' The fact that I had been able to investigate so interesting a problem through the white man's language gave me honorary citizenship. (Fanon, 1952: 38)

As you will note, he is speaking of French as the colonial power in his experience, and you could certainly write a book about the history of that language similar to the one I'm writing. The hierarchies are similar, the exploitation extensive, yet I choose English not only because of my own background but also because, if we are speaking of power, then English and its current reach are unparalleled. Maybe someone will need to write this book about Mandarin or Arabic in a century, or maybe we will have dispensed with imperialism, linguistic or otherwise, by then. One can dream.

For the moment, though, we need to contend with the empire building from which whiteness has benefited, and one of the starkest examples of the violence of imposed English is the treatment of indigenous children in boarding schools across North America. The settlers had spent most of the 18th and 19th centuries alternating between land theft and outright genocide, but once the space was fully stolen, there were still plenty of indigenous people around. While in the process of removing their food sources, eventually a plan was hatched to eliminate 'the Indian' by educating the tribal culture out of them, and the replacement of tribal language with English was a central component of this process (National Native American Boarding School Healing Coalition, 2020).

What's notable about this scheme is that I am certain if you were able to speak to the white men who built these schools, you would be told that it was absolutely for these children's betterment to be forcibly assimilated into their version of society. As I've mentioned before, racialized colonial subjects were not seen as fully able, so these children's families were thus unfit to be entrusted with their care. They could not be both 'Indians' and (white) men at the same time, for the two words were delineated according to the values the latter group placed upon the former. The imposition of English and all of the customs of the culture by which they were surrounded were important factors in their ability to be transformed into 'men', yet, as you will not be surprised to learn, even if this wasn't already a cruel practice in the first place, it also didn't work.

The litany of deleterious health and social impacts for the students and families subsumed into these types of boarding schools in what they themselves might not even have referred to as the United States and Canada is long, and when they struggled to heal from the trauma, they were given little support (Bombay *et al.*, 2014). Indeed, it's almost offensive for me to refer to them as merely 'boarding schools' or 'residential schools' given the treatment that transpired there. As Coates and Wade (2007: 520) explained: 'the most harmful and abhorrent acts of violence are represented in the most ordinary and benign terms. The conventionality of these terms endows violent acts with an air of acceptability and obscures their real nature from the victim's point of view'. When we consider stories like these, then, the line between linguistic violence and the type of violence we all recognize as such is blurred, and deliberately so, because the imposition of power upon others is, as the antisocial criterion states, a sign of *irritability and aggressiveness*, whether it's through the removal of one's language or physical assault. Imperial power is not only inherently violent but also in need of language to remain in place, and that language itself has been used as a weapon against those unfortunate enough to get in the way of this insatiable growth.

One of the reasons, I would argue, that these plans and other such stories from the past and present are so harmful to their subjects is that they are ultimately based upon a lie. Racialized people who do exhibit markers of 'order', which in this case means particular languaging, often have relatively greater opportunities, and for some, that marginal improvement is enough to chase these slim chances. There is, however, no real escape from racialization, so even the most well-bred, perfectly dressed and, yes, articulate racialized person will still exist inside of their imposed identity, thereby rendering them deserving of subjugation. We are told that if we work hard and demonstrate skill, we will rise, thereby proving ideologies of meritocracy, but there is little evidence to suggest that that is actually true, and in fact, there is counter-evidence suggesting that believing in meritocracy is harmful to racialized children once they find out the truth (Wiederkehr *et al.*, 2015). Indeed, whiteness built a maze for us and told us English was an escape, but it's really just a trap.

I can see a possible critique of the points made above being that, even if I focused on history in Part 1, this portion of the book is primarily about the contemporary practice of ELT, so, as bad as these events were, the present-day industry isn't engaging in the same behavior, and as such can and should be severed from the sordid past. This might be a fair point if ELT had actually stopped engaging in forced assimilation and other tactics that are difficult to delineate from colonialism. Macedo (2000) was clear in pointing out that recent campaigns to institute English-only policies shared many characteristics with the past. As he wrote:

> Colonialism imposes 'distinction' as an ideological yardstick against which all other cultural values are measured, including language. On the one hand, this ideological yardstick serves to overcelebrate the dominant group's language to a level of mystification (i.e., viewing English as education itself and measuring the success of bilingual programs only in terms of success in English acquisition) and, on the other hand, it devalues other languages spoken by an ever-increasing number of students who now populate most urban public schools. (Macedo, 2000: 16)

These colonial ideologies are how we ended up with English-only policies in our language classrooms around the world, and the harm of English-only policies has been a frequent topic in the literature, as many readers are probably aware (e.g. de los Ríos *et al.*, 2019; Marschall *et al.*, 2011). I certainly believed in these English-only ideals as a novice teacher, and I barred my students from their natural languaging, to my ongoing regret. I believed all of the arguments, that if the goal of the instruction was to help the students 'acquire the target language', then they needed to be 'immersed' in English, and provided with constant, 'comprehensible input'. And if they don't produce enough language at the start, we just say they're in their 'silent period' or perhaps that their 'affective filter' has been raised. I'm being glib here about terminology that many ELT folks adore, but there is a throughline for all of these ideas: We are excellent at coming up with new words to describe the fact that our students are uncomfortable, and in fact we have, as an industry, convinced ourselves that this sort of stress is unavoidable, and perhaps advisable, in language learning.

These restrictive classroom language policies don't actually cause the exceptional growth that is promised. Indeed, as I mentioned above, English-only classrooms are harmful and, for those who are more swayed by such things, costly (Anderson, 2015). An example provided by Menken (2014) elaborates upon the ideologies and motivations behind such policies.

As this principal indicated, the 'correct way' to learn English, in his view, is through English-only instruction. He believed that bilingual education programs use too much of the students' home language in instruction and, therefore, fail to teach English. Like many others in the sample, this school is labeled low performing by the state due to the performance of emergent bilinguals on English medium tests – a problem this principal sought to turn around by eliminating the bilingual education program. (Menken, 2014: 165)

The fact that he can justify his decision by pointing to test results is a reminder that finances and capitalism are never far from the discussion; however, leaving that aside for a moment, this is not a new or isolated phenomenon. The contemporary mindset that considers students' home languaging to be an obstacle to English is tied directly to the ideologies that supported the cultural destruction of the past. We can claim to be focused on building English skills, but the practice of ELT does not respect the languaging of our students. Sure, we might not be literally abducting children to boarding schools these days, but we do make sure that present-day children feel uncomfortable and isolated in their classrooms now, and we create jargon to justify their understandable reactions.

Even if some of the aforementioned English-only particular policies are specific to my home country, let us not fool ourselves into thinking these practices are confined to our imaginary borders. Boarding schools were just as prominent in Canada, and the exact same process, complete with language destruction and replacement with English, happened in Australia too (Reconciliation Australia, n.d.). We tend to think of settler colonialism as being focused on the theft of land, and that is central to the scheme, but the destruction of languages is vital to the system, and unfortunately we have chosen to extend these ideologies into our classrooms around the world to this day. When we think of language and violence, then, we have to consider every aspect of their connection, from how language can help facilitate or obfuscate violence to how language teaching itself can be the violence visited upon a people. And when we pull back to see how all of this destruction is in service of ensuring that certain people are closer to the top of the pyramid than others, then the antisocial nature of whiteness and the practices that uphold it are clear.

We have whole new ways of knowing, learning and teaching now, and no reason to continue to uphold these archaic notions of languaging. Banning languages other than English from an adult classroom might not seem as cruel as some of the stories above, but it is merely a different, softer means to the same end goal. It is imperative that we eschew language boundaries in our classrooms as well as in our epistemology, because in a world controlled by whiteness, capitalism and colonialism, these boundaries become hierarchies with only the softest push.

As harmful as this violence is, though, it is hardly the only way that our current practices are dangerous. Especially for adult learners, plenty of students choose to study the language with every intention of using it to their advantage rather than having been conscripted into doing so. We should absolutely respect these students' agency and provide them with what they seek. Unfortunately, however, the product we offer is unlikely to deliver them to their desired destination, and may well leave them stranded.

Criterion 5

Reckless disregard for the safety of self or others

In a class on research in language education, my classmates and I were once asked to discuss whether or not 'standard' English existed. Some of us had backgrounds in language education, and some of us were brand new to the topic, but our perspectives didn't necessarily correlate with our particular disciplines. In our small-group discussion, I found myself straddling the line between two opposing points of view, both of which I found somewhat compelling but neither of which I felt told the whole story. One classmate was insistent that there was absolutely a (region-dependent) 'standard' English, whereas two other classmates dismissed the idea of 'standard' English altogether. For a bit more detail, the person who supported the idea of 'standard' English often stuck out as more conservative than the rest of us, whereas the other two had espoused leftist talking points at various times. They were, however, all white, and I think that matters for what I am about to say.

Where I stood, and continue to stand, even if I wasn't quite able to articulate it during that discussion, is that 'standard' English, be it British, American, Australian or any other flavor, was invented out of linguistic flotsam and jetsam, not too differently from the processes that gave us whiteness. It both does and doesn't exist the same way that whiteness and race are not biological facts yet have great impact on us all. I disagreed with my one classmate in that he didn't seem to want to challenge the standard, but I disagreed with my other two in that they, like a lot of white peers in discussions about race, wanted to dismiss an invented but harmful concept without taking the time to actively dismantle it. In other words, we can't just get rid of 'standard' English, or the standard language ideology altogether (Lippi-Green, 2012), by saying we refuse to recognize its existence, because far too many people depend on its perpetuation for that tactic to be effective. We need to examine how, as the *Diagnostic and Statistical Manual of Mental Disorders* (DSM) criterion states, 'standard' English and those who uphold it are demonstrating a *reckless disregard for the safety of themselves or others* before we can have any hope of diminishing its immense power.

Mohamad and Deterding (2018) provided a brief history of the emergence of what many now think of as 'standard' English, from the Great Vowel Shift, to the invention of the printing press, to the social dominance of the languaging of elites in both London and growing Northeastern American cities in the 18th and 19th centuries. Broadly speaking, there came to be a handful of 'standards', yet even within these countries, very few people spoke the idealized way. Nevertheless, a handful of more powerful varieties emerged as models for language teaching and became classified as regional 'standards', despite the fact that, for example, it has been estimated that only 3%–5% of people in the United Kingdom demonstrate received pronunciation (RP) (Mohamad & Deterding, 2018). These relatively rare varieties are held up as 'standards' and promoted through the media despite the fact that they don't particularly correspond to common languaging practices, and you can find the same trends with what is known as general American (GA) in the United States. It is suggested that these uncommon accents are the easiest to understand, yet, as Mohamad and Deterding (2018: 208) noted: 'it is not necessarily true that an RP accent is the most intelligible way of speaking in many parts of the world, as clearly articulated English in countries such as India and Singapore produced by well-educated speakers is probably more easily intelligible in many places'. Though I might quibble with the 'well-educated' part of this, the point is that supposedly objective attributes such as 'intelligibility' are purely subjective and tilted toward those who uphold the status quo; if there weren't an RP or a GA for learners to aspire to, much of the field would have to change drastically.

As far as whether or not a 'standard' exists, either there are so many 'standards' that you would need to parse the definition into minuscule localized classifications – e.g. standard Brooklyn African-American English, standard Miami Cuban English – or you can dispense with the idealization implied by the word 'standard' and use different descriptors. If you want to be cheeky, you might call infrequently used varieties like RP and GA something like *model* English, both because of their artificial prestige and because, like a model home, they are pristine and unlike anything close to the reality of most peoples' lives. Or, you can do as I've done in this book and other spaces, and acknowledge the prominence of these small but mighty dialects by calling them versions of *standardized* English, because, for the time being at least, they do have a tight hold on our field, to the detriment of everyone except the small number of people at the top of the pyramid.

The strenuous effort involved in language standardization means that almost everywhere you look, you can find artificial hierarchies positioned as helpful to those who somehow manage to wind up on the bottom of the heap. Students' home languaging practices are disparaged if they do not match the standard put forth in their schoolwork, despite the fact that that very schoolwork often fails to meet its stated goals of bringing their languaging in line with said standard. As De Cuba and Slocum (2020: 379) noted: 'current research has shown that deficit approaches are ineffective in helping students acquire "standard" varieties and can cause real harm to students'. Students who can be very easily understood and who can convey their intended meaning in the desired language are still seen as lacking because they don't match a model against which they are unfairly measured.

'Standard' English isn't always referred to as such, of course. Among the many acronyms in the previous chapter, you can find English for academic purposes (EAP), in which the focus is often on 'academic English'. Now, I want to be clear in saying that what passes for clear communication in academic writing is usually deeply unpleasant to consume, and more concerned with data reportage than any sort of prose.[1] Despite being a 'native' speaker with however many decades in exclusive American schools, I still can't write in the style of most academic articles. Frankly, I think assessments of academic writing are more about gatekeeping than any sort of quality, even for those of us who haven't learned the language later in life. In other words, even for people who aren't classified as lacking in English, the people who judge academic writing aren't the best evaluators. With all of that said, though, academic English is ubiquitous as a goal for students, even at institutions that might give lip service to respecting their natural languaging. As MacSwan (2018) explained:

> While research on Academic English (AE) sometimes includes a note affirming linguistic equality, its focus on the discourse and structural characteristics of AE nonetheless conveys the impression, wittingly or not, that there are special 'cognitively demanding' features of AE that are absent from out-of-school varieties, and in so doing it reinforces and perpetuates standard language ideology in teacher education. (MacSwan, 2018: 5)

A student can be in full command of their own communication but if their decisions in expressing themselves do not match what is idealized, their languaging is not only seen as different but also inferior.

These ideologies are hardly harmless. As one example, Sung (2018) found that, in a school with a mix of Latinx, Asian and Black students, the only way to demonstrate progress was to exhibit academic English, meaning both that Black students, despite mostly speaking English at home, were punished for perceived struggles with languaging, as well as many immigrant students having trouble escaping certain 'tracks' for similar reasons. Academic English is also interwoven into national language assessments (MacSwan, 2018), thereby disadvantaging anyone who communicates differently, all with the implied justification that these students will need to use this uncommon dialect if they have any hope of being accepted by those who created it.

Lest we think this is a purely American phenomenon, Cushing (2020) found that the same ideologies are in use in the United Kingdom, even if the idealized forms are slightly different. In analyzing policy documents from English primary schools, he wrote the following:

> Policies here imply that (a) it is universally understood what is meant by '"standard" English', (b) all teachers and students are speakers of standardised (British) English and (c) and that this is the exclusively legitimate form of the classroom. Such policies fail to distinguish between the complexities of different genres and contexts of talk, with a blanket requirement for the use of spoken standardised English 'at all times'. Despite its textual prevalence, not a single policy offered their own definition of standardized English, and so consequently, teachers are permitted to enact any existing biases they may hold about standardised/non-standardised language in their classroom practice. (Cushing, 2020: 7)

This is not meant to point the finger directly at teachers, but considering we are all trained with these ideologies, then we are positioned as enforcers of linguistic hierarchies, even if we tell ourselves we are providing a service that benefits our students.

The word Cushing uses in that passage, 'legitimate', is important to consider, because ultimately what these ideologies do is render certain forms acceptable and others disposable and in need of correction. Yet, legitimacy is both power and context dependent. As Reagan (2019: 29) pointed out: 'a particular language variety may be considered "legitimate" in one setting, but less so in another. Standard American English (SAE) is "legitimate" in school settings, but may be marked and considered "non-legitimate" in some other settings – for instance, at a family reunion'. Notably, a family reunion or another similar context is likely to be a place in which people are comfortable. Nevertheless, we perpetuate the idea that the language demanded in *uncomfortable* contexts is the only language that we will allow ourselves to accept, and that the distance between this effortful languaging and whatever people choose without external pressure is evidence of a deficiency in a person (or a people), rather than the system that created the standards in the first place. Additionally, with so much of the scholarship from mainstream sources focused on assessment and 'improving' students' performance, it becomes a greater challenge to dispute these ideologies, because there is less supposedly empirical evidence for the legitimacy of unstandardized English. Yes, to speak and write and communicate in ways that diverge from the standard is to potentially risk worse performance on assessments, and because of this, many educators and schools fret about focusing on more affirming approaches to language teaching, an understandable approach created by the fear upon which those in power depend. I cannot honestly say there is no risk in choosing to ignore the pressure of 'standard' or academic English, but would it not be fair to say that continuing to perpetuate the status quo is risking students' well-being right now?

'Standard' English is a multifaceted attack on the languaging of the racialized, present as it is in both policy and practice, and despite its insistence on the construction of linguistic borders, it is hardly constrained by *national* borders. If we bring this back to our earlier discussion of English as a foreign language (EFL), then, we can see that these ideologies become a profitable international export, right up there with movies, music and missiles. Assessments in countries where standard American or British English is even more exceptionally rare still depend upon these forms as models. In South Korea, for example, standardized English tests determine economic futures to a disproportionate degree, and while these exams are considered technically sound (i.e. valid and reliable), there is little evidence that they actually correlate with improved skill (Kim *et al.*, 2019). Instead of the goal being linguistic development, the test score itself becomes the prize, as it is the only pathway to increased income, and with these students being well aware of this reality while also knowing quite clearly that 'standard' English has little bearing on their daily lives, they are often demotivated by this linguistic imposition. As Kim *et al.* (2019: 103) explained: 'The jobseekers objectify their learning results, and submit them into the neoliberal job market, waiting to exchange it with material profit. In the course of such score-building competition, the English tests turn into the ends in themselves and spawn stress and demotivation unconducive to learning'. Once again, even if the linguistic imperialism of the global EFL industry wasn't troubling from a moral standpoint, it also simply doesn't succeed at its stated goals. To put it another way, clearly these students are more familiar with a certain version of English than they would be if these tests weren't so impactful for their futures, but even if they do attain high scores, what many of them have developed is an antagonistic relationship with a language that they only need because they've been forced to depend upon it for the ceaseless growth that denotes professional success. You don't need 'standard' or academic English to live a modest life in a country where few people use the language at home, but you do need to be familiar with these uncommon forms if you want to compete on the global market. And isn't that what learning a language is all about, defeating and out-earning other people?

These exams are hardly unique to EFL contexts, of course. Universities in English-dominant countries also employ English tests for international students, whether it's the test of English for international communication (TOEIC), the test of English as a foreign language (TOEFL), the international English language testing system (IELTS) or some other version of alphabet soup. All of these exams are predicated upon the dual notions that there is an ideal form of the language and that students should be able to approximate and/or recognize it as such in order to be included in an educational community. It's not difficult to figure out why entrance exams are so tied to the idea of a 'standard'. As Jenkins and Leung (2019: 103) wrote: 'conceptualizing English as a stable and enduring phenomenon provides for a long(er) shelf-life for language tests as products, and obviates the need for regular revision and re-development, which are expensive'. You see, it's just cheaper and easier to stick with what's been making the system its money. In this way, English is less of a means of communication and more of a product to be purchased and refined. Surely, English has little to do with daily communication in many contexts where it nonetheless has a stranglehold on university entrance and particular career paths, and 'standard' English rarely comes into play even in countries where most use a version of English. We are required to support an ideal that renders most people inherently inferior by virtue of their identity, and even when people do manage to produce the requested forms without error, they might well be stigmatized based on the perception of their supposedly exotic accent (Orelus, 2020). For as long as standardized English reigns, there will be almost no escape from the way it pathologizes most languagers, and its prominence in the project of upholding both capitalism and whiteness is troublesome, leaving us with few options but to fight all three at once.

We have seen how 'standard' English is uncommon, often irrelevant and even demotivating, divorced as it is from peoples' daily needs. It represents, as the criterion states, a *reckless disregard* for learners' safety, since its centrality is more destructive than it is productive. For a moment, though, I want to briefly entertain a counterargument I have come across occasionally, namely the fact that, even despite all of this, it might still be useful for there to be a 'standard', just so that there are rules and regulations to impart to learners. What would be contained in textbooks and other course materials if there were no standardization at all? And, what language am I even using to write this book if not a version of standard American English?

It would indeed be messy and chaotic if we attempted to teach English without standardization. Assessment would be deeply challenging, perhaps rendered irrelevant, and jobs and schools would have to develop entirely new methods of evaluating suitability for hiring and placement. Without standardization, there wouldn't be much of a reason for countries to import 'native' speakers as language models, and indeed there might not be 'native' speakers at all. Technically, this means this book wouldn't exist, because my career options after college wouldn't have included going to South Korea to teach English without qualifications, and I thus would never have decided to pursue the field. Ultimately, though, when I think of why we depend on standardization, my suspicion is that we believe we need it because otherwise we wouldn't know what was the 'right' way to communicate in a given context; by extension, we wouldn't be able to point our fingers at who is 'wrong'. If an unstandardized language teaching field sounds preposterous to you, please do understand that what we're doing now barely makes sense unless you believe in the many harmful ideologies upon which our system is based. Standardization 'works' only insofar as it is successful at burnishing its own image and concentrating power in the hands of a few. If your hands have been among those few, as mine were when I was an unqualified 21-year-old teacher, then it's time we take the limited power we have individually and build collective power against the hegemony of standardization and all of the hierarchies it represents. And yes, I am indeed writing to you in what is mostly standardized American English, but I do what I can to make this language my own, and I reject the trappings and the jargon of academic English as often as possible; we can absolutely teach language students to do the same.

With all of this said, though, there is another dimension of standardization that I have only briefly mentioned here. Academic English in particular is largely focused on the written form, but when it comes to speech, perfect accuracy will get you nowhere if you live inside of a racialized body; you will always be seen as a member of the group into which you have been classified. One of the most insidious ways that the field of English language teaching (ELT) ensures the pathologization of the majority is through its treatment of accents and, even worse, its insistence upon silencing the authentic voices of those who just don't sound the right way.

Note

(1) Not that what constitutes 'good' prose is an objective measurement.

Criterion 6

*Consistent irresponsibility, failure to sustain consistent work behavior,
or honor monetary obligations*

Before I begin, I know I said I wasn't going to do this every time, but can we just pause and consider the absurdity of the wording of this criterion? Ignoring the fact that *recklessness* (from the previous criterion) and *irresponsibility* are essentially synonymous, the implication here is that anyone who *fails to sustain consistent work behavior* is that much closer to being classified as antisocial. I'm not sure I need to explain to you that members of particular groups are systematically excluded from the workforce, but by this metric, an assessment might be able to use a spotty employment history as evidence for what is considered a severe personality disorder. I understand the criterion in theory, as people who struggle to conform to professional standards are unlikely to stay employed, but said 'professional standards' are, in turn, constructed around an idealized identity. In other words, this criterion exemplifies the underlying point of this whole book, namely the fact that the people who are pathologized for one reason or another are then considered deserving of their oppression by those who are invested in maintaining the boundaries between order and disorder. Pathologization is an almost inescapable trap maintained by a system that is itself pathological when assessed according to its own parameters. But let's get back to language teaching, and a way in which it fails to *honor monetary obligations*. I think there are many examples of the ways that English language teaching (ELT) qualifies for this, but for this chapter, I wanted to focus on accents and the egregious, empty subfield built around eliminating them.

In looking for academic articles on accent reduction, the internet algorithms took over my browser and I started receiving ads for companies that promised to help me sound the right way. I really had been planning to build this around traditional sources, but I admit I had never actually spent time looking at what these companies offered their clients, and it seemed appropriate to investigate. What I found was that not only was accent reduction built on a faulty premise, but that also it is very expensive. Allow me to demonstrate.

If you visit the website for a company called 'Accent Advisor', you will be told[1] that there are three packages available. The 'best value' is $18 per 25-minute lesson, with lessons three times a week, or $54/week. The 'most popular option' is $19.50 per lesson, with lessons twice a week ($39/week). And the third option, called 'Lite', is $24 per lesson, once a week. If you can't make up your mind, the single lesson has a sad van in the background, the middle option has an airplane and the 'best value' has a satellite, because your accent will be reduced... astronomically? (Accent Advisor, n.d.). It goes without saying that despite their assurances that these prices are affordable, only a small number of people can afford to pay $25–$54 a week over several months to 'correct' what isn't actually a problem.

Consider what are they actually offering their clients. Their tagline is: 'We help people speak with an American accent'. I'm sure it's not a Chicano accent or a Southern Black accent, despite those being American. 'Speak Confidently', they promise. 'Many foreigners have a wide variety of speaking patterns that seem strange to Americans. Our coaches can help you understand these potential areas of difficulty. You'll learn a wide variety of tones that help you put the right feelings behind the things you say'. Yikes. But I can't just pick on 'Accent Advisor' because they are only one of ever so many.

'Accents Off',[2] with a tagline of 'Speech and Voice Improvement' (Accents Off, n.d.) commands its potential clients to 'Be clear, be confident, be heard', and says that by signing up with them, you can 'realize your potential in business and in life'. In business, eh? These companies feign toward equity, of course; it's bad optics if you don't. 'Accents Off' asks: 'What's wrong with having an accent? Nothing! Accents contribute to our global diversity'. But then they say: 'In today's competitive job market, clear communication is an asset high on every employer's priority list'. I hope you're noticing how frequently the language of capitalism appears in these promotions, not to mention the implication than 'an accent' is something that is inherently foreign.

There's a clue about the deceit at the core of this concept though. On the same page as the previous passage, 'Accents Off' includes the following: 'Your native accent will always be a part of who you are. You can switch back into your original accent whenever you want – but eliminating the "hard edges" of your non-native accent will make for a much smoother cultural and professional transition'. So, first of all, we are deeply mired in the native/non-native binary, but that is to be expected of companies in this space. Second, it's clear that this entire enterprise is based around the idea that assimilation into societal norms is the pragmatic approach. Third, 'hard edges' is a deeply stigmatizing way to describe someone's speech, and finally, the fact that they say clients can 'switch back into' their normal speech patterns is rather telling of the fact that, despite their name, they aren't actually offering to, in their parlance, take their accents 'off'. If anything, this subfield is, at best, teaching people how to perform a new accent, the way that a professional actor might when preparing for a role. For actors, they tend to call this *dialect coaching*, and that can absolutely be conducted in a respectful way; for these students, however, companies are preying upon their implied fears of financial instability to sell them expensive reinforcement of the fact that their own speech is less valuable, with zero engagement of the reality that it is, of course, the *white perceiving subject* (Flores & Rosa, 2015) who has done the devaluing.

There are further clues to the troubles with so-called 'accent reduction' throughout the websites of this company and other similar ones. 'Sankin Speech Improvement' pitches its services accordingly: 'Are you tired of people asking, "Where are you from?" Have people said, "Welcome to the US" even though you have lived here for over ten years? Are you often asked to repeat yourself? Do you feel that others are distracted by the way that you speak and therefore are not listening to what you are saying?' (Sankin Speech Improvement, n.d.). These are real, painful and all-too-common experiences for people who are classified as outside the boundaries of 'native' speech, but the solution is not for the people on the receiving end of this treatment to seek help for a problem that resides within them. Paying for someone to tell you what's wrong with your accent isn't going to make the white perceiver any more patient with you.

With all this said, these sorts of companies aren't actually the root of the problem. They are charging considerable fees based on the wrong issue, *failing to honor their monetary obligations* by stigmatizing certain accents without challenging the hierarchy upon which they depend, which will inevitably leave their clients vulnerable to the same raciolinguistic ideologies that have always been their true obstacles. Unfortunately, though, these companies are just branches of a larger tree. They wouldn't be able to promote themselves accordingly if there wasn't some sort of academic support for these practices, and indeed, it's not just private academies pushing 'accent reduction': universities do it too. Florida International University (FIU), located in a city (Miami) full of varied and valuable accents, offers these same services to 'students who are proficient in most aspects of English (reading, vocabulary, and listening comprehension) but who sometimes avoid speaking with native English speakers because they fear being misunderstood due to their foreign accents or pronunciation errors' (Florida International University, n.d.). It's one thing for private firms to try to make money in ways that I think uphold harmful ideologies, and quite another for a school to push the same concepts on their students. Even worse, they couch it in aspects of 'formal' linguistics, supporting their promotion with references to the phonetic alphabet, but, as ever, 'self-confidence' is centered in the pitch.

Best I can tell, the 'accent reduction industrial complex' formula seems to be:

(1) Remind potential clients of painful experiences they might have had.
(2) Promise them more confidence (and money) by learning to mimic a 'standard' accent.
(3) Give lip service to the fact that their normal speech is okay, but...
(4) Convince them that they have no chance without signing up and...
(5) Profit! (Even if you're nominally a non-profit educational institution, as the FIU program costs $649–$699.)

The specific case of Florida International was used in an article on the ways in which these endeavors reify the hierarchies among international students. The authors were even clever enough to use FIU's slogan of cheery stigmatization – 'Come Join Us and Lose Your Accent!' – as the title of their work. The authors demonstrate that the way that accent is conceptualized by FIU and other schools renders it something of a disorder, though one that the schools are clear isn't an official dis/ability, if only so they can ensure that financial support will not be provided. Nevertheless, these schools insist that students should not expect to be able to 'fix' their accents by themselves. As they explained: 'One consequence of accent being pathologized in ways described above is the impossibility of a natural or independent recovery. In other words, the implication of a "condition" as complicated as accent seems to be that it can only be treated under the supervision and guidance of a professional' (Ennser-Kananen *et al.*, 2021: 331). Not only do these students have an inherent deficit, but it is also a deficit that only the people who invented the deficit can resolve, which is actually true, in a fashion, because finding a solution to this pathologization is the duty of those responsible for the existence of the pathology.

It is important to note that this isn't merely an argument borne of the theories and frameworks I favor, nor just from my own experience. The ideologies that impact the treatment of the racialized have been identified empirically. Zheng and Samuel (2017) attempted to determine where the disconnect was when it comes to accent, that is, did people genuinely *hear* something different when they saw a racialized face, or did they *interpret* the same set of sounds differently? They took great pains to choose model speakers with voices of similar pitch, recorded them pronouncing the same set of words and then used three different kinds of software to equalize the sounds. The only things that were different about the recordings were the speakers' faces. At first, they found that the participants had sensed they were being tested on these biases, and had adjusted their responses accordingly, which is sort of funny. But, after conducting more than five different experiments, what they eventually found was the following: 'Collectively, in contrast with previous claims about how the ethnicity of a face affects the perception of accentedness, the evidence provided in the current study indicates that visual information influences people's interpretation of accentedness, but not their actual perception of accentedness' (Zheng & Samuel, 2017: 1857). The authors are using *perception* here to mean hearing, and contrasting it with what they are calling *interpretation*, in their words, *decision-level bias*. In other words, the participants don't necessarily see an Asian face and immediately think 'accent'; they hear an accent that is attached to an Asian face and make decisions accordingly. That, to me, is much more intractable than the alternative, putting the lie to any discussion of an 'unconscious bias'. Raciolinguistic ideologies aren't random or innate, and accent-based oppression is a conscious, cruel choice, one that all the deceitful 'accent reduction' courses in the world won't resolve.

There are significant consequences for those lower in the hierarchy of accents. Some of the consequences seem mundane, like the fatigue mentioned by the participants in one study. As Kim *et al.* (2019b: 79–80) explained: 'In addition to experiencing fatigue because of having to work in a language that is not their native one, nonnative speakers also experienced fatigue from constantly monitoring their own actions and thinking about how their actions will be interpreted or evaluated by others'. To paraphrase Morrison (1975) from Part 1, all of these axes of oppression are distractions; this sort of fatigue is hardly conducive to performing your very best at work. One can imagine quite clearly how feeling this fatigue could contribute to poor evaluations and thus lead to fewer opportunities for advancement, yet because nothing blatant or acute has been alleged, all observers might see is a person who is struggling and treated appropriately for it. That article goes on to share that so-called native speakers also feel fatigue, but not about their own identities; instead, they feel fatigue from having to strain to understand unfamiliar accents. One could easily choose to view this as a two-sided problem, but in fact, because of the inherent power differential, it will always be the 'native' whose fatigue is prioritized, and if it's too much work for them to have to understand the unfamiliar, it won't be them that suffer the consequences.

Vijay Ramjattan has done considerable work on accents and their connection to racialization in language education. In one article, Ramjattan (2018: 1) expands the concept of *aesthetic labor* – 'how the bodies of workers are styled by management in order to visually appeal to customers' – into the realm of speech, and particularly with respect to accents. As he wrote: 'even though it is rarely mentioned, ELT also consists of aesthetic labour in the sense of its workers needing to aurally appeal to customers' (Ramjattan, 2018: 5). Because ELT is as tied to capitalistic pursuits as any other field, certain accents are positioned as more marketable, and those who do not possess such accents are thus required to perform additional labor to be seen as equal to their white counterparts. Returning to the accent reduction branch of the field, Ramjattan (2019a, b) wrote of how, based on the perceived hierarchy of nations and names, both of which are, of course, tied to racialization, clients are urged, though never explicitly so, to reduce their accents in the hopes of counteracting their racialization. Companies and schools can market this process as a pure financial benefit, but because of the dishonesty inherent in refusing to grapple with the fact that the only actual problem with these accents is the unfamiliarity of the white listener, only the rare student who can effectively mimic the desired accent may yet see the boon they've been promised.

As with many of the issues I mention, my hands are not clean. Indeed, I once dabbled in trying to alter my students' accents. I didn't call it 'accent reduction' or anything, and I considered it teaching pronunciation, but there's a difference between showing students how words are commonly said and trying to change the way they're saying the words even if you can understand them just fine. I considered it my duty to provide them with this service, and I even came up with fun ideas for working on intonation and prosody. We practiced singing a Stevie Wonder song, and we learned the poem *The Night Before Christmas*, which in retrospect was not a great idea with respect to religious inclusion, but I thought they would enjoy it, and they seemed to. These were adult learners, mostly from China, and, as I understood it, they had enrolled in what was ultimately a shady, for-profit 'college' to try and acquire a certificate that they didn't yet know was meaningless. I had worked out by this point that the school was up to no good, but I needed the job, and I figured that the real value I could provide to the students was being innovative in the way I taught them how to pronounce words. Unfortunately, I really did evaluate them on how close they came to approximating what I considered a 'native' accent. I had them practice speaking into my phone's microphone and seeing how well the phone understood what they were saying. As you can see, I had yet to learn that the problem wasn't within these students, but in the phone manufacturers[3] having built their systems around a standardized voice. The problem wasn't within these students, but in the employers who may well have ignored their applications once they graduated. The problem wasn't within these students, but in the school that told them they were deficient, and in a field where that was the norm.

A lot of language teachers, myself included, read the work of Paulo Freire during their training, but I'm not sure how well we actually internalize his lessons. Most of us still seem to believe in what he calls the *banking system* of education (Freire, 1970), wherein we teachers are the sources of knowledge pouring ourselves into the empty vessel students. I know I once thought, much as I came to love and respect the students in my classes, that my accent was just a little 'better', and that I was setting a useful example for those who learned from me. So when it comes to accents, how many of us truly reject the idea that it is desirable for English learners to adopt a certain manner of speech? Even if we don't espouse it explicitly, our field still embraces these hierarchies, and as such, by not challenging these practices, by allowing otherwise respectable institutions to carry on making money off of accent-based fear, we remain complicit in one of the ugliest parts of ELT. We'll get to how to push back against whiteness in ELT in Part 3, but just know that the full eradication of not just the 'accent reduction' subfield, but the ideas on which it is based, is one of the most straightforward remedies for what ails our discipline. With that said, as nice as an ELT without 'accent reduction' would be, it would hardly be cured of the pathology of whiteness, because our field's issues are much bigger than any of what I've written in these six chapters. No matter what I have argued that the field has done and continues to do, much of this could be improved if the field was remorseful for its actions, yet, on the contrary, ELT is extremely proud of the damage it has done, and that is perhaps the most antisocial thing of them all.

Notes

(1) As of summer 2021.
(2) What a name!
(3) Who may well have been in China, of course.

Criterion 7

> *Lack of remorse, being indifferent to or rationalizing having hurt, mistreated or stolen from another person*

If you refer back to the 'Key Concepts' section of the Introduction, I explained why I believe it's best to avoid using the word 'minorities' when referring to racialized people, not only because it is often inaccurate, but also because it flattens the historical and present-day power differential between said groups. Well, the same argument can and should be applied to a few of the newer terms used to describe English. I referred to 'English as a lingua franca' in my chapter on acronyms, but this is also relevant for 'English as an international language' or even 'world Englishes'. All of these terms essentially classify English as a friendly bridge between people of different cultures or nations, the same way that, when people argue against the profit motive in English language teaching (ELT), others point out that English is, in fact, the language used in certain types of commerce. It's true that people with different home languages will sometimes use English to connect as peers, and it's true that certain types of business are chiefly conducted in English, but these facts gloss over the trauma involved in creating these scenarios, and even ignore the problem with any one language taking precedent over another. Sometimes we speak of this language as though it was handed down from on high and is thus a gift we are providing to students who are in dire need of access to communication, but nothing about the relative dominance of English is pure happenstance.

Someone once told me that they thought the teaching of English was inherently a racist act, and I was taken aback because it seemed impossible for the act of teaching to perpetuate such dire harm. The more I thought about it though, the more I considered it. Every time I traveled down a different epistemological corridor to debunk this incendiary assertion, I kept returning to the fact that ELT, as we know it, was a plan, and that the hierarchies under which we operate and which we are furthering, were orchestrated by those invested in the maintenance of the categorizations that rendered them more relatively powerful. Let's take a look at a particular aspect of language education that will hopefully demonstrate what I mean when I speak of orchestration, namely the practice of *language planning* that determines aspects of education policy at a national level.

Decades ago, Carol Eastman (1990) shared her assessment of how post-apartheid South Africa might best handle language instruction. Among other observations, she wrote: 'In post-apartheid South Africa, this would mean to opt for English as the medium of instruction while at the same time encouraging first languages in homes, neighborhoods, and regional activities. Functioning politically, official languages and languages used in the schools will be part of one's national identity regardless of an individual's level of proficiency' (Eastman, 1990: 8). That all sounds great, and part of her argument is that English is a better option than Afrikaans because of local citizens' preference for the former, but what we still have here is a *slightly* more entrenched colonial language being recommended as the primary means of official communication. She is not recommending that instruction be planned in local languages, even if she says they should be encouraged outside of school. As such, the colonial power spreads, even if it's British rather than Dutch. I mention this not so much to be critical of Eastman, considering it was 1990,[1] but to draw a throughline across decades of language planning in disparate contexts and nations.

A decade later, Jung and Norton (2002: 245) examined how the national policy on English instruction had evolved in South Korea, owing to, as ever, English's central role in 'current international trade and computer communication'. In the late 1990s, South Korea began to introduce the language to students earlier than it had been, and officials also changed the focus of their English instruction from grammar and writing to oral production, a policy change that I can't pretend didn't eventually lead to my own presence in the country. The authors asked teachers their opinion of the changes, and whereas many teachers saw English as *an* international language, only some saw it as *the* international language or a language deserving of its centrality in their curriculum. Additionally, as Jung and Norton (2002: 264) wrote: 'In schools with adequate support, and where teachers themselves believe that English instruction is important, the conditions for effective language instruction exist. For some, however, this success comes at a heavy price, if the Korean language and Korean educational policies are compromised'. Once again, English is essentially a financially valuable and intractable fact of life that can be approached from different angles but will remain centered because those in charge have determined that students need English to be included in the modern world, and other languages suffer accordingly. As Chen *et al.* (2019: 2) noted: 'This also leads to knowledge production that is dependent on English-speaking academia, so that English is colonizing the rest of the world'. Indeed, the fact that I am mostly writing within an academic space, and of course with largely standardized English, means I am to some extent contributing to this ongoing colonization project, as are all of your favorite journals and the tenure requirements upon which even the most radical of scholars might depend. I hope only that my work can serve as a bit of a 'poison pill' for English-dominant academia, so that editors will seek out reviewers from many linguistic backgrounds and begin to accept submissions in several languages, and people like me will later be forced to engage with other means of languaging to build their knowledge instead of being able to rest on the language they were born into.

The close bond between English and capitalism means that language planning and developmental aid are inextricable from one another as well. Donors and agencies from the Global North see funding English instruction as a way to 'help' colonized people, but, as Erling (2017) found when examining such practices in Bangladesh, this supposed aid does little to curb broader inequality, and may in fact reify the hierarchies that are already in place. As she wrote: 'we found that even in very rural Bangladeshi communities facing quite severe development challenges there were strong perceptions that English would be of value for people in terms of widening their economic and social opportunities' (Erling, 2017: 13). There isn't enough room in this book to provide a specific history of Bangladeshi colonization and exploitation,[2] but we see here the same pattern that has recurred in every instance of language planning that centers English: regardless of how it came to be so, English is seen as one of the best ways out of a bad situation, even for people who are unlikely to use the language in their daily activities. Erling (2017: 14–15) continued by adding: 'English should not be held up as a panacea for employability and poverty. How English may be accentuating gaps between the more and less privileged must be considered in further language planning initiatives and public debates about language policy if they are truly to contribute to holistic development'. As Erling makes clear, funding global English instruction can be helpful to *individuals*, but does not support full communities or groups of people. Ultimately, it creates a class of people who can demonstrate a certain type of languaging and are thus more deserving of support, and other people who, for reasons tied to various aspects of their identities and abilities, are meant to be left behind. Promoting English around the world essentially creates a lottery system wherein a few can hope to be given access to great opportunity and everyone else will be told they need to labor for the handful who have ascended more effectively than they have.

We have found ourselves in a situation in which it is unavoidably true that producing standardized English from inner-circle countries is potentially lucrative for individuals, and that those who do not demonstrate this capability have even less hope of the sort of rapacious economic growth that we promote as 'economic opportunity'. In places where

English has been positioned as the language of government – including education – being perceived as lacking in English is a significant obstacle, and even for those who acquire the proscribed forms, if an individual doesn't deliver the language in a way that pleases the unmentioned perceiver, it may thus remain a barrier to achievement. Unqualified emissaries of colonial powers are transported around the world to promote the language into which they were born, and are in turn exploited both by their employers who consider them interchangeable and by an industry that depends on their ascribing to the ideology that their identity makes them uniquely suited for the role. When confronted with potential issues, the field makes superficial, inconsequential changes to jargon and terminology, but continues to perpetuate the myth that it is beneficial to all who have little choice but to seek its aid, all the while ignoring the brutality of its past and present. A handful of people benefit financially, but at heart, the true beneficiary is the system that subsists upon that same pyramid of pathologization that renders so many groups disordered and subordinate to the ideal we are all urged to chase.

Individual English teachers surely feel conflicted about the impact of colonialism on their work, and not all of us are cheerleaders for capitalism or 'standard' English. There are many pushing against the field we've been given, plenty of whom are cited across these pages, and I have a certain amount of hope that these critical messages are traveling farther than they used to. However, even if you or I may indeed be uncomfortable with what English has wrought, can you honestly say that the broader field of ELT, what with its epistemology, its business model and its raciolinguistic ideologies, is genuinely remorseful for what it has become? I ask you this directly: would ELT ever change its ways naturally or, without us working against its harmful practices, would it not continue to perpetuate oppression without interruption? The truly antisocial part of our field isn't just that it leads to destruction, but that it has no remorse for the damage it causes for its own gain. Ultimately, I put forth to you that we may never be able to successfully challenge this power if we don't understand the fact that none of this would be possible if it weren't for the way that whiteness is centered in ELT.

Without whiteness as a silent but salient centerpiece, the power of the images and ideals promoted to students worldwide would be severely diminished, and the stigmatization of languagers would be far less effective without an oft-implicit point of comparison. Without the way that whiteness is tied into concepts of ability, we might struggle to convince people that their unstandardized languaging is evidence of a deficit. If whiteness weren't present, there would be much less pressure to suppress one's natural methods of communication and conform to an ideal that exists chiefly to shame, but because it is, our field remains an instrument of pathologization, positioned as a mythical respite for the people to whom it has provided no legitimate means of escape. We need to directly confront the structures of whiteness, in our field, in our classrooms and in our lives, if we have any hope of an ELT that loves the people it claims to serve. But how can one even conceive of attempting such a monumental task, and what would that even look like for language teachers? Well...

While I can't say I've come anywhere close to solving the problem, I have in fact been trying in my own small way. If you want to learn what I found out in working on issues of whiteness with language teachers, and are interested in taking the steps they did at their institutions, read on to Part 3.

Notes

(1) I am sure some of what I have written here will look silly in the 2050s. And that's good!
(2) Just ask yourself who is making your inexpensive clothes and why they are so inexpensive (Tripathi, 2015).

Part 3
Treatment...?

The Ezel Project

As many of you are surely familiar with, when you apply to most American doctoral programs, you are asked to write about a 'problem' you want to try and address. In our case, we had to write about it not only in our application but again when we arrived on campus for our group interview, for which my illegible handwriting was an obstacle, but apparently not enough of one to keep me from being accepted. In my case, I was a few years removed from my role managing the adult education program at a nonprofit,[1] and I thought I had a better chance of being accepted if I focused on some sort of numerical metric. Accordingly, I initially wrote about trying to improve attendance in free or low-cost community language programs, thinking, cynically, that if I could somehow figure out a solution to this phenomenon, every community language program would want to speak to me about how to address the issue. In our very first class, taught by our doctoral program's director, we were taught the basics of being Doctor of Education (EdD) students, and one of our initial lessons was to focus on articles published in the previous 10 years to ensure our citations were more relevant. While looking around for qualifying articles about attendance and community programs, I came upon an interesting piece of scholarship that got me thinking about this supposed problem from a very different angle.

Coming in just inside of the 10-year guidelines we'd received (this was the fall of 2018), Schalge and Soga (2008) interviewed students who had dropped out of a community education program to inquire about their reasoning, as well as interviewing their teachers and administrators. My own assumption up to this point had been that students left for logistical reasons (e.g. a lack of childcare), and that is indeed what the teachers and administrators in the study had assumed as well. As it turns out, according to the students themselves, many of them had left because they felt ignored and disrespected by the well-meaning staff, who, when presented with this information by the researchers, continued to dismiss this possibility. I found this interesting, and it got me thinking about why they'd refuse to engage with what their own dissatisfied students had said, but it was the only such article I was able to find, because tracking down students who have left free programs is understandably difficult.

It was shortly after this, in the next semester, that I was introduced to the concepts of raciolinguistic ideologies and translanguaging, and my lens began to expand, which led to my realizations about my students' having considered themselves 'bad at English'. Though too few doctoral programs encourage students to do such a thing, I started reaching out to scholars whose work I admired, and made a point of speaking to some of them in person when I went to a massive international education conference in Toronto. I didn't have a clue what I was going to do with all of the ideas that were starting to take root in my brain, but I knew I needed to start engaging with the public in some fashion.

For a class assignment, I created a very small-scale survey about race and language teaching, in which I asked some of my classmates from my old master's program if they included race in their lessons. A few said no, and a few said yes, but among the latter group, some instead referred to 'culture' repeatedly, which I took note of. Additionally, one of the questions asked if they had studied race in their training as language teachers, and many of the respondents said that they had, which surprised me, considering we had more or less the same training and we absolutely had not discussed race in our program beyond a stray essay by Franz Fanon. I began to feel like an epistemological boulder was closing in on me, and it was becoming clear, both from what I was learning in class and from the dispiriting conversations I was having with (white) language teachers, that there was something I needed to do that was bigger than improving attendance at community programs. There was such reluctance to even consider race – let alone racism – with almost every language person I knew, but I was reluctant to really focus on that intersection because I didn't want to be pigeonholed as a 'race guy'. Funny how these things turn out.

While I was at that same conference in Toronto, I went to a presentation about dis/ability and language learners, and part of said presentation included racist quotes from teachers who were study participants. With the scholar's permission, I posted a picture of a slide on Instagram, adding the caption, 'Wow, teachers can be gross'. As you can see, in this caption, there is nary a mention of race, but a friend's wife (a K12 teacher) materialized in my mentions to castigate me about the value of teachers, with the implication being, since I have mostly taught adults, that I was not one. Among her comments was the phrase, 'teachers work hard', positioned as a defense against the unstated implication that teachers can perpetuate racism. Now, you can decide for yourself why she might have felt the need to defend the honor of (white) teachers without being addressed, but that surprising encounter got me thinking about why someone's supposed hard work would preclude racism, which aligned with the Schalge and Soga article wherein the teachers positioned their good intentions as something of a shield from the students' criticism. And so there it was, a clear idea, and I began to write toward theorizing what you've seen me refer to as the *altruistic shield*, and I carried that idea, as well as the presentation, article (Gerald, 2020a) and eventually a full chapter (Gerald, 2022), into the next stage of my evolving scholarship. Inspired by *The Vocal Fries* and encouraged by my wife, who was tired of absorbing my random tangents, I also created a podcast (*Unstandardized English*) to talk out ideas surrounding race and language, and over time it broadened into a general examination of whiteness with occasional intersections with language teaching. While building a slightly larger presence online, I began to write a second article on decentering whiteness in English language teaching (ELT), which was desk-rejected from one journal and then readily accepted at another, and I was reasonably satisfied with my progress as an early-career scholar. And then 2020 happened.

In February 2020, my son, Ezel, was born, immediately rendering any work I was doing useless if it didn't have a substantive impact on the systems of whiteness under which he was likely to live and study. After the pandemic arrived just a few weeks later, I had a lot of time indoors to edit my now-accepted article on decentering whiteness, and as such it was published only a few months after I wrote it, which means, by chance, it was released in late May 2020, when, let's just say, a lot was happening when it came to public discourse on racism. Several white friends and associates had started peppering me with questions about 'what to do'. At first, I answered their questions dutifully, but I quickly grew tired of being a Helpful Black Friend, as I felt more like what Kendi (2017) would call a *Black exhibit*, visible but silenced. I decided that my scholarship did not go far enough. As Tuck and Yang (2014: 233) wrote, academia 'stockpiles examples of injustice yet will not make explicit a commitment to social justice', and I was not, and am not, satisfied with this. Despite the resonance of my many academic pursuits, my research needed to take direct aim at the centering of whiteness in our society. And so the Ezel Project was born.

The Ezel Project and Racialized Organizations

In July 2020, I began teaching a series of six-session synchronous online courses, for which I charged my clients an amount similar to that of a one-credit graduate-level class. These courses are called 'Decoding and Decentering Whiteness', and they aim to help the participants fully understand the different facets of whiteness, why it needs to be decentered and how they can collectively plan to make substantive changes within their organizations, or in their field, aiming to counter racism and redistribute racial power and wealth. For my research, I contacted course participants who identified as white and interviewed those who responded about how the course did, or didn't, help them decenter whiteness in their organizations, and what changes have occurred as a result of their subsequent efforts, both with respect to their organizations and the way they interact within whiteness; my dissertation includes narratives from a wider range of participants, but for this book, I have included only the narratives of white *language* educators. I wanted to understand how they felt that my course did or didn't alter their own relationship with whiteness overall, how it may or may not have supported their efforts to challenge whiteness in their organizations, and to learn what may have led them to become the type of white person who would be interested in such an undertaking in the first place, because it surely isn't every white educator who would choose to sign up for such a course.

Though I did not have a name for my approach when I began the courses, as they were created out of a sense of urgency, I have come to see my pedagogy as what I call a *mesotransformative praxis*, inspired by concepts described by Victor Ray (2019) in his previously cited article about racialized organizations. Ray (2019: 2) refers to organizations as the *meso* level,[2] and he wrote: '(1) racialized organizations enhance or diminish the agency of racial groups; (2) racialized organizations legitimate the unequal distribution of resources; (3) whiteness is a credential; and (4) decoupling is racialized'. Though it was not necessarily my original plan, the people who have taken my course thus far have mostly been white educators with small amounts of power within the racialized field of ELT, and the course would ideally support them as they respond to this unequal distribution of agency, resources and credentialing. In other words, the course would enhance their ability to seek a redistribution of racialized power, thereby helping to destabilize the pyramid and remove the hierarchies under which we all operate.

The work of John Diamond, for one, has taken a hard look at whiteness and the impact of white spaces on Black people in general and Black students in particular (e.g. Diamond *et al.*, 2020; Diamond & Anderson, 2021), and so my hope is that my own course and the reportage thereof (including this book) can challenge these structures directly. There are others offering classes under the umbrella of anti-racism or white supremacy, and books on race and racism have been extremely popular recently (Andrew, 2020). I value this work, and I am glad for people to engage, but I worry little will occur beyond performative social media posturing. I designed my course so that those who complete its sessions will have to, as a condition of the course, take concrete actions to make substantive changes to their organizations and/or field, and I am curious to see if my approach will prove to have resonated. I do not claim that this *meso* approach is better or worse than micro or macro efforts, but I know where I am best positioned to be of use, and chose this angle accordingly. And before you ask, yes, the class isn't specifically about language teaching but about whiteness overall, and the people I interviewed for this book were asked whether or not the focus on whiteness writ large was effective for their language education context. It's up to my participants, and to you, to determine if my approach was the right decision.

To that end, I think of my son at school with my own former classmates, any one of whom could have caused my destruction if they had so chosen – and who, nonetheless, perpetuated prolonged *spirit murder*[3] (Williams, 1987) – and anything smaller, even if well-intended, is not enough. I went to exclusive, expensive, 'elite' schools for most of my life, and even now, having finished what could be considered twenty-second grade, I am almost always one of the only Black faces around, and can count the Black educators I've had on one hand, an isolation which was no less true during my career in ELT. No matter which direction I have turned, whiteness has controlled my educational and professional experiences, and it is imperative I do whatever possible to make it so that that is not the case for my son. I felt that approaching whiteness through organizations was how I was best suited to protect him as he grew.

Accordingly, I do not believe in simply attempting such a task for my own profit. Even if I were to succeed at helping to change a considerable number of my clients' contexts, the reportage on the pedagogy and the praxis is just as important as the work itself. This research, whether I succeed or not, will hopefully serve as a narrative guide from inception to the necessarily unfinished conclusion of my mesotransformative approach to the decentering of whiteness, as applied to the experiences of the language educators you will soon meet.

To put this in standardized research terms, the purpose of the Ezel Project is to demonstrate whether or not a racialized and neurodivergent scholar can attempt to decenter whiteness through a mesotransformative approach, a two-pronged effort, as you will see below. First, the fact that it is a person with my specific positionality and background who has designed and led these courses, an endeavor from which I hope that anyone who reads my curriculum and my participants' narratives can take valuable lessons about the importance of being guided by their own identity and experiences. And second, this work represents an attempt to determine if, in the opinion of said participants, courses such as mine can effectively support their attempts to decenter whiteness in the racialized field of language education, thereby offering a possible way forward to dismantle whiteness as an overall system.

Accordingly, my research questions were as follows:

(1) How have my identity and my experiences as an educator and an academic within racialized organizations shaped the development of my mesotransformative decentering whiteness courses? (My own narrative answer to this question is what you're reading throughout this book.)

(2) How do white educators describe both the way that their experiences and prior relationship to whiteness influenced their decision to join a course on decentering whiteness, and the way that participation in this course shaped their efforts at substantively decentering whiteness in their language education context?

Before I share the narratives of a handful of my participants, though, I will walk you through the curriculum I developed for the course, so that you can have a greater understanding of the work I have attempted to do.

Course Design

It would be dishonest not to admit that the course was originally planned rather quickly. We all know that the events of May 2020 seemed to happen rapidly, particularly the back-to-back news stories about George Floyd and Amy Cooper. As traumatic as the former was (and remains),[4] it fit a more established pattern, sadly enough. I am not surprised at what the police are capable of, though the nonchalance involved was most likely what inspired so strong a public response. Nevertheless, it was the latter news story that really got under my skin, with no pun intended.

I know Amy Cooper. Not literally, but I know many people with precisely her profile. She is a financially successful white woman in early middle-age who by all accounts is politically progressive, yet will, as we all saw, endanger the life of a Black man when he tries to correct her behavior (Reuters, 2020). I do not have a large number of friends who are police, and truth be told, I also do not know very many people in circumstances as difficult as those of George Floyd. Suffice it to say that, as enraging as they are, each police murder affects me from a bit of a remove, because, although I worry about myself and my son, I do believe the chances are fairly low because I rarely drive and I do not live where they tend to patrol aggressively, which is its own commentary on class that I do not currently have space for.[5]

After the Amy Cooper video went viral, though, friends started sending me messages with questions. One friend, wary that alerting the authorities for any reason could be seen as similar to Cooper's actions, asked me if calling the police on a Black man wielding a knife was the wrong thing to do. Another person asked me what to do to help her daughter not be racist, an enervating question in many ways. These were, indeed, well-to-do women in their thirties and forties, and when I told my wife this was happening, she said that, were I a lawyer (like my mother), there would only be so much legal advice I would be willing to give out for free, and with these two as examples, I took the step of asking them if they would be interested in a class were I to put one together. The one asking for help with her daughter and racism ignored me (and has not spoken to me since), and the other, who had been worried about calling the police on a man with a knife, said she was open to it, and became one of my first students. This, of course, meant I had to actually create a class.

In designing the course, I had to think about a few things. First of all, what it would actually be, balancing what was realistic with what was necessary to actually accomplish something substantive. As mentioned above, I knew there would be a great deal of diluted diversity training popping up around the world, and that almost all of it would be offered online due to the pandemic. I decided immediately that I did not want to approach the course design from a gentle, patient perspective, because, truthfully, I was rather furious at a lot of my peers for their years of apathy on racism and whiteness. As I also mentioned above, my article, 'Worth the Risk: Towards Decentring Whiteness in English Language Teaching', had just been published in the *BC TEAL* journal, and I decided to build a course around some of the lessons contained in that work. Like I said, I did not limit the course to language teachers, but the general principles were the same.

There were a lot of aspects to consider, all of which I planned over a few days. I could have taken my time, but I thought it better to simply try something and then readjust for future courses. I also had no clue if anyone would sign up or not, even though my one friend had expressed interest. But at first, I needed to figure out the format. Online, yes, but how many sessions, and how long would each session be? And then, of course, what would be contained in each session, and what would the end goal be?

I initially decided on five sessions, both because it is a round number, and also because I had gotten it into my head that it would be pitched as the educational equivalent of a one-credit graduate course, three-credit versions of which often last about 15 weeks. Purely because of my own experience being tired of work calls and knowing I would have to plan around then-infant Ezel's own sleep schedule, I decided the classes would last an hour each, which would allow for extra time if needed in any given class. When I started to consider both the end goal and the actual curriculum, though, I changed my mind on the number of sessions.

I knew that any class I taught would be student or client centered, as this format aligns with the frameworks to which I ascribe, including *critical pedagogy* (Freire, 1970), which, as mentioned, eschews the belief in teacher-as-sage and student as empty vessel. I had no desire to try and plan out five full slideshows and lectures, and I simply do not believe that adults enjoy being talked at; most of the sessions would thus be structured as facilitated discussions. But I thought about the people who had approached me with whiteness questions before I offered them a class, and they, and anyone else I might offer the class, had come with very different levels of understanding about key concepts and terminology. If students signed up for the course and needed to be corrected or coached on the language repeatedly, disaster might ensue. So I decided that the first session needed to include an overview of the terms I would be using, and some of the concepts that would be central to the course. These terminology and concept slides then became the introduction to the conference presentations and invited talks I have given on decentering whiteness over the past few years,[6] as establishing a shared understanding of aspects of whiteness and racism is a central tenet of my public scholarship.

Consequently, this left me with a six-week course, five sessions and an introduction. Six hours is not actually that much time, and certainly not enough to completely invert someone's understanding of racism, but I figured that the material and activities I assigned would carry the remaining load effectively, and also I doubted anyone would sign up for a much longer commitment than that. Finally, it was time to actually plan the curriculum, and this was a task I undertook from the back, by which I mean that I had to answer what I wanted them to achieve overall before I could determine how we might get there.

In most of the bad trainings that I have attended, and even some I have been forced to design at a previous day job, participants are asked to make some sort of vague, undefined commitment at the end. No one follows up on these, and there is no reason to believe they will be completed. The concept of a commitment is not a problem, but the lack of weight is the issue. Researches in the field of behavioral design have shown that having people take the time to lay out the steps in a plan increases their chances of doing so (Datta & Mullainathan, 2014), as it was employed to great success in the most recent American presidential election (National Education Administration, 2020). With my goal of effecting organizational or field-specific change – though I did not come up with 'mesotransformative' until months later – I decided that the participants would be instructed to end the course with a workable, detailed and far-reaching plan to decenter whiteness in their institutions. Here is the final assignment as posed to the students at the end of the penultimate class:

- Final Assignment: A collective action plan
  - Dates, times, parties involved
  - How will you know you've succeeded?
  - What happens if you don't?
  - What happens if you do? Do you stop?

Working backward from this destination, I asked myself what they would need to know in order to create a workable plan.

I went back to review literature I had encountered during my studies and in the process of writing my articles. I dove into the many extant analyses of whiteness, building my own pedagogy through both conceptual arguments and empirical findings. Among the latter, I read, first, about the whiteness of teaching and how challenging it is to discuss this explicitly (Picower, 2009), with teachers falling back on any other portion of their identity they can find (e.g. religion, ethnicity) in order to distance themselves from being complicit in whiteness. I reminded myself of how popular culture creates – and certification programs reify – an image of a heroic white educator 'making a difference' in racialized communities (Cann, 2015). The issue of presumed altruism has recurred in my work, and it is one of the topics that I am always concerned will be left out of any such courses on whiteness, allowing educators 'off the hook', so to speak, because of their supposed good intentions. I also read of how self-described liberals exhibit a particularly insidious form of racism mixed with intense denial thereof (Zamudio & Rios, 2006), which resonated strongly from my own experience in a series of nominally progressive schools. I felt I had to ensure that my courses directly addressed these possible issues with white educators in some fashion.

Finally, though, I came across what eventually pointed toward some possible paths forward for the assignments in my course. I encountered the idea of assigning white learners a racial autobiography (Ullucci, 2012), as many have never explicitly considered their own whiteness and its impact on their context. Similar to Picower's (2009) findings above, Ullucci wrote:

> Culture was the more salient component for many students; unraveling how being white functioned was more of a hurdle. More than a few students mentioned that they didn't have racial backgrounds – that other components of their identity were more important. While this may feel true to a particular individual, it also exposes a gap in this assignment. Being white matters. (Ullucci, 2012: 97)

When I looked for a way to build a course curriculum, this seemed a natural place to begin. Also helpful to me was learning of the fact that challenging whiteness can be classified as *transgressive white racial knowledge* (Crowley, 2016). Among his participants, Crowley found not only a sense of ambivalence and a lack of confidence, but also an ability to understand racism and whiteness on a purely intellectual level, and I thought that there was something to work with there. Taken together, the findings above led me to take note of a few themes that had emerged from this subsection of the literature, namely what I saw as a strong desire to distance oneself from whiteness and racism, an urgency to position oneself as a savior and the need for white educators to come to a fuller understanding of how whiteness has shaped their lives and careers and to have a supported space where they could build toward concrete action instead of remaining understandably uncertain of a way forward. And so, with the first week set for an introduction and the final week for participants to share and discuss their action plans, I wanted to address the remainder of these ideas in the four unoccupied sessions and the assignments in between.

I decided that the primary idea was connecting aspects of whiteness related to individual experience to the broader organizational impact of whiteness. I used the idea of the racial autobiography as a starting point, and then decided I would 'zoom out', as it were, to have the class address the impact of white leadership in organizations, followed by an exploration of white spaces, and finally a week in which they would take what they had learned so far and tie it to their own contexts. Below, you will find weekly the curriculum and assignments, with details about each session.

Decoding and Decentering Whiteness
Course Outline and Curriculum

- Session Zero: Introduction and Terminology
  - Agenda:
    - PowerPoint presentation
  - Assignment(s):
    - Racial autobiography
- Session One: White Leadership
  - Agenda:
    - Recap/sharing of racial autobiographies, discussion of disconnect between white leadership and employees of color
  - Assignment(s):
    - Readings on 'Sundown Towns'
    - Instruction to research racial exclusion in participants' childhood hometown/current location, as well as reviewing racial identification of leadership at places of employment
- Session Two: White Spaces
  - Agenda:
    - Discussion of readings and findings from research about hometown racial exclusion and leadership at place of employment
  - Assignment(s):
    - Podcast on exemplar of white saviorism (Renee Bach)
    - Instruction to detail the many factors that allowed the woman in the above episode to get away with what she did
- Session Three: White Saviors
  - Agenda:
    - Discussion of Renee Bach and, more importantly, her enablers, and how not to be a white savior in addressing issues
  - Assignment(s):
    - Four of six (their choice) of 'classic' Black authors writing about different aspects of racism and whiteness
    - Instruction to connect chosen readings to their own context

- Session Four: Contextualizing
  - Agenda:
    - Discussion of their chosen readings and their connection to their own context
  - Assignment:
    - Final Assignment (see above)
- Session Five: Action Plans
  - Agenda:
    - Sharing (and interrogation) of action plans

Session Zero

As described above, this first week is called 'zero' because it's a different format from the others and an establishment of key concepts and ground rules. Most of this session is comprised of a PowerPoint presentation I developed for my talks on decentering whiteness in language teaching, with the difference being that, in my talks, I delve more deeply into the language-based concepts in my article, whereas, for this session, we veer off into course goals and a preview of the rest of the curriculum. Participants introduce themselves briefly, but full detailed introductions are saved for the following week because the assignment at the end of this session is the aforementioned 'racial autobiography'. I end by explaining the fact that all assignments will be emailed to them within an hour of the end of the class, and that ultimately, the course is for their benefit, so the amount of time they choose to spend on the assignments will determine how much they will get out of them.

Session One

This session has often been the most challenging one for me, because it represents the transition from an instructor-led lecture format to a facilitated discussion. We begin by discussing the participants' racial autobiographies, which I caution them should only last around five minutes each after the first group spent almost the entire hour sharing their stories, leaving us no time to discuss anything new.[7] After these discussions, we turn our attention to white leadership, and the disconnection between the image that racialized organizations put forth and who actually makes the decisions. I often use the website of a well-known chain restaurant with particularly cringeworthy messaging and an all-white leadership corps with racialized frontline workers, but you can use just about any company, or indeed just about any school, considering how many deans are white at schools that claim to care about Black lives. I end by assigning a few readings, most notably the introduction to the book *Sundown Towns* (Loewen, 2005), in preparation for a discussion on the impact of white spaces. Participants are also instructed to review the websites of their own institutions for the demographics of leadership, along with the racial composition of the towns and cities where they have lived.

Session Two

We begin this session by discussing what participants have learned about their own institutions, hometowns and places of residence, and by examining the potential impact of said whiteness not only on the racialized but also on white children (and adults). This week is usually, from my vantage point, where the class begins to 'click', as the somewhat disparate topics start to coalesce into a clearer understanding of the ubiquity of whiteness and the harm that can result. For language teachers especially, the consideration of how whiteness pervades almost all public spaces allows such participants to analyze how their students might be impacted by these unmentioned expectations and by the ideal against which they will be measured. I end by assigning a different sort of task, a podcast episode about a particularly egregious white savior named Renee Bach, a young adult who established a clinic in Uganda without medical training and allowed 105 children to die (Aizenman & Gharib, 2019).

Session Three

The point of including the Renee Bach story is not so much to horrify (although it's horrifying), but to help participants resist the urge to respond to the issues we've discussed by trying to play the hero and center themselves in resolving the issue. In discussing her story, we examine the structures that had to be in place in order for her to cause the damage she caused, which means we discuss mission trips, nonprofits and whiteness as an automatic symbol of gravitas. By the end of this session, participants are meant to be prepared to consider their own contexts and how one can possibly effect change without playing the hero. Accordingly, at this point, I consider the students prepared to read 'classic' Black writers, and give them the choice to read four selections from a group of six texts, texts which capture a range of eras, topics, author positionalities and styles. Again, in adopting this curriculum, you are free to choose different texts, but the point is to choose carefully. Providing participants with a choice went over well, and all were able to find work that spoke to them. The texts are from Baldwin's (1955) *Notes of a Native Son* and *Stranger in the Village* (1955); Fanon's (1952) *The Negro and Language*; Davis's (1982) *The Approaching Obsolescence of Housework*; Lorde's (1981/2007) *The Uses of Anger*; and, for the ambitious, DuBois's (1935) *Transubstantiation of a Poor White*. The DuBois chapter is nearly 80 pages, and only one person has chosen to take it on. I commend her!

Session Four

Because my participants were predominantly language teachers, the Fanon essay has been the most popular discussion point among all the options, but ultimately this session is designed to allow the participants to draw connections across different axes of oppression in conjunction with the binary between whiteness and all it holds in opposition. I ask simply that participants consider where they might be able to substantively change their context, and they are given the final assignment without any other reading to consider for the last session.

Session Five

In this final session, everyone shares their plans, and I, along with the other participants, ask pointed questions to help these plans come closer to the clarity necessary to actually put them in place. With only one or two exceptions, every participant has been engaged in the work and returned for the final session prepared to enact some sort of change in the context around them, and with many of my participants in the language space, there is a chance that if they all succeed in the long term, this course will have had some small role in shifting the field. But that will depend on whether or not the participants feel the course was influential in their ability to decenter whiteness, and that will be determined through the narratives contained in both my dissertation and in the chapter that follows.

Every final session is bittersweet for me because I really do enjoy the class, and it feels, from my perspective, as though I really do have the chance to have an impact on whiteness in language education, and in education more broadly for the other participants. I had no idea as to whether or not this would work when I planned it. I am also, as a teacher, pretty allergic to lesson plans, so aside from the start and finish, I wanted to remain flexible and dynamic, and indeed, I altered the curriculum over time, particularly with respect to the six final reading choices. What was important to me as I planned the course and led my first groups through it was that I gave as compelling a tour of whiteness as I could. They could spend years reading the many books on whiteness, but, in their six weeks in my class, I wanted these students to see the threads connecting their own racial identity, their workspaces, where they had been raised and where they were choosing to raise their children, and how little has changed since titans like Baldwin and Lorde were writing about these issues. The best I can say about this curriculum is that it was an educated guess. But, though you will be able to judge this for yourself as you read the participants' narratives in the next chapter, it seems to have resonated with the people on the course, so perhaps I guessed pretty well.

Before moving on to the participants' narratives, though, it must be noted that a significant factor in this course is my own presence, not so much because of any skill I possess but because the facilitated discussion format requires me, as the instructor, to be open and direct with the participants about how whiteness has impacted my own life. In other words, though I think this curriculum can and should be used by others, I warn you that you'll have to adapt it to your own positionality and experiences instead of trying to take this 'off the shelf' and put it to use without doing the work. You can do it, but you need to employ it with care. With that said, you are welcome to visit my website and contact me if you'd like to use it or adapt it, as I will gladly help you do so. Anyway, on with the participants and their narratives, so you can learn from their experiences.

Michael[8]

Michael is a high school teacher originally from the Boston suburbs. His hometown is overwhelmingly white and generally affluent, the location of one very exclusive university and down the road from a few more. According to him, he was largely unaware of his whiteness as a child, a fact that was common among the white participants in my classes and a sharp contrast from the handful of participants of color, who were often able to pinpoint their racialization within some early memory. Similarly, when his elementary school did import a handful of Black students from Boston proper, his classmates delineated between the kids from his town and the 'other' kids, though they rarely if ever explicitly mentioned that these other students were racialized. When he was growing up, he and his immediate family often visited his grandparents, who lived in the Midwest, and were members of a country club. On one of these visits, his older sister pointed out to him that all of the people being served were white while all of the servers were racialized, something he hadn't taken note of himself. He also remembers the fact that, when driving through certain areas with largely Black populations, his grandmother would be sure to double-check that her car doors were locked, even when they were out in broad daylight, complete with a *click* that Michael could always hear. It's easy enough to shrug these things off, and to some extent Michael must have in the sense that he didn't confront his grandmother at the time, but it's worth asking yourself, if you're white, how many of these seemingly small moments happened in your life. Nevertheless, Michael didn't become any kind of racial justice crusader while eating with his grandparents, and it ultimately took him a lot longer to make the choice to confront these issues, as these anecdotes were blips in the background of a life that gave him little occasion to examine his whiteness.

These days, he draws a throughline from his grandparents, who were closer to what one might call 'overtly' racist, to the people in his politically progressive but still very white hometown, who would never embarrass themselves by supporting anti-Black violence, but still took great pains in recent years to prevent the construction of public housing in their community, under the guise that there would be an increase in traffic... in a town with only 25,000 people. If you understand racism only as outright hostility, you can delineate the more obvious action of locking your car doors from the more 'respectable' act of enforcing the boundaries of a community that just happens to be very white. Only with a more nuanced and more accurate understanding of whiteness can you see that both actions have a similar result of creating and defending white spaces.

Michael now works as an English language composition (i.e. writing) teacher in a city about 90 miles west of his hometown, having studied sports journalism in college and essentially grown bored of covering college football among people who treated the game as a religious experience. Since his mother was a teacher, he had always kept such a career as a possible fallback and, a few years ago, applied to and was accepted into a prestigious overseas English education program, which placed him in a Balkan country. His description of his so-called 'training' reminded me of my own in Korea, as he was essentially taught how to keep his students' attention and what to do when they didn't understand him, all of which he knew was sorely inefficient because he'd completed student teaching at home by this point and was thus more experienced than others in his cohort. Many of the others in the program were not trained teachers but people who saw the overseas experience as a professional feather in their caps that they were likely to use as a springboard to a political or diplomatic career, whereas Michael was indeed planning to teach long term, and tried to make the best out of what was ultimately a bit of a strange situation. He was often contacted last minute and asked to travel to different schools around the city where he lived, tasked with speaking to the students who were the most 'advanced' in English. In his estimation, both he and the students found their conversations rewarding, and they had complex discussions about a wide variety of topics that the students were rarely exposed to in their normal schooling, which Michael says that even the local teachers considered antiquated. There is only so much benefit a group of students can get from an unfamiliar teacher temporarily parachuted into the classroom, even if the discussions were fun, and though Michael enjoyed his experience, it was clear that, had he not been trained in advance, as was the case for many of the others in his group, he would have merely been a friendly 'native speaker' face that the state government could point to as proof that they'd provided their students with a benefit, and that the American government could continue to celebrate as a product of its generosity. Michael took note of the flaws in this system, and did the best he could, and then his time was cut short by the arrival of the pandemic and he returned home.

With this experience in his recent past, Michael applied to all of the larger school districts in his home state, particularly because he wanted to teach in schools with bilingual students. He's interested in education policy, and he had learned, from both his student teaching experience and his brief English as a foreign language (EFL) sojourn to Europe, that there were a lot of problems in these districts and also in the practice of language teaching. He was eventually hired at a school that's only 6%

white and, while stuck at home and working on his ongoing master's studies while teaching full-time, he came across my article, taking an interest in the intersection of whiteness and language teaching as avenues along which he could ultimately effect change. I can't say definitively that the above anecdotes are the reasons why Michael was inclined to sign up for the course, but it is clear to me from our discussions that he has long been slightly uncomfortable with the trappings of whiteness around him, even before he was able to put such a feeling into words. As we'll see with the other narratives, the seeds to challenge whiteness started early for Michael, even if they didn't grow into something more visible until adulthood.

Michael had come to understand the fact that white teachers in general, and white language teachers in particular, have the capacity and tendency to cause harm, and wanted to find a way to counteract this in himself and in his practice. He told me about a principal at a school where he had once worked and their insistence on students producing acceptable academic English as a measure of success, which aligned with state testing metrics. Indeed, said school had attained the title of a 'turnaround' school because of its improvement with respect to standardized measurements, and the principal credited what Michael classified as their policing of student language as a factor in this change. He was also keenly aware of the fact that students classified as 'English learners' would often write what he would consider very strong essays but, because their languaging fell outside of the expected norms, they were seen as deficient writers. Michael also took note of the fact that any discussion of the harm caused by the reliance upon such standardization was absent from all of his teacher training, and that he had had to seek out other resources to become better versed in the impact of whiteness on his practice. His observation was important, because in truth, there remains very little explicit discussion of whiteness in language education; at one point after my article was released, it remained one of the only such academic publications, a trend that is likely to have changed by the time you read this, but was certainly the case when he came across the work I was trying to do independently and without any official academic appointment. In other words, from his life experiences to his early career in both Europe and Massachusetts, he had realized something important was missing from what could make him into a genuinely great teacher of language, and once I started advertising my class, he contacted me fairly quickly.

Michael was in my sixth cohort of participants, the majority of whom were white language teachers. Unlike some of the other groups, none of these individuals knew each other beforehand, and as such, the initial sessions required a bit more time for introductions and cohesion, at least in my opinion. What was unique about this group was that one participant specifically contacted me during the course to request that we spend more time on language teaching specifically; as you saw in the curriculum, the course is open to anyone but mostly attracts white language educators because those are the people who see my presentations and so forth. As such, it was important that I strike a balance between my broader goals regarding whiteness and individual participants' requests, since they were paying clients after all. That was the only time I received an explicit request regarding the more general nature of the material, and it wasn't from Michael (nor was it done publicly), but I mention it here both to acknowledge that some folks reading this might find the lack of explicit language teaching material in the 'Decoding and Decentering Whiteness' curriculum to be a bit of a hurdle and to mention that Michael was a part of the cohort where my facilitation shifted the most intentionally during the course. From the third week on, after I received that request, I built more of my discussions around the structures of language teaching and their connection to whiteness as opposed to my usual strategy of focusing on whiteness and allowing participants to draw more of their own connections to their contexts and organizations, and it seemed to work well both for the person who requested the shift and for the other participants. Ironically, the cohorts of mine that were entirely comprised of language teachers never made such a request, so there's no real way to predict how people will respond, and if anyone hopes to use the curriculum, an ability to adapt between cohorts or even between weeks is vital.

By the end of the class, Michael had, as assigned, considered his position within the broader field. He told me that, among all of the aspects of whiteness we had discussed, the related concepts of white saviorism and presumed altruism particularly resonated with him, as he remembered having thought that traveling to teach in an impoverished European country was inherently prosocial, and he later understood the harm that can be caused by such a belief. He also knew, as a fairly new classroom teacher, that he had an immense amount of responsibility to his students but not a particularly large amount of power. Whereas some of the participants have been powerful university provosts, some, like Michael, were best positioned to effect change in the classroom itself, as well as among their peers. Consequently, he felt it was vital to change the way his future students' assessment and evaluation were conceptualized, separating standardized and academic English from what would be considered 'good' writing; essentially, taking rigid forms of prescriptivism out of the way he reviews student writing.

He shared with me a story of an author having visited his school (virtually) and speaking to his class, during which he was speaking to one of his students using the chat function, a student whose writing he finds to be vibrant and creative. He communicated to her that she should continue to develop her unique writing voice, despite the fact that it breaks the 'rules' that K12 students are often given in American schools (e.g. avoiding first person).[9] He acknowledges that the state tests will still require certain types of language production, but for this student and others, he wants to separate how they view the quality of their writing from the wholly different skill of test score achievement.

This wasn't all that he planned to pursue after our class, though; he wanted to build toward collective action with his colleagues and across his school, and he identified a handful of other teachers he felt would support him in this work. In his estimation, even with a theoretically supportive administration, only so much was possible if he tried to go it alone, and, after our course finished, he planned to approach people, feeling hopeful and full of ideals he wanted to achieve. And then he ran into some obstacles. Regarding these obstacles: you'll find that all of these participants ran into issues, and indeed that's why the final course assignment is inclusive of the fact that obstacles are likely. If these types of efforts were simple, we would have been rid of whiteness a long time ago, and ELT wouldn't be the sort of field that it is. The key is what you do after you run into trouble, and how you continue to forge ahead over what will likely take several years.

In Michael's case, two of the teachers he trusted and knew best, and with whom he expected to be able to build, quit their jobs toward the end of the school year, one of them citing treatment by the administration as her reasoning for doing so. And, of course, the thing about building a team to challenge oppression within your organization is that people don't tend to stay with said organization for a long time if there is oppression worth challenging. For the white participants I've worked with, and for any white educator reading this, it's important to avoid being the white savior, which means that one needs to work with minoritized colleagues in some fashion to successfully redistribute power. Yet, if the organization is as unkind to minoritized employees as many organizations are, said colleagues might just up and leave, as is their right. So all this left Michael without any colleagues he knew well enough to be able to expect that they'd be interested in the work he wanted to find a way to do outside of his own classroom.

Eventually, he was left with just one other colleague who taught ninth-grade writing, and he began to gently engage with her on these topics, sharing articles and resources and coming to a place of mutual understanding on, at the very least, the harm of language instruction relying upon prescriptivism. More time will be needed before the two of them can accomplish more substantive shifts in school policy on language instruction, but he's somewhat hopeful. More hopeful, though, is that he has developed a very productive relationship with his direct supervisor, and has felt able to be explicit and direct about the ideologies underpinning the way writing is assessed in their school. His supervisor has been receptive if uneasy, considering the school's ballyhooed reputation for student test score improvement, but instead of obstructing his efforts to push against the standardized assumptions of what constitutes 'good', she has encouraged him to continue on his path.

Michael half-joked that he failed at rallying his colleagues considering that two of them quit almost immediately after he finished our class, and before he even got to try to build what he wanted to. He presented me with an informal metric of success for his long-term plans, saying that if he were to be extremely successful, over the next 10 years the school would fully break from the mandated standardized testing that continues to keep the administration in a stranglehold financially and ideologically, and would revolutionize their writing and language curriculum. He would also be satisfied if the rest of the school's teachers, who are visibly disengaged during professional development sessions on racism and other axes of oppression, were interested in changing their practice to challenge the hierarchies codified into their work. It would be a moderate success to merely get the administration on board with subtle shifts in the framing of language instruction; that is, essentially staying out of his way as he made whatever small changes he is able to pursue. And, worst-case scenario, he just gives up and quits after getting frustrated in a few years, which is always technically possible; I will check in on him after this book comes out.

He thinks that, although he stumbled into a better understanding of some of these things through his experiences and then the self-education he actively pursued, the field would greatly benefit from including mandated courses on whiteness and/or anti-Blackness in language education while teachers are being trained, not just as a vague sense of awareness but as a practice that was then a required component of fieldwork before teachers were sent off into classrooms full of racialized students in whose harm they would thus become complicit. Of course, as he admitted, this would require changing hearts and minds in the teacher licensure space, and who knows how possible that is, though that doesn't mean we shouldn't try.

Michael's story is unfinished, both in terms of whiteness and language teaching, and also as an educator in general. That's not a particularly dramatic way to end his narrative, but unless and until the field itself undergoes substantive shifts, all of our efforts will remain incomplete, slow and prone to the sort of pitfalls he ran into immediately. The point, though, is that people who come from exclusive and affluent white enclaves, complete with relatives who are scared of Blackness altogether, are not destined to remain ignorant of the harm whiteness perpetuates, even if they take a while to learn how best to challenge what's around them. In other words, if Michael can push against all he's been given, then so can you.

Andie

My intention in choosing these three narratives to share with you is not so much to find the 'most successful' participants – you will not find a single one that conquered whiteness! – but more to present you with different versions of white people in different parts of the language education field, all of whom came upon my class and then tried to push against whiteness in some fashion. So, since Michael is a K12 writing teacher, I wanted to include a more academic perspective, as I'm sure that many of you are in that space. Andie is a teaching English to speakers of other languages (TESOL) professor at a public university in the Midwest, and, as a child, was actually bussed from her whiter neighborhood to a minoritized area when forced integration was a common practice in the 1970s. Like Michael, she grew up in broadly the same geographic region where she now works, but the Midwest is large, and she teaches several states away from where she spent most of her young life, which in her case was near Minneapolis. I could be more circumspect about which state she's from, but it will become relevant later when her interest in my class is mentioned, because her personal familiarity with the location where George Floyd was murdered is important to the story. But I'll get there later.

Andie describes her parents and grandparents as genuinely welcoming people, which I am sure many people would say, but I do think it's important that she never once used the word 'nice' to describe them. They may well have been nice, but Andie's done enough work to know that niceness and racism are hardly antonyms, and indeed the appearance of the former is not nearly enough to preclude the latter. What she meant by this was that, quite literally, her family took efforts to welcome others into their homes, regardless of their background. So when she was eventually bussed into different areas and then looked back years later to realize she was one of only a few white children in class pictures, these experiences had not been presented as either remarkable or detrimental to her. She hardly remembers now how much she must have stood out at the time. With all that said, though, her family did end up in a white suburb, and even if it wasn't, as far as she is aware,[10] an explicit attempt to avoid various groups of people, she does acknowledge that her parents were focused on what they perceived as 'upward' mobility, up to and including their eventual retirement to the Southwest, and no matter how kind they may well be, it's not a coincidence that moving 'up' usually does mean moving closer to whiteness. But that's a bigger issue than her own family, and one of the reasons the course has a session on the construction of white spaces.

Andie mentioned a few experiences when explaining her gradual transition from having grown up in a largely homogenous space, and a general assumption early in her now decades-long career that, like Michael, her work was inherently altruistic, to the urgency she feels now to transform our field. First, she was witness to the way her ex-husband was treated by various agents of the state and bureaucratic processes. Her ex-husband was a brown-skinned man from Mexico who was questioned and doubted constantly just for attempting to live his life. Whether it was the police, or the bank, or just people she knew from her hometown, she came to see how a place that could feel so warm and welcoming to her could be oppressive to others she cared about. From people I've spoken to for this book and others in my class, it often does seem to take a close peer relationship with a person categorized as a threat to whiteness to see that everything we're trying to tell you isn't just some sort of fable, and it would be nice if white children were taught about whiteness explicitly so this didn't have to keep happening, but considering how many people still deny it even after seeing it up close, better she learn from what she saw than ignore it. She started to pull away from spending her time and money in white spaces, and became generally distrustful of white strangers after seeing how they could treat her so differently from someone she loved.

Later, when she pursued a mid-career shift to academia and moved to a majority-Black city (Atlanta), she was responsible for working with young, white future teachers around the time that Michael Brown was killed and the protests in Ferguson, Missouri, started. She noticed that said teachers were mostly unequipped to grapple with the daily onslaught of news while trying to teach English to their own students, who were mostly adult refugees denied access to schooling in their home countries. It probably would have been easier to just try to ignore what was going on, but, despite what the field might think, adult learners aren't lacking in intelligence, and they can see the news, so no matter how high-minded the practice of English teaching may perceive itself to be, it was clear to Andie that she and these young, white teachers were going to have to figure out how to talk about racism in their classes. She was, by this point, in her forties, and with many years in the field already, she knew she'd have to do a lot better than she had done based on her initial training. She and said students wrote about the process of trying to build a more effective pedagogy regarding American racism, which was published in conference proceedings, though she now thinks she would write this project up very differently, since she hadn't yet done nearly as much work on the topic as she since has.

The area where she now teaches is economically depressed, a former Rust Belt boom town devastated by shifts away from unionized manufacturing jobs. She told me once that, because there's so little traffic downtown, the city has transformed portions of wide boulevards into a flourishing bike-lane system, which is sort of sweet. And then, in May 2020, she, like much of the rest of the world, watched as a Black man was killed on camera, but for her it happened to be in her hometown. The way she described this and other instances of public anti-Black violence is that it was clear that people will literally die if she and other white educators don't do the work they need to do. It's easy enough to dismiss police violence as disconnected from one's role as an educator, even if you have the wherewithal to condemn it appropriately, but the location of the Chauvin murder made it impossible for her to ignore its connection to her own life, and how she could choose to either make it easier or harder for such events to continue.

I'll pause again to point out that, yes, we as humans shouldn't need such horrific events to push us forward, but if they do happen – and they do – then the only hope is that some people step up their game after the fact. Considering that some white folks went back to sticking their heads in the sand and others decided to expend their money and energy on trying to shove *everyone else's* heads back into the sand, I will take whatever the inspiration happens to be, though your mileage may vary on this. This is not meant to absolve white folks of the fact that they are coming to these revelations as adults with decades of upholding the pyramid in their past, but we can't pretend that everyone is ready to confront these issues as an adolescent because (white) schools and (white) parents, no matter what country we're from, have left most of us unprepared for what we need to do, which in turn is because they were poorly taught themselves. Education as we know it is hardly a panacea, but it can be a balm if applied correctly, as we all know it surely is not.

Anyway, as I've said several times by now, my article came out a week later. Andie came across it once it began to make the academic rounds, and then she took the step of recommending me to review an article, something I had rarely done before at that point. Because I am nosy and was still mostly unaware of how academia worked, I asked the journal editor where my recommendation had come from, and he told me who it had been, which led to my reaching out to her and building a scholarly relationship. That friendship is probably why I can say things like, 'we as humans shouldn't need such horrific events to push us forward' about her, but that doesn't make it any less true. I am telling this story for a few reasons, including the fact that, much as I have been critical of the journal system, I can't pretend that my presence in a peer-reviewed publication didn't catch peoples' attention, which is all the more reason that they need to be finding much more challenging material to proliferate instead of the same old tired scholarship that's written without humanity and upholds hoary old hierarchies. Additionally, because if there are any students reading this, you really should be nosy and inquisitive about the aspects of the unnecessarily opaque system you've decided to enter. There's no reason you can't get a friend (and a student) in places you wouldn't expect.

With all of that said, not everyone who finds me or my work compelling has been willing to sign up for my class, and once I started offering sessions, she expressed an interest in enrolling. At first she said she wanted to try and convince some of her colleagues to join alongside her, but no one did, which didn't surprise me, and by the fall, she was part of a cohort. By the end of our course, she had come up with a comprehensive action plan that she seemed to be very excited about, and I was hopeful it would come to fruition.

She had told me, around the time that the class started, that she was trying to work with her predominantly white TESOL trainees on issues of whiteness and language teaching, and, at the time, had been encouraged by their initial interactions. Unfortunately, by the end of the semester, one of the students had complained about her class to another professor, and she was worried about retaliation that might ensue. She did not yet have the protection of tenure, and, teaching at a public university in a time of considerable racist backlash, there was certainly a chance that her approach might have come under fire. From what she had told me, very few people in her school's area saw TESOL as a viable career, and so the few that chose said path may not have been open to being challenged on their complicity in a broader system that they wouldn't have had any prior reason to associate with language teaching, especially considering that her students were not generally wealthy and may not have considered themselves to be powerful. Thankfully, though, nothing ended up coming of said complaint, and she was free to pursue her action plan, along with the study she was set to conduct during a sabbatical. The spring of 2021 was looking bright, and she'd even decamped to her parents' home over the winter since she was still working remotely, and you can probably guess by the way I'm framing this that things didn't go as planned.

Andie's plan was to create a teacher pipeline, engaging with local public school teachers to help identify high school students who might have an interest in the field and building toward ways to support them in their education and professional development over several years, thereby helping to diversify the local teaching pool while also, presumably, continuing to challenge the white teachers who came into her own classroom. For reasons that any of us can understand,[11] public school teachers in the year 2020–2021, despite seeming open to her ideas, were simply overwhelmed with obligations and changes and pressure, and asked her to bring her idea back to them at some later date, which is certainly a setback but a perfectly reasonable one. She even offered to help them in whatever way she could, but they never got back to her, again for reasons that make sense – no racialized public school teachers wanted to do some well-meaning (white) professor's extra project that year, even if it might have helped in the long run. Around the same time, she hit some roadblocks with her own research, which she chalked up to, as she understands it, people being reluctant to include those they see as outside of their group, the old emic/etic divide that many of us doctoral students learn about when we begin our programs. In her case, it wasn't a racist exclusion, but, one presumes, a view that a professor couldn't possibly be worth trusting and welcoming, which is interesting considering the lessons she was raised with and how she learned that her own community was prone to treating the racialized the way she'd been taught not to treat anyone. All this left her stuck.

One of the reasons she had wanted to help build a pipeline was the sorry state of language education in her school's area, which is to say that, even within the paradigm of a field that is already rife with harmful practices, it was notably worse. Based on what she told me, the schools barely knew what English language teachers did or why they were even necessary, and the language teachers were forced to expend considerable energy trying to prove their value to their places of employment, all the more reason why they might have not had the time to help her with her pipeline idea. But she heard about something that initially seemed promising and hoped to find some support for the plan she had put together.

Her own statewide union, which includes both K12 teachers and the faculty of her school, held a meeting in late spring to announce a mentorship program for racialized teachers, not just of language but in the profession overall. At this meeting, the racialized teachers who were present had many critical questions for the leadership, asking what sort of training any interested white mentors would have to undergo, and exactly at what point they would be considered safe mentors for racialized teachers. She found herself unsurprised that the union was as unprepared as they seemed to be to answer their questions, though she was impressed by the teachers and their refusal to be dismissed. She herself asked how they were recruiting interested mentees, and if they had thought of looking for racialized and bilingual high school and college students who might want to become language teachers. As she expected, the union hadn't even considered this, which, to her, underscored how easily the field and the students within it are forgotten. She had entered the meeting with hope that she might find a way to get somewhat closer to bringing her idea to life, but left disappointed once again. As a reminder, not one of these action plans is likely to go off without a hitch, because the systems in place and the people who support them are too invested in the status quo to make it easy for individuals to effect any significant change.

Eventually, though, she learned of a local foundation that she was told might be interested in supporting something akin to a pipeline idea, though they'll need the plans to be fleshed out and very specific before they consider financing her. She is wary of falling into the white savior trap, of course, and so she decided she would wait until the racialized K12 teachers' lives had calmed down enough to have space for her to connect with them, because she wants to be sure that these teachers take the intellectual lead on whatever ends up happening. Yes, she's the professor, and she's the one who would be doing the legwork of writing grants and tracking down whatever funding, but she wants the power and the real logistical know-how to come from the people on the ground, the people who would ultimately be supported by any pipeline that comes to fruition. The closing chapters of her story have yet to be written, but, like some scholars tend to, Andie has an extremely detailed spreadsheet prepared, complete with dates months and years into the future to ensure that something worthwhile comes of the work she's trying to do.

After the scare of her student complaining, it turns out that, on balance, her efforts to challenge the language ideologies of the TESOL field had actually had a positive impact on several of the people in her class. She suspects that part of this is because it was clear how hard she had worked to make their program as comfortable as possible for them in other ways, including convincing an associate dean to give these students additional flexibility in completing their field hours, a potentially instructive lesson for white academics who are interested in challenging the epistemology of their discipline; the discussion of whiteness is likely to be uncomfortable, and there's little to be done about that, but perhaps students will come along for the ride if they otherwise feel supported, even if one of them whines to another professor. Ultimately, Andie is still evolving, despite having already spent decades in the field. She has a long way to go, but for you reading this, if you happen to have been in the language space for a long time, there's absolutely no reason you have to stay stuck in place if you come to understand that there is this much work that needs to be done. It's up to you.

Josefina

I know what you're thinking. 'That's not an Anglo name!' And you're right, it's not. Yes, it's a pseudonym, like all of these, but her real name is of the same type, a Mexican name that is very close to a standardized Anglo name. And now, you might be thinking, 'if she's Mexican, how can she be white?' But yes, there are absolutely white people in Mexico, and not just of the traveling gringo sort. I wanted to include Josefina because her experience shows the malleability of racial categorization, and her conditional classification as white, both as a child in Mexico and then here in the United States and working in other countries, has given her a different perspective from the others written about above.

I assumed, incorrectly that because her family moved to Texas when she was young, she wouldn't actually remember how she had been seen in Mexico, but I was wrong. As a child, even though her hair was actually light brown, she was often called *la guerita* ('blondie'), despite not actually understanding what it meant and being annoyed by the nickname. As she explained it, it was common for her relatives to comment on newborns' skin tone upon first sight and, at least in her experience, they always valued lighter children over darker ones. I'm not the right person to say whether or not Mexicans conceive of said colors as being of different 'races', but being placed into the category she now understands as something akin to whiteness affected her even before she moved to a country that was much more explicit about who does and doesn't get to be white.

Her family moved here with the hope that studying in English would help her and her sister have a better chance at professional success in the long run. She remembers encountering Black and Asian people for the first time, after having only seen them on TV or reading about them in books. Attending a predominantly Black and Brown school, she graduated from her status as *la guerita* in Mexico to being called 'the white girl' in Texas, even if many Americans would automatically classify her as something other than white because of her nationality, name and languaging. Unlike Michael and Andie, who were firmly ensconced within whiteness and had to learn to push against it, Josefina has always had an uneasy relationship with her racialization, pushed around from the inside to the outside of whiteness against her will; she even dyed her hair darker eventually, partially to move away from being *la guerita*. I will note here that these experiences are unfortunately inevitable with the system of pathologization created to support whiteness and its ideals, for you can match one aspect of whiteness while always remaining somewhat distant from its supposed benefits if you don't have everything it wants.

Later, she moved to a different (and whiter) school, where few of the students were bilingual, and she saw her sister mistreated because of her darker complexion. She remembers being grateful that she was closer to whiteness because it allowed her to avoid the same fate, and she even attempted to mimic the way her peers sounded to escape being classified as foreign, immigrant, other. She watched TV and tried to match how the characters spoke. And the thing was, *she was good at it* – she produced an impressive facsimile of her white peers' accents, and people complimented her on 'getting rid' of hers.[12] It troubles her to reflect on this next part, but she also recalls the distinct deficit mindset she had about her former classmates at the more diverse school, people who continued to speak Spanish at home while her family didn't. She pitied their lack of opportunity to be part of a school environment where they might have a chance to change the way they spoke like she had. As she moved through her high school and college years, she chalked up her peers' academic struggles to their supposedly inferior English and was happy she'd come much closer to what she at the time considered the standard. And indeed, it did work out, because, by this point, she's had a fascinating career in ELT, being sent on assignment to several countries, and she probably wouldn't have done so if she hadn't come closer to the identity into which she had been placed as a child.

As you can probably gather, though, she doesn't agree with the way she once thought of her peers, and she sees her previous mindset as a sad example of internalized raciolinguistic ideologies, something that not every person with her experience moves away from. She could easily have continued to believe she'd pulled herself up by her linguistic and academic bootstraps, but she had a series of experiences that changed her mindset. At one point, she was employed at a university's intensive

English program (IEP), which, for the uninitiated, are programs that international students with supposedly inadequate languaging skills are often sent to when they enter their undergraduate or graduate studies. She was still very judgmental of unstandardized English, but then she found herself surrounded by (white) colleagues who would poke fun at students for their supposed struggles, and her experience as someone who had struggled to find a version of acceptance led her to empathize with the students instead of the instructors. Actually, no, she wasn't merely more empathetic to the students – she got angry at her colleagues, and the anger hasn't abated since. The other teachers made racist comments that were disguised as well-meaning efforts to help the students assimilate into the 'culture', and, being a young, novice teacher at the time, she didn't feel she had enough of a voice to speak up. All she was left with was a pile of anxiety and fury, and, though at first she channeled it into becoming an advocate for the students who were unfairly maligned, she carried those feelings with her, hoping to gain herself a seat at the table where her voice couldn't be ignored anymore.

Over time, she started weaving discussions of racism into her teaching, particularly when it came to her international students who were being introduced to the country for the first time and were not completely aware of the dynamics at play. She recalls one African student who, although easily classified as Black by white Americans, had not considered herself part of this racial category until she spent time here, and she expressed appreciation for Josefina's approach after having returned home. Essentially, this student had learned, both by living here and from discussing these topics in class, how much oppression was still present even in a country that is so heavily mythologized around the world, and how she wouldn't be spared no matter how she herself identified. Though I've heard (white) TESOL people express the sincere belief that they ought to keep 'politics' out of their classrooms, all this does is uphold the extant ideologies that need to be fought, and so long as the field pretends to be apolitical, it will continue to reify the harm in which it is complicit. She hadn't received any such instruction on teaching about issues of racism during her own teacher training – which should not surprise you by now – but her ability to draw upon her own experience as both insider and outsider compelled her to ensure that these issues remained front and center in her pedagogy.

As her career progressed and her employment became more secure, she began to seek out member organizations, both what I've referred to as Big TESOL and the state-based affiliates around the country. She was quickly appalled by the language ideologies on display, particularly with respect to students' 'incorrect' writing. One member had written in a public forum that she was going to give a student a harder assignment as, essentially, punishment for her deficient languaging, and Josefina was deeply disturbed by this sort of bizarre vindictiveness and cruelty. After all, she figured, if the student had been able to express their thoughts clearly, then what did it matter that it didn't match the 'standard', and why on earth were they thus deserving of punishment? But these were the sorts of attitudes that were on public display among the membership of the most prestigious and powerful organizations in the field. She thinks that if she hadn't been someone who had expended such effort on their own languaging, she might not have understood how harmful these ideas were, and so she resolved to continue to push the field and the people within it whenever she could.

Eventually, the spring of 2020 came around, and, like the other two people above, she and her close friend, another TESOL practitioner, found my article and reached out to me together. Once again, it's not so much that my article was transcendent but that, as Josefina told me, it put into words what she and a lot of other people had been thinking but had yet to express in the literature. With that said, though, I don't know that these articles aren't being written so much as that they haven't been published. The editors need to change what they're looking for, but all the rest of us need to ignore the advice I once received to dilute our own passion into the standardized, supposedly apolitical work that we are told will get us published – lest we perish – and keep our voices front and center in our work. Imagine an ELT field, an academia in general, where my short little essay wasn't seen as novel. I don't want to be one of the only people writing about whiteness and language teaching, at least not until we actually do something about it.

Josefina was particularly drawn to the discussion of altruism, and when she and her friend finally did take the class that fall, the white savior week resonated quite strongly with her. She also responded the week we spent on the harm that can be caused by all-white leadership, and she told me that, in many of her workplaces, including her current one, she's often felt resistance from top leadership against any sort of change she might try to develop. She thinks she needs to get to a much higher level to have any chance of genuinely disrupting the status quo, because there's too much invested in things remaining as they always have been. As much as she would like to believe that the individual instructors can make all the necessary changes alone, she thinks that leadership buy-in is essential, and of course, if the leaders haven't been trained or taught not to fall for these harmful ideologies, they will not be willing to challenge what they're so used to. It's rarely outright malice, just that people are generally more interested in what they think will help them, and they're not wrong to believe that they, individually, might reap more benefits from a system where they've amassed a certain amount of power, even if we'd all be better off if power weren't within the hands of so very few. It's hard not to keep trying to climb up the pyramid.

By the time her course with me ended, she was prepared to approach her contacts in Big TESOL to push for changes within that very organization. Josefina is someone who people have come to know among the aforementioned affiliate organizations, and she hoped that her years of working toward greater influence would serve her well. But, and we're three-for-three now, that's not what happened, for reasons that were both internal and external. Externally, her job informed her that she was being sent on an assignment to teach in South America, which meant she had to arrange her life to travel internationally during a pandemic while also preparing for the work she'd have to do. And internally, she simply got overwhelmed by everything that was happening, to the point where she had to take an extended break from social media and current events just to feel capable of focusing on her work obligations. She told me that she felt somewhat traumatized by her experience, and, combined with her shift in roles, she didn't feel it was the right time to try and approach TESOL with her concerns. In a way, she thinks she failed at her original plan to have a broad impact, but that doesn't mean she didn't make any progress at all.

Josefina eventually decided to use her experience to influence her direct colleagues, even if it meant holding off on challenging Big TESOL itself. At first, she attended several very bad 'diversity' trainings sponsored by her employer, during which she noticed that the facilitators had not been trained or supported in how to deliver the material, and that they were usually volunteers instead of individuals paid for their time. The facilitators would often publicly pose personal questions about experiences with racism in the workplace, and then wonder why no one was willing to speak up. Josefina grew frustrated and complained to her organization about how harmful these practices could be. She told me that our discussion about white leadership, in the second session, had helped her prepare for this eventuality, as, despite her annoyance with these trainings, she wasn't surprised to see how flimsy they were when she considered who had been responsible for offering them. She told her organization that they needed to take these issues seriously, a sharp contrast to how meek she had felt early in her career when presented with the same sort of injustice.

Essentially, she started to weaponize the fact that she is well-liked and respected, and became something of a persistent nuisance to a small number of her (white) colleagues, sending them articles and links and explicitly connecting the materials to their experiences at work. I'm sure we've all known a colleague or friend who sends us 'interesting' articles without any context, but she's made it nearly impossible for her colleagues not to see the connection between what she sends them and what they do. Her colleagues aren't the type who would have chosen to take my class – she made a point of telling me that one is married to a Republican operative, though they're divorcing – but because of the goodwill she has built, they don't dismiss what she says as readily as they would if it were coming from, say, me. There's an interesting point to be made here about who gets to take on this sort of role as someone who pushes people's buttons on issues of oppression, and Josefina is well aware of the unique identity and experiences she has had that allow her to speak as an insider with respect to both whiteness and her students' perspective. She knows how she's gotten to be precisely who she is and considers it her responsibility to use that to push against what she knows is causing her students harm.

She also knows that her colleagues have limits, and she puts a lot of effort into trying to walk that tightrope where she doesn't let them off the hook but doesn't push so hard that they shut her out entirely. These women are parents, and she has often approached them by reminding them of how these oppressive ideas might have affected their children, which is certainly tugging on their heartstrings, but if whiteness can use the same parental fear to inspire all sorts of hierarchization, she might as well use the same playbook in the opposite direction. According to her, some cracks are starting to emerge in these women's facades, and she's hopeful that they're taking these lessons to heart. On a more personal note, she's also taken the time to pass these lessons along to her nieces, which has little to do with her work obligations but is a gratifying experience, and she has watched as they have, in her view, surpassed her in passion and capability. She is convinced that the younger generation, with a bit of support from those who've spent years in the midst of the mess, will prove to be more powerful than any of us know.

There's certainly some cynicism in what Josefina told me about her career and her goals. She can't see herself staying in her current role long enough to rise to the level of power she thinks she'd need to make all of these types of changes herself, and frankly she doesn't want to be as far removed from the classroom as she'd have to be to personally redirect policies. A lot of the people she's spoken to are at the same level of hierarchy as she is, meaning policies are still controlled by people far higher up the ladder (or, you know, the pyramid). If she gets several other instructors to change the way they teach, that's not as much as changing the entire organization or field, but it will have an impact on their students and the ideologies that are presented to them, and that's more than just doing the same in her own classes, where she changed her pedagogy long ago. She's seen enough to know she shouldn't expect the field to undergo a revolution tomorrow, though that doesn't mean she believes in being satisfied with incremental change. Even with her hiatus from social media, she keeps herself plugged into the news of the field and has contacts worldwide from her work and her various pursuits. She is capable of turning up the volume on the weaponized nuisance dial whenever she sees fit, and those same feelings she found in herself as a novice teacher who worried about the way her students were treated will continue to push her forward, no matter what country she's sent to in any given year.[13] She has come to revel in the fact that she doesn't fit into any of the boxes that people have always wanted to confine her, and she's going to use that to help all of us knock down these structures, one hesitant, white colleague at a time.

I hope you didn't think these narratives were anti-climactic. I did write that they represented what I *tried* to do to challenge whiteness in the field, and indeed, along with my endless list of ongoing projects, the course is one attempt to offer something substantive to counter what's currently in place. None of my participants 'solved' whiteness in their corners of language education, and I actually can't say that any of them work in contexts where whiteness has been decentered. With the possible exception of Josefina, even their classrooms are still, to some extent, built on white language expertise because of their own identities, and until more of their organizations are willing to grow and evolve, that will remain the case. I am hopeful that they will continue to push, and that they will maintain the energy needed to persevere through the sort of setbacks you learned about in their stories, and I hope for the same with the other people who have come through my class thus far. But, though I appreciate their taking the time to catch up with me and share their stories for this book, it's a bit dispiriting to see that so many of their big plans were altered by the simplest of things. Job departures and overwhelmed potential collaborators are going to happen; the issue is that these were essentially individuals working alone to build toward something more substantial. Now, if we check back in a few years, maybe Andie's grand plans have come to fruition and there's a pipeline in the city where she works. Maybe Michael's school will have eliminated standardized testing for languages. And maybe Josefina will have found a way to bend Big TESOL to her will. But, as much as I can take some small amount of pride in the people who have set out around the ELT world to try and chip away at a massive superstructure, it's an uphill battle that we're all trying to fight.

These three individuals came from very different backgrounds and work in different parts of the language world. Their relationships with whiteness are varied, and the reasons why they've decided to no longer embrace the pyramid scheme are just as dissimilar. I do think it's fair for me to say that they all realized, one way or another, that even if it brought them certain temporary benefits, whiteness and all of the ideas that flowed from it were not beneficial to them as language educators, or to them as people. If we think all the way back to some of the ideas we've discussed earlier, they learned that, even if being seen as white might confer additional power and credentials, whiteness as a system and a concept did not converge with their own interests and morals, and they've since sought means to pull it down from its perch atop the field, even if they've only made a certain amount of progress thus far.

As long as whiteness continues to use language teaching as a means of pathologization, through its policies, its practices and its pedagogy, we're all just tossing rocks into the ocean and hoping the ripples turn into a wave. So much needs to happen before we can consider this work to be complete that it's almost silly to imagine. There are plenty of people who find the decentering of whiteness in our field to be of utmost importance, and plenty who put forth considerable effort in trying to discredit the work we are doing. Far more troubling, though, are the many who don't much care either way and just keep their head down to try and eke out a living in a field that isn't particularly set up for such a thing. I don't really care about the people who actively hate the sort of work that you and I are trying to do; I say 'you' there because I really am writing this for the people who are intrigued by these ideas but hopefully just need a push to take action. We don't need our enemies to come over to our side here. We just need everyone who might be on the fence to come down off of it and work together with us to change this field.

But that's quite enough of my diagnosing what currently exists. We went through seven chapters on the many concepts and ideologies that I believe led us to the current field of ELT, then seven more on ways in which its practices can be mapped onto the criteria of antisocial personality disorder due to its adherence to whiteness and the resultant callousness, corruption and cruelty. Part 3 is called 'Treatment…?', not just because of the narratives from my participants but also because of what follows, a prescription for a healthier version of ELT. I've written a whole lot about what's wrong with all of this, and shared with you not just my own experiences in the field, some of which I've never shared with anyone, but also the stories of three people who saw these issues and tried to work with me to find a way forward. In the remainder of Part 3, then, I'm going to finally tell you what I think needs to be done to make ELT into a field we can all be proud of, one that produces the sort of love that is missing from a system that exists primarily to other and stigmatize. I commend any one of you who is trying to do your part to disrupt what's currently in place, but it's just not going to be enough without a massive surge of support for a new way of thinking, learning and teaching. Accordingly, I offer you here my best ideas for what we need to do to create a better version of ELT. I hope this can be taken, considered and built upon, as I have no expectation that my ideas will remain useful without needing improvement over time. Nevertheless, here is my way forward.

Notes

(1) Refer back to the 'Bad at English' chapter in Part 1 for more on that experience.
(2) As opposed to *micro* (interpersonal) and *macro* (societal).
(3) The psychological violence that results from a lack of care for others who depend upon us.
(4) I still have never watched the full video because I cannot subject myself to these things anymore.
(5) Which is not to say I haven't been hassled by the police several times.

(6) And you can find much of the information from these slides in the Key Concepts section in the Introduction.
(7) Adjusting on the fly has been key to the success of these courses.
(8) Names are pseudonyms; participants were interviewed via Zoom and transcripts were generated from the recordings.
(9) Rules that I also have little patience for, which you can probably tell by now.
(10) She mentioned that she thought it was worth asking her parents about it now.
(11) For anyone reading this far into the future who doesn't know when the COVID-19 pandemic began, I hope there hasn't been another one.
(12) Florida International University would have been proud!
(13) They sent her to Japan a few months later.

Prosocial Language Teaching

The following are seven recommendations for creating a new version of English language teaching (ELT) where whiteness is no longer centered, and where the hierarchizations under which we all live are challenged and ultimately demolished. This is not meant to be a definitive list, and I encourage you to add to it, and reach out to me with any additional ideas you have. Why seven? It's a number that's recurred throughout this book, so it just made sense to add to the pattern. These are in no particular order of importance other than the fact that I'm trying to start with a wider scope in addressing issues that impact the whole field before gradually narrowing into ideas regarding classroom teaching. Alright, on with it, then.

What We Call What We Do

As you know by now, I've been using 'English language teaching' throughout this book, mostly for the sake of convenience and also because I think it's the most accurate of the available descriptors. That doesn't mean I actually think it's a good term, though, and any new version of our field is going to need a new name altogether. If you remember the acronym chapter from Part 2, one of my chief complaints was not so much the existence of acronyms but that they're used to paper over unresolved issues and don't actually address the oppression that still courses through the field. Any phrase that is going to be used to describe something as complex as what we do is not only going to need to be honest about how we often reify harmful language ideologies, but should also point toward a more productive path forward. Consequently, I propose we dispense with 'ELT' and instead admit that what we really are is *teachers of standardized English* (TSE). This would serve several purposes. First, it would broaden the scope to include people like Michael, who currently teaches what his school calls 'composition', but, were he not the type of person he is, he would simply be reinforcing raciolinguistic ideologies all the same, even if he isn't tasked with introducing the language to his students. Second, it would bring standardization front and center, and we would no longer be able to ignore its centrality in our field.

These names matter. My master's degree is in teaching English to speakers of other languages (TESOL), and by definition, no matter how my students language, they are mere 'speakers of other languages'. Similarly, 'English language teaching' suggests that there is, indeed, one version of English that is meant to be conveyed to others. By reframing our work as the teaching of standardized English, we give ourselves the option of either continuing along the same path of upholding these ideologies but nonetheless doing so more honestly or being a TSE who challenges that standardization. This also acknowledges that, at least for the time being, there's no getting away from the prominence of standardized languaging, but if it can be framed as one, rare, constructed option among many, then it might lose some of its power. Indeed, the fact that standardized English is able to hide under the name of 'the English language' is part of why it's so hard to dislodge. By bringing standardization front and center in our conceptualization of our work, we can start along the path of decentering it, like removing the curtain to reveal that there's no wizard after all, just a small, petty version of a much grander language. We need to push schools to update their programs to be explicit about the centrality of standardization in the way they conceive of the language, and I bet you'd actually see them change their curricula to move away from these ideologies before they admit that they're complicit in the broader practice of linguistic stigmatization. And speaking of schools and their curricula...

A More Comprehensive Training

All of the people I interviewed agreed that their own training had been lacking. My own experience was similar. So much of the way we attempt to build ~~English language teachers~~ teachers of standardized English is tied to the dry nuts-and-bolts practice of carrying out lesson plans, and far too many of our conferences and talks are based around 'teaching tips'. Though I suspect this is changing because so many of us have spoken up about it, you can still sit comfortably in your career as a TSE without having to consider any of these issues. You can graduate and get certified without understanding why, say, accent reduction is harmful, and then it's really up to you to make the choice to learn all of this. I had less than zero incentive to challenge my initial notions of English teaching during the years I was actually in the classroom; as you've read above, much of my evolution came after I left, though it was tapping into ideas that had long been gestating. Understandably, many teachers, no matter the genre, are overworked and underappreciated, so relying upon their rare free time to develop into the type of educator who is willing to challenge these ideologies is just a way for the system to remain in place. This all needs to happen from the moment they first take any sort of education class, be it in undergraduate studies, a master's program or an external certification.

A new version of training needs to include a deep engagement with all of the issues I've raised here, from racism, anti-Blackness and whiteness, to the intersection of ableism, concepts of intelligence and language ideologies. It's necessarily messy, but so is the work of education, and this is how we have to build our future teachers. You shouldn't be able to step into a classroom without having a clear concept of all of these different types of oppression, and, if you are in any way responsible for programmatic decisions, you need to ensure that you're not producing any more graduates who are lacking in such ways. I'm not particularly sure what to do about the existing teacher corps that isn't the type to sign up for classes like mine – nor do I think my very short class is enough – but I doubt you can force the resistant ones to grow. Our best bet is to replace them over time, so that by the time toddlers my son's age are old enough to consider this field, the ones who worship at the altar of enforced standardization and raciolinguistic ideologies would be in the distinct, disempowered minority, which is to say, they will have finally been *minoritized*. Without much more comprehensive training, we'll keep having to scramble and backfill the missing knowledge for the handful of eager people who want to seek something different, and it's high time that stopped being the way we went about building teachers.

Purposeful Purchasing

These same schools need to use their purchasing power to select vastly different materials for their developing teachers. It's one thing for me to tell individual teachers to spend their money more wisely, but that's not the problem, really, because that will hardly hit them where it hurts. It wouldn't take a program director very long to scan a given company's materials for harmful language ideologies and evidence of pathologization in practice. At this point, the school could either choose materials from a different company, or pressure said company to evolve. They could even combine with other schools to alter the standardized English teaching materials that are most commonly disseminated. In the case of programs where professors are given the freedom to choose their own curricula, schools can still recommend more anti-oppressive companies after having done their preliminary research. The only reason that the publishers continue to create materials that reify these harmful ideas is because they think it's the most profitable way to operate. Even though we are currently stuck existing within racial capitalism, we do still have the power to band together to affect the almighty market. When it comes to the materials that are given to novice language teachers, then, the institutions responsible for their development are dropping the ball if they don't put their weight behind finding alternatives.

On a related note, school districts need to change what they buy as well. Textbooks and other materials are hardly the only problem in our field, but they are perhaps one of the most visible, and it will take nothing more than a little bit of time and extra effort for those with the power to make purchasing decisions to find better options. I am well aware that, depending on the context, the companies responsible for said materials might have long-existing relationships with the institutions and their leadership, which is why I think it might be likelier that they pressure their current supplier to alter their output. Institutions can make themselves quite annoying if they so choose, to the point where it might be less stressful for a publisher to change than it would be to continue to be harangued by unhappy customers. For better or worse, right now, institutions that make large publisher purchases are indeed customers first and foremost, and they have the right to demand better products lest they take their business elsewhere. Similarly, students absolutely have the power to band together and demand better materials in their own programs, and I don't know if any such students will ever read this, but you don't have to suffer through the bad textbook if you don't want to. All of us lower on the pyramid are told that these decisions are out of our hands, but we have a lot more hands than they do, and the fact is, the only thing that motivates said companies is income; they'll make a glittering textbook on countering raciolinguistic ideologies if they think it'll make them more money than the same old song they've been playing.

Upending EFL Prerequisites

As of now, in many countries, all you need to become an English as a foreign language (EFL) teacher is a particular passport and some level of schooling. Yes, they prize whiteness, but, as you know by now, whiteness isn't just light-colored skin; you have a much better shot at the type of job you might want if you can get closer to the ideal in both look and sound. In Part 2, we've discussed how the very concept of nativeness, whether they call it that or not, is detrimental to both the students and the teachers. Honestly, we probably just need to pull the whole of EFL apart and start from scratch, but in lieu of that, the countries and companies that do this hiring need a whole new set of prerequisites for their recruitment. Forget about what type of passport people have or even if (standardized) English was the language in which they studied. Forget about how they sound and look. Yes, teachers should be capable of teaching, which is hardly an objective metric, but the way EFL teachers are hired now is rarely based on any sort of skill.

I instead submit to you that if teachers were hired based on how well they could demonstrate care for the culture and language of the students they would be teaching, they would be far more successful than the stray 'native speaker' or representative of whiteness. Schools might blanch at losing the ability to market idealized specimens to their potential clients, and there would surely be many holdouts to what's being proposed here.

But the teachers would have a better experience traveling to countries for which they had a documented affection and respect, and the students would have a better chance of connecting with their teachers. Yes, this would have prevented my own career from starting, as I knew less than nothing about South Korea or Korean when I was 21, but maybe it would have inspired me to sit down and study the place and the people I hoped to meet.

There is certainly a risk that this would lower their scores on the standardized English exams that far too many are forced to take, but I don't actually think that that's a given. This may seem like a digression,[1] but there's a rather large study which suggests a correlation between Black students' graduation rate and the presence of but a single Black teacher in elementary school (Gershenson *et al.*, 2017), which is more Black teachers than I ever had at that age. Now, this doesn't mean that Black teachers are inherently more skilled, and of course, Black teachers can uphold anti-Blackness just as much as anyone else, but it's reasonable to state that, because of the way that Blackness is often treated, they have shared some experiences with their students, and might have a chance at connecting with their students more effectively. To be clear, this is a correlation and not a causation, but to return to the EFL discussion, the field is afraid to move away from the native model because it fears losing income, and that loss of income is tied to the specter of lower test scores and other related metrics. If EFL teachers were sourced via their connection to the places to which they hope to travel, I can't say that the students would do *better* on the tests, but I think that they'd be much happier, and that's what a new version of our field would seek.

Testing Transparency

So. Look. Best case scenario, we'd be done with using proficiency tests as a means of entry into exclusive institutions, or, indeed, having exclusive institutions at all. The fact is, it's marginally harder for white perceivers to understand people who test below a certain level, and that extra work just isn't seen as worth it for a lot of places. With all of that said, this book is being released in 2022, and there's zero chance that we've done away with the entire testing apparatus by that point, or any of the several years afterward. Similar to my recommendation regarding what we call the field, then, my suggestion here is to get transparent about what tests are and represent.

There are two streams of testing that I want to address. There's the way students are prepared for tests within their normal schooling, and there's the external test-prep world, which is its own monster I'll get to in a second. Regarding the former, we need to be honest with our learners. The tests are narrowly tailored around a mostly unreasonable and unrealistic set of constructed standards that only tangentially apply to the way they are likely to language, and they are, for the time being, tied to various types of access and cultural capital. They can choose to put considerable effort into attaining a specific score, like a video game with stakes that are far too high, but we can also make clear that these metrics do not define them or tell any sort of story about their value. The students who are classified as deficient in languaging should have the testing portion of their education separated from their normal day, and schools should frame this as a misguided obstacle that has been placed in front of them for as long as it continues to exist. You might be thinking that this would demotivate them, but what we're doing now hardly engenders enthusiasm, so what could it hurt to be transparent? Indeed, I think we might see better results if the students were told that the tests were harmful but that they ought to prove they could outmaneuver the system anyway. It's worth a shot.

As for the global test prep system, your tests of English as a foreign language (TOEFLs) and your tests of English for international communication (TOEICs) and what have you, it's already separated from the school day, of course, and, as far as I can tell from people who've worked within it (including Josefina), it's presented fairly neutrally, as a necessary series of steps to attain entry into a new educational and/ or professional world. Ultimately, these organizations need to be very careful in removing harmful ideologies from how they present the language, and stick to an honest description of what's on the tests, as well as making it easier for those with less money to afford the preparation. If the tests exist and determine students' future, then someone should be available to support them, but they can't reify the students' classification as linguistically deficient in the process, and they can't exclude the poor from the picture. Mostly they're trash and should just go away, but that's not actionable advice, is it?

Membership (Re)Organizations

When I started my doctoral studies, one of the things they told me was to look at a big, long list of professional organizations and join the ones that suited my interests. As most of you know, even the 'student' rates for these organizations are rather expensive, and unfortunately, almost all of these organizations are in sort of a bind, in that they have to make the decision to either push their field forward or remain beholden to their least progressive members. I'll leave it up to you to determine whether or not your own organizations straddle this line effectively, but the largest ones are often too fearful to push the envelope, and they stay stuck in a hand-wringing loop. I've made my issues with Big TESOL clear, but this is no less true at other similar organizations, and even if a new, progressive leader is elected to a powerful position, it's rare that they're fully surrounded by people who share their vantage point. It's hard to suddenly reverse course on a big ship, which is something you could say about the field in general, and society more broadly, though, as I've said before in this book, that's no reason not to try.

The same point can be made of academic journals, many of which are, of course, tied directly to these organizations. You will certainly find a really compelling article in the occasional issue of the 'most prestigious' journals, but you will still find publications about the 'achievement gap' and 'learning loss' alongside this important work, so it's always one step forward, one step back. I don't blame any scholar, particularly not a scholar of color, for trying to get their name into one of the big journals, because you need jobs and that's how the system currently works, but this isn't how it should be. We need to do whatever we can to starve the big journals of our best ideas, and we need to ensure that these new ideas are easily disseminated. More than anything about its quality, I think that the biggest factor in the relative popularity of my 'Decentring Whiteness' article was the fact that the journal it was published in, *BC TEAL*, is open access and, from what the editor told me, eager to publish new ideas.

Do what you have to do, writers, to get your jobs. Hopefully that will change someday, and I expect it will soon, given how unsustainable this current paradigm is. But it's time for all of us who care about a different language education field to do our own thing. We need several new, open-access avenues of publication that directly challenge the status quo. We need new organizations with explicit commitments to decentering whiteness and countering anti-Blackness in the field. The old ones do not exist to serve the people who want a different field, and we need them to see that they can't hold onto the power they've amassed without the people who want something more. They've always been inhospitable places for us to try and thrive, and we need to finally make them feel that same level of pressure. And then, if they are willing to really do the work, we can let them join what we've built. Or we can let them wither away to nothing.

Shifting Classroom Power

Finally, we turn to the classroom, as I'm sure some of you would like a recommendation for how you might change your pedagogy right this minute. Truthfully, little we do in front of our students will matter all that much in the long run if the field remains mired in its old ways, but there are always things we can build toward. More than anything else, then, more than a fun way to teach verbs or a clever pronunciation lesson, the best thing we can do is to consider our power in the classroom.

As I've said, one of the reasons Freire (1970) criticizes what was, and remains, the dominant form of pedagogy was the fact that it presents the teacher as a fountain of knowledge ready to fill the students who are waiting as empty vessels. No matter how nice or fun you are, if you position yourself as the sole authority on English in your room, you are perpetuating this system, and the many ideologies we've discussed here are tied to this hierarchization. You can know everything about the connection between dis/ability, racism and language, but if your (perhaps unexamined) mindset in the classroom is that you are the sole linguistic authority, you have to find a way to break free from that. There are, absolutely, experiences and skills of yours that your students are unlikely to have had, but you must find a way to treat them as intellectual equals.

In an article I co-authored with Vijay Ramjattan and Scott Stillar (Gerald *et al.*, 2021), we presented the idea of what we called *counterprescriptivism*. As we explained:

> Racialized students should be empowered and encouraged to challenge their white teachers if and when they are told the way they are using the language is incorrect. Meaning-making is ultimately a negotiation of power, and if a student can convey the meaning they seek, they should be able to assert their intent in the face of possible correction. (Gerald *et al.*, 2021: para 6)

This is but one idea. If reading that can help you come up with your own, I hope that you can develop some and run with them. The point is to explicitly share linguistic power in the classroom with your students, and accordingly work together toward a version of languaging that supports both them and you.

This is not meant to be the full list of changes that need to occur to turn our field from antisocial to prosocial. We have a gargantuan amount of work to do, and we needed to start several decades ago, but tomorrow will have to suffice. The fact is, we believe we're the good guys, but we're, by and large, upholding what others have put in place, and unless we finally get honest about the hierarchization we're pushing onto our students and onto everyone who engages with English without being fully included into whiteness, we'll continue to play our roles as pawns in the pattern of pathologization that we desperately need to break. I hope that what you've read thus far has been convincing enough to get you thinking about what you can do differently in the language education space, and if not, my apologies for falling short. But this battle is going to be fought, one way or the other, and considering how many people are continuing to have English pushed on them, it's up to all of us who are part of the field to make it one that brings love and support instead of stigmatization and harm. It is fully within our power to change English language teaching, and anyone who tells you otherwise is beholden to the only system in which they feel comfortable existing.

My larger hope for all of us is that we not only push whiteness out of the center of our field, but also that our field can play a central role in the demolition of whiteness overall. This is not a silly pipe dream, though, but a real goal in which you yourself can play a part. Accordingly, we have just a bit more to discuss.

Note

(1) How rare for me!

Conclusion

Pathologization Dependency

In Michael Mechanic's (2021) book, *Jackpot*, he spends time with individuals in the orbit of extreme wealth. I say 'in the orbit' because most of the ultra-rich people with whom he wanted to speak were unwilling to sit for open discussions involving their own wealth. Yes, we all have the image of flashy celebrities, but those are exceptions; most of the people with hundreds of millions of dollars (or more) are not people you've ever heard of. What Mechanic found, among other things, is that these people are unbelievably stressed and anxious about their own wealth. These are the people at the very, very top of the pyramid we've discussed throughout this book, and they're actually pretty miserable. This is not to say that wealth doesn't confer significant advantages, including, as he outlines in his book, a deeply immoral international concierge health care system, but if you think about what everyone is being told to admire, you can see that there really isn't anything worthwhile at the top of the heap. The public discourse in our system favors ceaseless growth at the expense of others, but all of it to what end? The small number of people with more power and wealth than you can imagine are forced to spend much of their time or that same money on protecting their own fortunes and legacies, and in turn the rest of us have considerably less because they're so preoccupied with themselves. There is great reason to try and escape from poverty, but the message we all receive isn't just to get to a comfortable place, which is rare enough, but rather to just keep trying to move up and up. And *why*?

It's simple enough to say that people buy into the story they've been sold of reaching the top, something from which few of us are immune, but I think there's more to it than wanting to win at a proverbial competition. I think, for this fantasy to have become persuasive enough to power our global society, we don't just need to want to win, we need to want other people to lose. What I mean by this is that, as Mechanic points out in his book, since we tend to compare ourselves to the people in our own circles, if everyone around us suffers a blow that we are able to absorb, it can provide us with the same boost as if we'd been the only one to hit the lottery ourselves. Yet, we live in a world where upward mobility is rare (Song *et al.*, 2019), and indeed, when it comes to axes of oppression, few of us will live long enough to move from an oppressed social group to a dominant one. This is a long way of saying that it's a lot easier to feel better about your station in life because you see the flaws in others than it is to expect you'll actually reach the top, and in order for these flaws to remain front and center, we need to ensure that we engage in a constant practice of pathologization. Without there being something genuinely wrong with the people below you, all that's keeping you afloat might in fact be a global system of oppression that happens to value the groups of which you are a member. Whiteness and all of the concepts tied to it depend upon this pathologization to function effectively, and most of us do too, even if we don't realize it. The only way we'll ever get out of this, then, is to take apart this system of pathologization, and demolish the structure of whiteness overall.

What we call English language teaching is a perfect tool to further this pathologization, because, unlike some other axes of oppression, you do have a certain measure of control over the way you produce language, even if you can't control how people perceive you. As just one example, the related field of second language acquisition expends considerable effort on boiling its namesake process down to formulas that hardly take the individuals and their identities involved into account, rendering any supposed struggles a more personal failing than they truly are. We think white polyglots are either preternaturally gifted or extremely hard workers – and surely some of them are – but the racialized people who move through several named languages in ways we consider 'imperfect' are nonetheless deficient and in need of correction. We almost need to believe in our treasured language ideologies in order for our hierarchies to be maintained, and this ties into all of the concepts that have been weaved throughout this book.

Without the stigmatization of unstandardized English, we'd have no effective way of oppressing people who were otherwise perfectly competent but communicated in ways we found less than ideal. A former colleague of mine was routinely disrespected by our clients, who clearly didn't like being told they couldn't do certain things, yet who frequently complained about the fact that she, in their view, didn't 'speak English'. My former students have always been forced to apologize for the way they language, when truth be told, the public was inhospitable to their incontrovertible distance from whiteness. In a way, language gives people a wonderful excuse to dismiss people they were never going to respect in the first place, but because it's seen as so anodyne and neutral, and within a person's control, we're happy to use it to push people down.

Speaking of control, in a previous ideological lifetime, I was the co-presenter of a presentation that involved some of everyone's favorite buzzwords, including *grit* (Duckworth, 2016). I was convinced that if I just found an innovative way for my students to gain control over their languaging, they'd soon reach great heights in English. We cited evidence that suggested that a person with *an internal locus of control*, a belief that they could influence their own circumstances rather than the other way around (Joelson, 2017), stood a better chance of succeeding, yet what this and other similar research often fails to ask is who is allowed to believe they can control their circumstances. Ultimately, once you've been pathologized through the way you communicate, it's difficult to find support in any way other than suggestions to improve said communication.

People who are viewed as unable to clearly communicate or process English are positioned as lacking in ability overall. At another previous job, in employee training, we were told to create curricula at a 'fifth-grade reading level', despite the fact that all of the grown adults who worked at this particular government agency could communicate with one another just fine. All of the normal regulations about diversity and discrimination were posted around the office, but the way we viewed these workers' languaging was a window into the way that unstandardized English is tied to conceptualizations of ability. Workers whose notes on the agency's unwieldy database were written outside of enforced norms were routinely corrected, and my colleagues and I were occasionally tasked with helping these grown adults with years or decades of experience compose emails that the agency viewed as acceptable when we were in our training sessions together. People expressed anger at 'ungrammatical' notes the workers wrote, despite the fact that the most incomprehensible thing about them was the inter-agency jargon and abbreviations they were told to use. This wasn't an English academy by any means, but the fact that, at some point before my tenure, they had decided that their staff couldn't fully be trusted with communication undermined their tendency to hire people from many different racial and linguistic backgrounds. It was gratifying to see that, unlike so many other types of work, racialized users of unstandardized English could indeed be hired into salaried positions that paid enough to provide them with comfortable lives, but the way their languaging was viewed was an indication of how little they were ultimately respected by their leadership, very few of whom were representative of the same linguistic diversity I mentioned. That environment was an example of how conceptualizations of language are tied to the way we view ability and dis/ability, and though they'd be sued immediately for an actionable example of racism, we can still use language as a tool to pathologize those we don't actually value.

I should add, by the way, for those who are unaware, 'fifth grade' in the United States is usually for children ages 10–11, and this reading level was explained to me repeatedly as, essentially, 'don't use big words in your materials', despite the fact that most agency missives were written in impenetrable legalese that even I don't understand. These adults had full access to context clues, the internet and each other, if they really needed to find out what something meant, but ultimately, it suggests to me that the agency felt their workers were about as capable as children because of their languaging, which ties all the way back to the beginning of the book when we touched on the fact that colonized people were often seen as childlike. It's hardly a coincidence that so many of these workers hailed from countries colonized by English-speaking nations.

Let's bring it back to the settlers here. No matter what they did (and still do), no one wants to be seen as the villain. It is presented as neutral now, but pushing English and other colonial languages onto the people who lived in countries that were 'settled' was seen as a gift for the poor, uncivilized natives. I haven't spoken all that much about religion in this text because I simply haven't spent the time in theological spaces to offer much valuable insight in that respect, but there's not much difference between so-called mission trips and the way whiteness is exported around the world through English teaching, and this goes back centuries to much less benign campaigns. You can recall the residential schools, you can recall the treatment of the enslaved, whichever action you prefer, conquest is never complete without linguistic imperialism, and this is justified by the pathologization of the imperial subjects. Yes, they ultimately want money and power and land, but for the individual members of society, who are likely to never have all that much of said power, the conquest is shared with them by virtue of rendering the colonized as deficient. For people at my or your level, the disorder contained within the exploited allows that exploitation to continue unabated, and we are comforted by exclusion from the exploited group yet constantly anxious about our possible descent to the target level. It's not economics that trickles down, but the feeling that others are inferior, and whole industries, including our own, can and do power themselves off of this emotion.

Not every country has a large number of people we'd classify as Black, but we're all swimming in the water of anti-Blackness, even people like me who always knew they were Black and were mostly happy about it. Anti-Blackness, even if rarely made explicit, colors much of this perpetual pathologization process, because reminding whiteness of the dark projection it has created is a reason for deep-seated fear. It's no wonder that many of the workers I mentioned above are called out for their languaging when it's evocative of Black cultures, and it's no wonder that they are then seen as childlike. It's no wonder, as I said way back in Part 1, that I still, several months after I wrote that previous chapter, get 'slang' as a result when I google 'African-American language'. It's no wonder that to embody Blackness in your languaging is to be seen as deficient, no matter how strong your command of your communication actually is (Baker-Bell, 2020). The more that some white folks say that my writing resonates with them, the more I wonder how true that would remain if I didn't tend to write fairly close to standardized norms, and, like this book, much of your favorite scholarship is still written to appeal to a white audience using language that they won't dismiss as inferior.

There are a lot about my anxieties regarding my own language in this book, as you've seen by now, but I include it because, since part of this work is autoethnography, analyzing my identity with respect to the subject is part of the methodology involved in the work that I do, and is part of the reason it can be powerful for scholars of color to employ (Hernández-Saca & Cannon, 2019, 2021). I can't really spend however many pages talking about anti-Blackness and languaging without explicitly considering how this has impacted me. I also include these concerns because I want to be clear that this policing of Black languaging doesn't just impact the people who are excluded but is also harmful to the people you might expect are included in the version of English that whiteness would welcome. By making clear that how I speak and write is often perceived as not just separate from but superior to the racial category into which I've been placed and with which I have identified, there is an internal bifurcation that people in my position have to carefully navigate. Frankly, I gave up a while ago, and I stopped trying to either distance myself from or match my peers, but I only have that choice because of all of the other ways in which I'm closer to the ideal.

One of those ways, of course, is my class status. Less about my own income than about the fact that my parents had degrees from exclusive institutions, I didn't have to navigate a lot of the obstacles that other Black people my age had to when considering what to do after high school or even after college. My whole English teaching career happened partially because of my nationality, yes, but the second requirement was a college degree. I got to do what I got to do because we were closer to the top of the pyramid in the first place, though as I've learned more about how unbelievably wealthy my classmates actually were, clearly we were several rungs below them. We've discussed many times how the concept of nativeness is harmful for language teaching, but the fact that I was able to get the job with a college degree but without any sort of expertise in teaching recalls our early discussion of the *aristogenic* intent of the eugenics movement. Even leaving the most egregious aspects aside, they explicitly wanted to create environments through which a better class of people would be built, and with the particular types of 'native' teachers who were hired, a better class of English user can be created. Recall that it was only my similarly exclusive degree that allowed the Korean officials to overlook my Blackness and its negative linguistic associations.

My parents were and are exceptions to what was expected of their peers, especially considering the era in which they themselves were raised. Had we been different types of people, they would be precisely the type that devotees of racial capitalism would point to as counterexamples when people like me try to demonstrate the oppression inherent in this economic system. If there's one or two Black people who can escape their expected fate, then the rest of us deserve what we get. To 'succeed', as racial capitalism would define it, is to defy the pathology of Blackness rather than to disprove its validity. Any individual who can do it proves that the others just didn't try hard enough, an infuriating cycle of justification but an illustration of why pathologization is so integral to the perpetuation of this hierarchization. There will always, always, always be something wrong with the people who don't rise and, as ever, academic literature will be there to support this pathologization dependency, because academia depends on it too. Go and do a quick search to see how many articles you can find that compare performance between white and Black students (i.e. studies about *race*) without actually mentioning *racism*. Indeed, through every search I do, a group of search terms + 'race' brings exponentially more results than the same search terms + 'racism', even though no one's race has ever caused a problem without the presence of racism. I am sure that many of the researchers comparing racial groups are attempting to support the racialized, but if you're not inclined to see the humanity in Blackness and other racialized groups, it's just more evidence for our status as fundamentally disordered. Accordingly, we, along with the dis/abled and those who speak unstandardized English, are mashed together into a stigmatized stew and told to fight each other to see who can get the closest to the top of a pyramid that still leaves its victors bereft of joy. What are we even doing here?

This is all just a race to the bottom, pun fully intended. You can't 'win' unless everyone else not only loses but is proven to be deserving of their loss, and you have to profit, literally or figuratively, from the pain of countless people if you want to get anywhere close to the mythical ideal. Language is a powerful tool, but it's not the only one, and whiteness will continue to slam us all against each other so long as we allow it to exist. We stand little chance to extricate ourselves from this, then, unless a large enough portion of white people not only grow uncomfortable enough with this system to read these books or sign up for whiteness classes but actively reject the lessons they've been taught. What white people need to do, really, is to become heretics.

Heretical Whiteness

What exactly is wrong with 'fine'?

As an aspiration for us to push on people, we sell the exceptional, the transcendent, but there is plenty of power to go around for everyone to be *just fine* if that's what we actually want to have happen. Think about it for a second: if you snatched most of what the people at the very top of the pyramid are hoarding and spread it among everyone as evenly as possible, we'd all be better off. Even the people who fancy themselves exceptional would be rid of the anxiety of dealing with their extreme wealth and the fear of slipping down levels of the pyramid. I understand why we all fall for this – I play the lotto sometimes too and imagine what I'd do if I hit the jackpot. I've also imagined what it would actually be like if whiteness really were demolished, and my family and I could live without having to assert our legitimacy every day. And in my view, as fun as revenge fantasies are for the many people harmed by whiteness, what it would really look like is that everyone would be… fine. Everyone would have enough food, shelter, health care and love, and they'd all be fulfilled in how they choose to spend their time. Despite all my rhetoric, what I do is ultimately about this sort of love that many of us are prevented from enjoying. What whiteness does, through its many related ideologies and stigmatizations, is stand in the way of the type of love that we absolutely need as a species if we have any interest in continuing this whole civilization thing. I'm not saying whiteness is the primary reason we're hurtling toward global disaster, but I am saying that, with regard to language teaching, the ongoing climate refugee crisis is more of a feature than a bug for the institutions that want a surfeit of subordinate clients (United Nations Refugee Agency, 2021). We lack humanity when we depend upon the pyramid, and so few people benefit that we're ultimately endangering everyone just so that we can prove that certain groups deserve their position at the bottom. In our pursuit of pathologization, we do nothing but harm ourselves. But there's no reason this has to continue.

Now, I don't assume all of you reading this are white, but this last part here is for white readers. Specifically white readers with a small amount of power or money, at the least, since I have no desire to give advice to people who are struggling to get by. But the rest of you, you've got work to do, in all aspects of your life. I also realize that some of this might be seen as an individualist approach to a systemic issue, but individuals buy and read books, and there are choices you can and should make in your daily lives, even as you begin to work with me and others on challenging structural oppression.

So, you must consciously and explicitly reject the oft-unspoken trappings of whiteness. You can't just reject racism, which is a good first step, but the equally powerful concept that you are unavoidably connected to. You have to look directly at whiteness and say that you don't believe in its value, and you need to live this every day. If you've already started, if you've taken some classes and done some reading, that's good, you should keep that up. If you have already extricated yourself from proudly racist family members, that's also good, and if you haven't, go do it now. You do not have time for your uncle or your mother to get it together, unless they show signs they're willing to do the work alongside you, and they're bad for your kids, if you have any. With that said, make sure you are ready to push your more liberal friends who get uncomfortable when people talk explicitly about whiteness, but don't position yourself as the Good White Person while you do it. It's hard to toe this line, but you have to. Sorry.

In fact, who are your friends? Have you chosen well? Are they people who will support you as you challenge whiteness, or will they withdraw from such a pursuit? Can you trust them to choose heresy over the god of whiteness, or do you need to find different people to rely on? I don't say this lightly – I had to remove a considerable number of people from my life when I focused more intently on this work, and of course, I'm not actually white myself. It might be easier for you to just let your indifferent white friends slide, but as long as they're around, your work will be all that much harder.

Money is a big part of whiteness, of course, and where you choose to spend yours matters. Try taking a break from donating large amounts of your money to well-funded, white-led institutions, if you have the funds to make such a choice in the first place. Look up every place you choose to donate and volunteer, and see who they allow to actually make decisions on their behalf. Is the staff diverse, or is it 'diverse' with racialized frontline staff and smiling white board members and directors? Maybe skip out on the galas celebrating the world's truly antisocial thugs, people who pilfer from their populace and only give back to avoid paying taxes and scrub their consciences clean. Put your money into the hands of the people who actually need it instead of other white people who believe they know more about the racialized than the racialized do about themselves.

If you live in an extremely white area, don't just sit there and accept that that's how things are. Look into the history of why it's so white and who was pushed out to make it that way, then ensure that everyone in your community knows where they really live and whose land they're on. And when one of your neighbors pushes back after you give them this information, don't let up. Be the one person on your block who speaks up when neighbors express discomfort with changing demographics, and get other supportive neighbors on board.

If you have children, and you moved someplace to put them into 'good' schools, interrogate what that actually means and how those metrics are determined. Who are the schools good *for*? And what exactly would happen to the students in 'good' schools if they were forced to attend a 'bad' school? Would they truly suffer, or would they, in this system built around them, actually be just fine? Or is it more that they would 'fall behind' and stand a lower chance of securing their own place in the pyramid later on, thereby affecting your own standing? Just think about it. Does your child 'need' the test prep that other people can't afford, or would they, horror of horrors, end up at a perfectly fine school if they didn't excel? I'm not saying no one at all needs support, but I *am* saying that if you have the option to choose an unnecessary leg up, you shouldn't. What this is about, really, is relinquishing that extra push that whiteness wants to hand you. If you don't consciously turn against it, it will find you and support you anyway. And when your friends ask you why you've made these choices, you need to be honest with them, despite the awkwardness that might ensue.

Speaking of said awkwardness, you need to talk about that. Whiteness thrives in silence and you need to reject that silence. And if you need support in doing so, build a community, though without burdening any racialized friends you might have, unless you're willing to compensate them fairly for their labor. Find some white friends who are willing to push against hand-wringing resistance, and talk about how to address each instance together. Construct yourself a heretical whiteness support group if you need to, and seek the paid guidance of racialized experts. Also, please don't pretend you yourself are above being called out when you inevitably screw up. That's a big part of this process, too, reaching the point where you are confident enough to know both that you will make mistakes and that you'll continue to improve. So find some people to work with so you're not challenging whiteness alone. The people I've worked with have all gotten over that initial fear that challenging whiteness will make others uncomfortable, because they understand that it is part of the responsibility of heretical whiteness that you will upset people. You will need support in doing so, and you should seek it out proactively.

Finally, when it comes to language, I've said about as much as I possibly can about how to challenge whiteness in English language teaching (ELT), but this goes for every place where opinions about communication are expressed. Do the people you know criticize poor grammar and spelling frequently? How are accents viewed and framed by your friends and colleagues? Do you actually value all ways of communicating, and in what ways could you improve?

For people who are ensconced in whiteness and all it has to offer, those who are outside of its chilly embrace are seen as neither legitimate nor fully capable. To exercise your perfectly reasonable right to make a request or to occupy space is to challenge their own identity as the only people who represent order. To dare to live the same way that they do is to step outside of our status as disordered, and to attempt to speak their language is no more feasible to them than an animal learning to talk.

When you subscribe to the pathologizations that whiteness depends on, there is a very narrow sliver of humanity that is deserving of respect, support and love. To truly value everyone is to turn away from the hierarchies that have been built on the backs of so many. If you are ready to choose heretical whiteness, to reject what you've been taught to believe, you will be committing an act of immense love, from which there is no turning back. It will be scary, and messy, and ultimately joyous, and it's just about our only chance.

For me, this entire project has emerged from a realization that the only way out is through. This idea has become something of a mantra for me over the past few years. Whether it's my gradual realization and eventual diagnosis of my neurodivergence, the mood disorders that I struggled with, or, most importantly, the way I tried to pretend I hadn't been deeply harmed by racism, it all ends up in my scholarship. There are willing participants in my research, but as a writer, I pretty much always write about the way I experience the world, yet I think that's what every writer is doing – the only difference is whether or not they're honest about it. I offer you a final story about how I've tried to address the harm of whiteness through my public scholarship, in the hope that more of you will join me in these efforts.

In the fall of 2021, I participated in a livestream for an offshoot of the British Council, a recording of which is on YouTube if you're curious. We were basically talking about a lot of the ideas you've read in this book, and overall, we received extremely positive feedback. Several thousand people have apparently watched the livestream by now, and I worked with British Council again a few months later.

Two people didn't like it, though. One was a Black teacher who commented during the stream that 'diversity in language teaching isn't necessary'. Always disappointing when Black folks uphold hierarchies that keep us down, and particularly given I said nothing about 'diversity' at all. We sort of told her why what she was saying was harmful, and frankly it was fun getting to really dig into why the work I do matters. I figured that was the end of it, and I encouraged people to email me if they wanted to discuss the issues further. That may have been a mistake, because a couple days later, I got an anonymous email from someone calling themselves 'Leftenant Dan', and, well. Brace yourself, I'm just going to post the email here.

He wrote:

> *First off, you aren't even fucking black. Next off, if you dare talk about 'ending whiteness' one more fucking time, you sick racist fakenigger, I'm going to walk on over and 'end your jaw' with a swift fucking cracking KO that will leave you slurring like a real nigger for the rest of your fucking miserable life. Do this: go enter yourself into a permanent mental asylum before you get yourself or others hurt, you dumb fcking crybully.*
>
> *Sincerely,*
Your betters.

I told the guy who organized the event, he was outraged and contacted the email server, the email server shut down the guy's account, whatever. I'm not worried about him and the bridge he lives under. I'm a writer and I like to talk about racism so let's talk about it. It's all data.

Let's start at the beginning.

'First off, you aren't even fucking black'.

So, this guy saw my livestream and clearly saw my face, but he says this. Based on what he says after this, the only thing I can conclude is that he thinks I'm too 'articulate' to fit his conception of Blackness. If anyone doubts the reality of raciolinguistic ideologies…

'*Next off, if you dare talk about "ending whiteness" one more fucking time…*'.

Okay, he's British ('next off'). I never said 'ending whiteness' on the livestream, because I knew it was a less radical audience than my twitter followers, so he's just making things up. But, let's be clear, whiteness is the cause of this guy, so whiteness can go.

'*…you sick racist fakenigger, I'm going to walk on over and "end your jaw" with a swift fucking cracking KO that will leave you slurring like a real nigger for the rest of your fucking miserable life*'.

That's not a typo on my part by the way. He spelled it 'fakenigger' without a space. Yes, there's a threat in there, but who cares. 'Slurring like a real nigger' is the crux of this analysis, and ties all the way back into the history I included in Part 1. This man's ideology is such that Black languaging is classified as worthless and unintelligible – we are not allowed to speak clearly and forthrightly in this guy's mind, and to do so is to become a '*fakenigger*'.

'*Do this: go enter yourself into a permanent mental asylum before you get yourself or others hurt, you dumb fcking crybully*'.

I have no idea why he censored 'fcking' there. But, anyway, just for good measure he calls me mentally ill. Language, race and dis/ability, all together. I wish someone I knew based their entire body of work around that intersection…

I have written a book that argues that language variety, racialization and the conceptualization of dis/ability are all intertwined and positioned as pathologies subordinate to whiteness, and here comes this guy to prove my point. What a wonderful present this man gave me! This happened between the first and second drafts of writing this book, and I was so glad to have an ending that tied the three major ideas together. A generous soul, this troll.

Was I scared? I mean, I considered being scared, and of course, white nationalists are terrifying when they're in power, but this is clearly some useless individual who isn't even in the same country as I am. Hell, most of the people who watched the livestream were in far-flung locales, so he's probably a white English as a foreign language (EFL) teacher who can't handle the fact that he's not qualified for his job.

I'm making jokes here, but I want to be clear that this sort of nonsense just isn't something certain scholars have to deal with. I'm using it as data, as fuel, but although I'm glad I can do that, I shouldn't have to. With that said, if I'm going to be out in the public, some folks aren't going to like it, and if this is going to be part of it, then the only way to deal with it is to address it head on.

This man was clearly threatening me to try to get me to shut up, and you all know quite well by now, this is just going to make me louder. So, thanks, 'Leftenant Dan'. I'm never going to run out of fuel at this rate.

And for all of you who've read this far, keep talking, people. They can't stop us.

Acknowledgments

As you might gather from all the pages you just read, I don't believe that either the language education field or academia are constructed to affirm the work I am trying to do. As such, to have had any chance of putting a book like this together – while working a full-time job and finishing a related but separate dissertation – I needed the support of a great many individuals, each of whom played different but vital roles in my development, and in the development of my thinking and writing.

First, it was the eventual chair of my dissertation committee who told me she thought that a short essay I was writing about whiteness and ability had the potential to be expanded into something larger, and so when the publisher inquired about working with me, I believed in my work enough to submit a version of that same introduction you read as a sample that turned into this book. I've worked with Catherine Voulgarides on several writing projects now, and without her encouragement to step into bolder epistemological territory, I expect I'd have given up long ago on writing anything interesting. I also have to thank the other two members of my committee, Anthony Picciano and Davíd Hernández-Saca, for their guidance and their critical analysis of my schoolwork, and their patience with my own impatience. I also have to thank the staff and peer reviewers at Multilingual Matters for not only releasing the book, but also accepting a proposal from a new author and being supportive of the unorthodox direction I told them I wanted to travel.

Zooming out a bit to my broader school community, I had several influential professors during my time as a doctoral student at Hunter, not all of whom I have the space to list. In particular, in addition to the classes with two of my committee members, I found my thinking pushed and challenged by Maite Sánchez, David Connor, Rosanne Kurstedt and Laura Baecher, and I have to tip my cap to the program's director, Marshall George, who not only taught us for several semesters but also kept the whole ship running through a time when we all know a lot of adjustment was needed. Marshall was also the one who told us, back in our very first class, that it was important to find our voice in our writing, and

I took his lesson to heart, as I hope you can all see by now. I also have to acknowledge our dean, Michael Middleton, who took a meeting with me a few weeks into my very first semester (and a few more times after that), and mostly just gave me room to talk and feel like my ideas mattered, though I'm not sure either of us realized it would lead to a book like this one, so maybe he'll regret it.

Though I have obviously grown frustrated with English language teaching (ELT), my years in the field did lead me to the point where I felt this work was necessary, and if I hadn't met valuable people in my pre-doctoral times, I wouldn't have bothered to make this attempt to improve the whole thing. In particular, I have to thank the years of support from Lesley Painter-Farrell, Scott Thornbury and Gabriel Díaz Maggioli, all of whom at some point metaphorically sat me down and told me to take my work more seriously. Hopefully, they'll read this and think I've listened. Also fitting into this category would be Rob Sheppard, a past, present and future collaborator whose passion for the field is unrivaled.

I have been supported by academics and educators who have considerably more experience than I do, and without whose honesty and generosity I would likely have doubted myself too much to push forward. These people span several disciplines, hardly limited to language, and they range from people I have collaborated and thought with directly (e.g. Clara Vaz Bauler, Mira Debs, Kisha Bryan, Maria Rosa Brea, Jennifer Delfino and Elizabeth King) to people whose work I admired that I reached out to for discussions that helped me along the way (e.g. Jonathan Rosa, Subini Annamma, Victor Ray, Kerri Ullucci, Ryan Crowley, Jessica Calarco and Neda Maghbouleh), to the wonderful experience of having Cheryl Matias serve as editor for a separate chapter I wrote during this process, to Nelson Flores supporting me when an older white academic kept following my work around the internet to try and discredit me.

There is the group of people I tend to refer to as Trojan Horses, aka not particularly senior white academics and educators who, as far as I can tell, are attempting to make things more difficult for the white environments in which they exist (e.g. Nicole Pettitt, Caitlin Green, Monica Baker, Betsy Sneller, Erin Nau, Johanna Ennser-Kananen, Melissa Baese-Berk, Tyson Seburn, Tim Hampson, Nick Ironside, Brent Warner and Alison Oatsdean). And then there are the people I consider to have been striving alongside me, who were (or are) new to scholarship but are fully unable to rest as they challenge the structures around them. I certainly cannot list every peer of mine whom I admire, but among the very many are Scott Stillar, Kelly Wright, Chu May Paing, Tasha Austin, Selena Carrión, Ixchell Reyes, Maureen Kosse, Keisha Weil and Kelsey Swift; my schoolmates, especially Andrew Wintner, Daniel Hernandez, Inna Kruvi and Abdul Siddiqui; and, despite being on his own trajectory to great respect within the field, Vijay Ramjattan, for not being too busy to sit down with me at a conference in 2019 and help me work toward coherence with my then-nebulous ideas. Additionally, everyone I've met through the Scholars of Color in Language Studies group deserves to be commended for the work they're doing and the support they always show to me and to one another, and I would be remiss if I didn't thank everyone who has appeared on my podcast, *Unstandardized English*, and made it what I consider to be an important little slice of scholarship. And on the podcast tip, mine only exists because of the work of Carrie Gillon and Megan Figueroa on *The Vocal Fries*, who have also become good friends and co-conspirators.

Outside of all this, I've still needed the people who knew me as Justin long before I started publishing under 'JPB', and though my group of friends has shifted and evolved over the years, knowing that they'll be around even if no one actually reads or likes this book is always valuable. I need to thank the Alli/ysons for holding me down at my previous workplace when I was struggling, as well as Nader, Steve, Theresa and their partners for being supportive of me at different times and in different ways. Ultimately, though, I must give particular attention to my Mr French, Keith Stewart, for all of those Friday night Zoom calls where I babbled about my work during the time when we were all stuck at home.

My family, who will probably learn some interesting facts about my experience in the pages of this book, would love me even if I never wrote a single word, and I've gained a whole new family through my marriage, all of whom have been cheerleaders for what I've been trying to do. I thank all of them, from my sister and Kyle, to my many siblings-in-law, to Suzanne and Ron and Benita, to my father, who was my first teacher, and my mother, who was my first champion.

He won't be able to read this until at least the end of kindergarten (ha), but my work took on so much more urgency when a little ball of energy named Ezel came into our world just before we were all cut off from one another in early 2020. He's going to be bored of hearing about what was happening in his first years of life very soon, but none of this happens if I don't know I have a Black boy to try and protect from the ravages of whiteness, and I hope someday this proves to have made a difference in his life.

No single being has spent more time close to me while writing this book than our rambunctious Lagotto Romagnolo, Neptune, who knows exactly when I need silent support and loyalty, and who doesn't quite know when to *just stop*, but we love him anyway, most of the time. And finally, I'm nothing without Alissa Margaret Tyghter-Gerald. Nothing good, anyway. That's all there is to it.

Thanks for reading. Now close this book, or turn off your tablet or computer, take stock of your own context, consider what changes you might be able to make and look up my contact information on my website, because if you read all the way through this and found my arguments compelling, I probably want to work with you, too. Whiteness and ELT can handle each and every one of us if we work alone, but they don't stand a chance if we do this together.

    Let's get to work.

References

Accent Advisor (n.d.) See https://english.accentadvisor.com/.

Accents Off (n.d.) See https://accentsoff.com/.

Aizenman, N. and Gharib, M. (2019, August 9) American with no medical training ran center for malnourished Ugandan kids: 105 died. See https://www.npr.org/sections/goatsandsoda/2019/08/09/749005287/american-with-no-medical-training-ran-center-for-malnourished-ugandan-kids-105-d.

Alim, H. and Smitherman, G. (2012) *Articulate while Black: Barack Obama, Language, and Race in the U.S.* Oxford: Oxford University Press.

American Psychiatric Association (2013) *Diagnostic and Statistical Manual of Mental Disorders* (5th edn). https://doi.org/10.1176/appi.books.9780890425596.

American Psychiatric Association (2017) Intellectual disability. Parents and Families. See https://www.psychiatry.org/patients-families/intellectual-disability/what-is-intellectual-disability.

Anderson, C. (2016) *White Rage: The Unspoken Truth of Our Racial Divide*. New York: Bloomsbury.

Anderson, M. (2015, November 2) The costs of English-only education. *The Atlantic*. See https://www.theatlantic.com/education/archive/2015/11/the-costs-of-english-only-education/413494/.

Andrew, S. (2020, June 3) Amazon's best sellers list is dominated almost entirely by books on race right now. CNN. See https://www.cnn.com/2020/06/03/us/amazon-best-sellers-books-race-trnd/index.html.

Annamma, S. (2018) *The Pedagogy of Pathologization: Dis/abled Girls of Color and the School Prison Nexus*. New York: Routledge.

Annamma, S., Connor, D. and Ferri, B. (2013) Dis/ability critical race studies (DisCrit): Theorizing at the intersections of race and dis/ability. *Race Ethnicity and Education* 16 (1), 1–31.

Appel, I. and Nickerson, J. (2015) Pockets of poverty: The long-term effects of redlining. *Social Science Research Network*.

Baker-Bell, A. (2020) *Linguistic Justice: Black Language, Literacy, Identity, and Pedagogy*. New York: Routledge.

Baldwin, J. (1955) *Notes of a Native Son*. Boston, MA: Beacon Press.

Baldwin, J. (1963) *The Fire Next Time*. New York: Vintage.

Bell, D. (1980) Brown v. Board of Education and the interest-convergence dilemma. *Harvard Law Review* 93 (3), 518–533.

Beneke, M. (2020) Mapping socio-spatial constructions of normalcy: Whiteness and ability in teacher candidates' educational trajectories. *Whiteness and Education* 6 (1), 92–113.

Berne, P., Langstaff, D., Morales, A. and Invalid, S. (2018) Ten principles of disability justice. *Women's Studies Quarterly* 46 (1/2), 227–230.

Block, D. and Gray, J. (2015) 'Just go away and do it and you get marks': The degradation of language teaching in neoliberal times. *Journal of Multilingual and Multicultural Development* 37 (5), 481–494.

Bombay, A., Matheson, K. and Anisman, H. (2014) The intergenerational effects of Indian residential schools: Implications for the concept of historical trauma. *Transcultural Psychiatry* 51 (3), 320–338.

Bonfiglio, T. (2002) *Race and the Rise of Standard American*. Berlin: Mouton de Gruyter.

Bourdieu, P. and Wacquant, L. (1992) *An Invitation to Reflexive Sociology*. Cambridge: Polity Press.

Breshears, S. (2019) The precarious work of English language teaching in Canada. *TESL Canada Journal* 36 (2), 26–47.

Bryan, K. and Gerald, J. (2020, August 17) The weaponization of English. *Language Magazine*. See https://www.languagemagazine.com/2020/08/17/the-weaponization-of-english/.

Canagarajah, A. (1999) *Resisting Linguistic Imperialism in English Language Teaching*. Oxford: Oxford University Press.

Cann, C. (2015) What school movies and TFA teach us about who should teach urban youth: Dominant narratives as public pedagogy. *Urban Education* 50 (3), 288–315.

Charles, Q. (2019) Black teachers of English in South Korea: Constructing identities as a native English speaker and English language teaching professional. *TESOL Journal* 10 (4), 1–19.

Chen, X., Dervin, F., Tao, J. and Zhao, K. (2019) Towards a multilayered and multidimensional analysis of multilingual education: Ideologies of multilingualism and language planning in Chinese higher education. *Current Issues in Language Planning* 21 (3), 1–24.

Chude-Sokei, L. (2006) *The Last 'Darky': Bert Williams, Black-On-Black Minstrelsy, and the African Diaspora*. Durham, NC: Duke University Press.

Clemetson, L. (2007, February 4) The racial politics of speaking well. *New York Times*. See https://www.nytimes.com/2007/02/04/weekinreview/04clemetson.html?fta=y.

Cloud, N. and Bernstein, T. (2005, September) Difference or disability? TESOL International Association. See https://www.tesol.org/read-and-publish/journals/other-serial-publications/compleat-links/compleat-links-volume-2-issue-3-(september-2005)/difference-or-disability-.

Coates, L. and Wade, A. (2007) Language and violence: Analysis of four discursive operations. *Journal of Family Violence* 22 (7), 511–522.

Crenshaw, K. (1990) Mapping the margins: Intersectionality, identity politics, and violence against women of color. *Stanford Law Review* 43 (6), 1241–1299.

Crowley, R. (2016) Transgressive and negotiated White racial knowledge. *International Journal of Qualitative Studies in Education* 29 (8), 1016–1029. doi: 10.1080/09518398.2016.1174901.

Cushing, I. (2020) 'Say it like the Queen': The standard language ideology and language policy making in English primary schools. *Language, Culture and Curriculum* 34 (3), 1–16.

Datta, S. and Mullainathan, S. (2014) Behavioral design: A new approach development policy. *The Review of Income and Wealth* 7–35.

Davis, A. (1982) The approaching obsolecence of housework. In A. Davis (ed.) *Women, Race, and Class* (pp. 1–271). London: The Women's Press Ltd.

Davis, L. (1995) *Enforcing Normalcy: Disability, Deafness and the Body*. New York: Verso.

De Cuba, C. and Slocum, P. (2020) Standard language ideology is alive and well in public speaking textbooks. *Proceedings of the Linguistic Society of America* 5 (1), 369–383.

de los Ríos, C.V., Martinez, D.C., Musser, A.D., Canady, A., Camangian, P. and Quijada, P.D. (2019) Upending colonial practices: Toward repairing harm in English education, *Theory Into Practice* 58 (4), 359–367. doi: 10.1080/00405841.2019.1626615

Delpit, L. (1995) *Other People's Children: Cultural Conflict in the Classroom*. Chicago, IL: The New Press.

Diamond, J. and Anderson, K. (2021) School safety for whom? The negative consequences of school policing and punitive discipline for Black students. *Green Schools Catalyst Quarterly* 8 (1), 38–51.

Diamond, J., Posey-Maddox, L. and Velazquez, D. (2020) Reframing suburbs: Race, place, and opportunity in suburban educational spaces. *Educational Researcher* 50 (4), 1–7.

Dixson, A.D. (2018) 'What's going on?': A critical race theory perspective on Black Lives Matter and activism in education. *Urban Education* 53 (2), 231–247. https://doi.org/10.1177/0042085917747115

DuBois, W. (1897, August) Strivings of the Negro people. *Atlantic Monthly*. See https://www.theatlantic.com/magazine/archive/1897/08/strivings-of-the-negro-people/305446/.

DuBois, W. (1935) Transubstantiation of a poor white. In W. DuBois (ed.) *Black Reconstruction: An Essay Toward a History of the Part which Black Folk Played in the Attempt to Reconstruct Democracy in America, 1860–1880* (pp. 211–288). New York: Harcourt.

Duckworth, A. (2016) *Grit: The Power and Passion of Perseverance*. New York: Scribner.

Dunbar-Ortiz, R. (2014) *An Indigenous Peoples' History of the United States*. Boston, MA: Beacon Press.

Eastman, C. (1990) What is the role of language planning in post-Apartheid South Africa? *TESOL Quarterly* 24 (1), 9–21.

Emejulu, A. (2016, June 28) On the hideous whiteness of Brexit. Verso Books. https://www.versobooks.com/blogs/2733-on-the-hideous-whiteness-of-brexit-let-us-be-honest-about-our-past-and-our-present-if-we-truly-seek-to-dismantle-white-supremacy.

Ennser-Kananen, J. (2021) 'My skin is hard': Adult learners' resistance to racialization and racism, *Nordic Journal of Studies in Educational Policy* 7 (3), 179–189. doi: 10.1080/20020317.2021.2008113

Ennser-Kananen, J., Halonen, M. and Saarinen, T. (2021) 'Come join us and lose your accent!': Accent modification courses as hierarchization of international students. *Journal of International Students* 11 (2), 322–340.

Erling, E. (2017) Language planning, English language education and development aid in Bangladesh. *Current Issues in Language Planning* 18 (4), 388–406.

Fanon, F. (1952) *Black Skin, White Masks*. New York: Grove Press.

Ferber, A. (2007) The construction of Black masculinity. *Journal of Sport and Social Issues* 31 (1), 11–24.

Flores, N. (2019) Translanguaging into raciolinguistic ideologies: A personal reflection on the legacy of Ofelia García. *Journal of Multilingual Education Research* 9 (5), 45–60.

Flores, N. and Rosa, J. (2015) Undoing appropriateness: Raciolinguistic ideologies and language diversity in education. *Harvard Educational Review* 85 (2), 149–171.

Florida International University (n.d.) Accent reduction. Florida International University – English Language Institute. See https://eli.fiu.edu/programs/community-outreach-program/accent-reduction-classes/.

Fong, S. (2019) Racial-settler capitalism: Character building and the accumulation of land and labor in the late nineteenth century. *American Indian Culture and Research Journal* 43 (3), 25–48.

Freire, P. (1970) *Pedagogy of the Oppressed*. London: Continuum.

Galton, F. (2015) *Memories of My Life*. New York: Routledge.

Garcia, C. (2019) Why teach for America teachers don't belong in low-income schools. *San Diego Union Tribune*. See https://www.sandiegouniontribune.com/opinion/story/2019-04-12/teach-for-america-teachers-ban low-income-schools.

Garcia, O. and Vogel, S. (2016) Translanguaging. In G.W. Noblit and L.C. Moll (eds) *Oxford Research Encyclopedia of Education* (pp. 2–21). Oxford: Oxford University Press.

Gerald, J. (2020a) Combatting the altruistic shield in English language teaching. *NYS TESOL Journal* 7 (1), 22–25.

Gerald, J. (2020b) Worth the risk: Towards decentring whiteness in English language teaching. *BC TEAL Journal* 5 (1), 44–54.

Gerald, J. (2022) The end of altruism: Moving from white hero discourse to racial justice praxis. In C. Matias, P. Gorski and T. Jackson (eds) *The Other Elephant in the (Class)room: White Liberalism and the Persistence of Racism in Schools*. New York: Teachers College Press.

Gerald, J., Ramjattan, V. and Stillar, S. (2021, May 17) After whiteness (Part One). *After Whiteness (Part One). Language Magazine*. See https://www.languagemagazine.com/2021/05/17/after-whiteness/.

Gershenson, S., Hart, C., Lindsay, C. and Papageorge, N. (2017) *The Long-Run Impacts of Same-Race Teachers*. Berlin: IZA – Institute for Labor Economics.

Gillborn, D. (2015) Intersectionality, critical race theory, and the primacy of racism: Race, class, gender, and disability in education. *Qualitative Inquiry* 21 (3), 277–287.

Goodley, D. (2014) *Dis/ability Studies. Theorising Disablism and Ableism*. New York: Routledge.

Graeber, D. and Wengrow, D. (2021) *The Dawn of Everything: A New History of Humanity*. New York: MacMillan.

Harris, C. (1993) Whiteness as property. *Harvard Law Review* 1707–1791.

Henry, C. (2008) Obama '08: Articulate and clean. *The Black Scholar* 38 (1), 3–16.

Hernández-Saca, D. and Cannon, M. (2019) Interrogating disability epistemologies: Towards collective dis/ability intersectional emotional, affective and spiritual autoethnographies for healing. *International Journal of Qualitative Studies in Education* 32 (3), 243–262.

Hernández-Saca, D. and Cannon, M. (2021) The gift of disruption: Feeling and communicating subverted truths at the intersection of racist and ableist practices. In C. Mullen (ed.) *Handbook of Social Justice Interventions in Education* (pp. 1–24). Cham: Springer.

Hernández-Saca, D., Gutmann Kahn, L. and Cannon, M. (2018) Intersectionality dis/ability research: How dis/ability research in education engages intersectionality to uncover the multidimensional construction of dis/abled experiences. *Review of Research in Education* 42 (1), 286–311.

Hudson, J. (1995) Scientific racism: The politics of tests, race, and genetics. *The Black Scholar* 25 (1), 3–10.

Hunter College School of Education (n.d.) School of education graduate admissions. TESOL PreK-12 program overview. See https://education.hunter.cuny.edu/admissions/graduate-programs/teaching-english-to-speakers-of-other-languages-tesol/tesol-prek-12/.

Ignatiev, N. (1995) *How the Irish Became White*. London: Routledge.

Jenkins, J. and Leung, C. (2019) From mythical 'standard' to standard reality: The need for alternatives to standardized English language tests. *Language Teaching* 52 (1), 86–110.

Joelson, R. (2017, August 2) Locus of control. *Psychology Today*. See https://www.psychologytoday.com/us/blog/moments-matter/201708/locus-control.

Jung, S. and Norton, B. (2002) Language planning in Korea: The new elementary English program. In J. Tollefson (ed.) *Language Policies in Education: Critical Issues* (pp. 245–265). Hove: Psychology Press.

Kachru, B. (1997) World Englishes and English-using communities. *Annual Review of Applied Linguistics* 17 (1), 66–87.

Keep, William W. (2020) The Federal Trade Commission and Multi-level Marketing: Connecting the Dots. *seekingalpha.com*. Accessed May 12th, 2022. See: https://seekingalpha.com/article/4380462-federal-trade-commission-and-multi-level-marketing-connecting-dots/

Kendi, I. (2017) *Stamped from the Beginning: The Definitive History of Racist Ideas in America*. Philadelphia, PA: Bold Type Books.

Kendi, I. (2019) *How to be an Anti-racist*. New York: One World.

Kim, M., Choi, D. and Kim, T. (2019a) South Korean jobseekers' perceptions and (de)motivation to study for standardized English tests in neoliberal corporate labor markets. *The Asian EFL Journal* 21 (1), 84–109.

Kim, R., Roberson, L., Russo, M. and Briganti, P. (2019b) Language diversity, nonnative accents, and their consequences at the workplace: Recommendations for individuals, teams, and organizations. *The Journal of Applied Behavioral Science* 55, 73–95.

Kim, W. and Garcia, S. (2014) Long-term English language learners' perceptions of their language and academic learning experiences. *Remedial and Special Education* 35 (5), 300–312.

Kubota, R. (2015) Race and language learning in multicultural Canada: towards critical antiracism. *Journal of Multilingual and Multicultural Development* 36 (1), 3–12.

Kumaravavidelu, B. (2016) The decolonial option in English teaching: Can the subaltern act? *TESOL Quarterly* 50 (1), 66–85.

Lee, I. (2009) Situated globalization and racism: An analysis of Korean high school EFL textbooks. *Language and Literacy* 11 (1), 1–14.

Leonardo, Z. and Broderick, A. (2011) Smartness as property: A critical exploration of intersections between whiteness and disability studies. *Teachers College Record* 113 (10), 2206–2232.

Lippi-Green, R. (2012) *English with an Accent: Language, Ideology and Discrimination in the United States*. London: Routledge.

Loewen, J. (2005) *Sundown Towns: A Hidden Dimension of American Racism*. New York: The New Press.

Lorde, A. (1981/2007) The uses of anger. In A. Lorde (ed.) *Sister Outsider: Essays & Speeches by Audre Lorde* (pp. 124–133). Berkeley, CA: Crossing Press.

Macedo, D. (2000) The colonialism of the English only movement. *Educational Researcher* 29 (3), 15–24.

MacSwan, J. (2018) Academic English as standard language ideology: A renewed research agenda for asset-based language education. *Language Teaching Research* 24 (1), 1–9.

Maghbouleh, N. (2017) *The Limits of Whiteness: Iranian Americans and the Everyday Politics of Race*. Stanford, CA: Stanford University Press.

Marschall, M.J., Rigby, E. and Jenkins, J. (2011) Do state policies constrain local actors? The impact of English only laws on language instruction in public schools, *Publius: The Journal of Federalism* 41 (4), 586–609. https://doi.org/10.1093/publius/pjr003

Matias, C. (2013) Tears worth telling: Urban teaching and the possibilities of racial justice. *Multicultural Perspectives* 15 (4), 187–193.

Matias, C. (2016) *Feeling White: Whiteness, Emotionality, and Education*. Rotterdam: Sense Publishers.

Matias, C. and DiAngelo, R. (2013) Beyond the face of race: Emo-cognitive explorations of white neurosis and racial cray-cray. *Journal of Educational Foundations* 2 (1), 1–20.

Mansfield, K. (2015) Giftedness as property: Troubling whiteness, wealth, and gifted education in the United States. *International Journal of Multicultural Education* 17 (1), 1–18.

McKelvey, T. (2019, March 22) Pete Buttigieg: Why would an American learn Norwegian? BBC News. See https://www.bbc.com/news/world-us-canada-47587540.

Mechanic, M. (2021) *Jackpot: How the Super-Rich Really Live: And How Their Wealth Harms Us All*. New York: Simon & Schuster.

Menken, K. (2014) Restrictive language education policies and emergent bilingual youth: A perfect storm with imperfect outcomes. *Theory Into Practice* 52 (3), 160–168.

Metzl, J. (2019) *Dying of Whiteness: How the Politics of Racial Resentment is Killing America's Heartland*. New York: Basic Books.

Mills, C. and Lefrancois, B. (2018) Child as metaphor: Colonialism, psygovernance, and epistemicide. *World Futures* 74 (7–8), 503–524.

Milner, H. (2008) Critical race theory and interest convergence as analytic tools in teacher education policies and practices. *Journal of Teacher Education* 59 (4), 332–346.
Mohamad, N. and Deterding, D. (2018) The fallacy of 'standard' English. In O. Kang, R.I. Thomson and J.M. (eds) *The Routledge Handbook of Contemporary English Pronunciation* (pp. 203–217). New York: Routledge.
Morris, M. (2016) *Pushout: The Criminalization of Black Girls in Schools*. New York: The New Press.
Morrison, T. (1975) Black Studies Center Public Dialogue. Portland State University, Portland, OR.
Motha, S. (2014) *Race, Empire and English Language Teaching: Creating Responsible and Ethical Anti-Racist Practice*. New York: Teachers College Press.
National Education Administration (2020) Make a plan to vote. EdVotes. See https://educationvotes.nea.org/presidential-2020/make-a-plan-to-vote/.
National Native American Boarding School Healing Coalition (2020, August 3) 'Kill the Indian, save the man': An introduction to the history of boarding schools. National Native American Boarding School Healing Coalition. See https://boardingschoolhealing.org/kill-the-indian-save-the-man-an-introduction-to-the-history-of-boarding-schools/.
Nielsen, K. (2012) *A Disability History of the United States*. Boston, MA: Beacon Press.
Omi, M. and Winant, H. (2014) *Racial Formation in the United States* (3rd edn). New York: Routledge.
Orelus, P. (2020) Other people's English accents matter: Challenging 'standard' English accent hegemony. *Excellence in Education Journal* 9 (1), 120–148.
Owen, P. (2020, August 13) *Tucker Carlson: BLM Protesters Are 'Thugs With No Stake in Society'*. The Wrap See: https://www.thewrap.com/tucker-carlson-blm-protesters-are-thugs-with-no-stake-in-society-video/.
Painter, N. (2011) *The History of White People*. New York: W.W. Norton.
Pennington, J., Brock, C., Palmer, T. and Wolters, L. (2013) Opportunities to teach: Confronting the deskilling of teachers through the development of teacher knowledge of multiple literacies. *Teachers and Teaching: Theory and Practice* 19, 63–77.
Phillipson, R. (1992) *Linguistic Imperialism*. Oxford: Oxford University Press.
Phillipson, R. (2008) The linguistic imperialism of neoliberal empire. *Critical Inquiry in Language Studies* 5 (1), 1–43.
Picower, B. (2009) The unexamined Whiteness of teaching: How White teachers maintain and enact dominant racial ideologies. *Race Ethnicity and Education* 12 (2), 197–215.
Pulido, L. (2016) Flint, environmental racism, and racial capitalism. *Capitalism Nature Socialism* 27 (3), 1–16.
Ramjattan, V. (2015) Lacking the right aesthetic: Everyday employment discrimination in Toronto private language schools. *Equality, Diversity and Inclusion: An International Journal* 68 (3), 692–704.
Ramjattan, V. (2018) Raciolinguistics and the aesthetic labourer. *Journal of Industrial Relations* 61 (5), 726–738.
Ramjattan, V. (2019a) Racializing the problem of and solution to foreign accent in business. *Applied Linguistics Review* 1–18.
Ramjattan, V. (2019b) The white native speaker and inequality regimes in the private English language school. *Intercultural Education* 30 (2), 126–140.
Ray, V. (2019) A theory of racialized organizations. *American Sociological Review* 84 (1), 1–28.
Reagan, T. (2019) *Linguistic Legitimacy and Social Justice*. Cham: Palgrave Macmillan.
Reconciliation Australia (n.d.) What is reconciliation? Reconciliation Australia. See https://www.reconciliation.org.au/what-is-reconciliation/.
Reilly, P. (2015) Eugenics and involuntary sterilization: 1907–2015. *Annual Review of Genomics and Human Genetics* 16, 351–368.

Reuters (2020, July 6) Canadian woman charged for calling police on Black bird-watcher in N.Y.C. *National Post*. See https://nationalpost.com/news/world/white-woman-who-called-police-over-black-bird-watcher-in-nyc-is-charged.

Ricento, T. (2013) Language policy, ideology, and attitudes in English-dominant countries. In R. Bayley, R. Cameron and C. Lucas (eds) *The Oxford Handbook of Sociolinguistics* (pp. 524–544). Oxford: Oxford University Press.

Robinson, C. (1983) *Black Marxism: The Making of the Black Radical Tradition*. Chapel Hill, NC: UNC Press.

Roediger, D.R. (2005) *Working toward Whiteness: How America's Immigrants became White: The Strange Journey from Ellis Island to the Suburbs*. New York: Basic Books.

Rosa, J. (2016) Standardization, racialization, languagelessness: Raciolinguistic ideologies across communicative contexts. *Linguistic Anthropology* 26 (2), 162–183.

Rosa, J. (2018) *Looking Like a Language, Sounding Like a Race: Raciolinguistic Ideologies and the Learning of Latinidad*. Oxford: Oxford University Press.

Rosa, J. and Flores, N. (2017) Unsettling language and race: Toward a raciolinguistic perspective. *Language in Society* 46 (5), 621–647.

Ruecker, T. and Ives, L. (2015) White native English speakers needed: The rhetorical construction of privilege in online teacher recruitment spaces. *TESOL Quarterly* 49 (4), 733–754.

Sampson, T. (2020, August 24) The UK in a changing Europe. The UK economy: Brexit vs. Covid-19. See https://ukandeu.ac.uk/the-uk-economy-brexit-vs-covid-19/.

Sankin Speech Improvement (n.d.) Sankin speech improvement. See https://www.sankinspeechimprovement.com/non-native-speakers-accent-elimination-and-modification/.

Sayej, N. (2018, April 21) J Marion Sims: Controversial statue taken down but debate still rages. *The Guardian*. See https://www.theguardian.com/artanddesign/2018/apr/21/j-marion-sims-statue-removed-new-york-city-black-women.

Schalge, S.L. and Soga, K. (2008) 'Then I stop coming to school': Understanding absenteeism in an adult English as a second language program. *Adult Basic Education and Literacy Journal* 2 (3), 151–161.

Schenck, A. (2020) Examining the influence of native and nonnative English-speaking teachers on Korean EFL writing. *Asian-Pacific Journal of Second and Foreign Language Education* 5 (2), 1–17.

Schissel, J.L. and Kangas, S.E.N. (2018) Reclassification of emergent bilingual with disabilities: The intersectionality of improbabilities. *Language Policy Journal* 17 (4), 567–589. https://doi.org/10.1007/s10993-018-9476-4

Schissel, J.L., Leung, C. and Chalhoub-Deville, M. (2019) The construct of multilingualism in language testing. *Language Assessment Quarterly* 16 (4–5), 373–378. https://doi.org/10.1080/15434303.2019.1680679

Short, D. (2020, June 22) *Race, Identity, and English Language Teaching: A Joint TESOL Quarterly and TESOL Journal Publication*. Wiley Online Library. See https://onlinelibrary.wiley.com/doi/toc/10.1002/(ISSN)1234-5678.race-identity-and-english-language-teaching.

Smiley, C. and Fakunle, D. (2016) From 'brute' to 'thug': The demonization and criminalization of unarmed Black male victims in America. *Journal of Human Behavior in the Social Environment* 26 (3–4), 350–366.

Smithsonian Institute (n.d.) Blackface: The birth of an American stereotype. National Museum of African-American History and Culture. See https://nmaahc.si.edu/blog-post/blackface-birth-american-stereotype.

Song, X., Massey, C.G., Rolf, K.A., Ferrie, J.P., Rothbaum, J.L. and Xie, Y. (2019) Long-term decline in intergenerational mobility in the United States since the 1850s. *Proceedings of the National Academy of Sciences* 117 (1), 251–258.

Staples, B. (2019, October 12) How Italians became 'White'. *The New York Times*. See https://www.nytimes.com/interactive/2019/10/12/opinion/columbus-day-italian-american-racism.html.

Straubhaar, R. (2015) The stark reality of the 'White Saviour' complex and the need for critical consciousness: A document analysis of the early journals of a Freirean educator. *Compare: A Journal of Comparative and International Education* 45 (3), 381–400.

Sue, D. (2010) *Microaggressions in Everyday Life: Race, Gender, and Sexual Orientation*. Hoboken, NJ: Wiley.

Sung, C. (2011) Race and native speakers in ELT: parents' perspectives in Hong Kong. *English Today* 27 (3), 25–29.

Sung, K. (2018) Raciolinguistic ideology of antiblackness: Bilingual education, tracking, and the multiracial imaginary. *International Journal of Qualitative Studies in Education* 31 (8), 667–683.

Tarter, B. (2020, December 14) Vagrancy Act of 1866. Encyclopedia Virginia. See https://encyclopediavirginia.org/entries/vagrancy-act-of-1866.

Taylor, Y. and Austen, J. (2012) *Darkest America: Black Minstrelsy from Slavery to Hip-Hop*. New York: W.W. Norton.

Tripathi, S. (2015, April 9) Mind the gap: As companies and governments dither over compensating Rana Plaza workers, victims suffer. Institute for Business and Human Rights. See www.ihrb.org/commentary/rana-plaza-factory-collapse-two-year-anniversary.html.

Tuck, E. and Yang, K. (2014) R-words: Refusing research. In D. Paris and M. Winn (eds) *Humanizing Research: Decolonizing Qualitative Inquiry with Youth and Communities* (pp. 223–247). Thousand Oaks, CA: Sage.

Ullucci, K. (2012) Knowing we are White: Narrative as critical praxis. *Teaching Education* 23 (1), 89–107.

United Nations Refugee Agency (2021) Climate change and disaster displacement. UNHCR. See https://www.unhcr.org/en-us/climate-change-and-disasters.html.

United States Holocaust Memorial Museum (n.d.) *Holocaust Encyclopedia*. The Biological State: Nazi Racial Hygiene: 1933–1939. See https://encyclopedia.ushmm.org/content/en/article/the-biological-state-nazi-racial-hygiene-1933-1939.

US Department of Education (2015) Identifying and Supporting English Learner Students with Learning Disabilities: Key Issues in the Literature and State Practice. Institute of Education Sciences.

Vitale, A. (2018) *The End of Policing*. London: Verso.

Voulgarides, C. (2018) *Does Compliance Matter in Special Education? IDEA and the Hidden Inequities of Practice*. New York: Teachers College Press.

Walsh, P. (2019) Key concepts in ELT: Precarity. *ELT Journal* 73 (4), 459–462.

Wiederkehr, V., Bonnot, V., Krauth-Gruber, S. and Damon, C. (2015) Belief in school meritocracy as a system-justifying tool for low status students. *Frontiers in Psychology* 6, 1053. https://doi.org/10.3389/fpsyg.2015.01053

Williams, A. and Emamdjomeh, A. (2018, May 10) America is more diverse than ever – but still segregated. *The Washington Post*. See https://www.washingtonpost.com/graphics/2018/national/segregation-us-cities/.

Williams, P. (1987) Spirit-murdering the messenger: The discourse of fingerpointing as the law's response to racism. *University of Miami Law Review* 42 (1), 131–153.

Willoughby, C. (2018) Running away from drapetomania: Samuel A. Cartwright, medicine, and race in the Antebellum South. *Journal of Southern History* 84 (3), 579–614.

Wolfe, P. (2006) Settler colonialism and the elimination of the native. *Journal of Genocide Research* 8 (4), 387–409.

Yoon, I. (2019) Haunted trauma narratives of inclusion, race, and disability in a school community. *Educational Studies* 55 (4), 420–435.

Zamudio, M. and Rios, F. (2006) From traditional to liberal racism: Living racism in the everyday. *Sociological Perspectives* 49 (4), 483–501.

Zheng, Y. and Samuel, A.G. (2017) Does seeing an Asian face make speech sound more accented? *Attention, Perception, & Psychophysics* 79, 1841–1859. https://doi.org/10.3758/s13414-017-1329-2

Index

Academia – 36, 37, 82, 106, 107, 133, 134, 140, 160,
Accent Reduction – 98, 99, 100, 101, 102, 103, 104, 147
African-American Language/African-American English – 53, 158
Altruistic Shield – 57, 80, 115
Annamma, Subini Ancy – 3, 37, 38
Anti-Blackness – ix, 5, 7, 17, 18, 32, 35, 39, 40, 55, 131, 148, 150, 152, 158, 159
Antisocial Personality Disorder – 1, 10, 58, 59, 82, 144
Aristogenic – 42, 43, 159

Baker-Bell, April – 4, 158
Baldwin, James – 1, 31, 32, 41, 124, 125
Brexit – 8, 25
Broderick, Alicia – 41, 42
Bryan, Kisha – 81

Carlson, Tucker 1, 2, 9, 58
Cooper, Amy – 118
Critical Race Theory – 3
Cushing, Ian – 94

Davis, Angela – 124
Deskilling – 72, 74
Diagnostic and Statistical Manual of Mental Disorders – 1, 67, 74, 91
Dis/Crit – 3, 4
Drapetomania – 35, 36, 37
DuBois, W.E.B. – 31, 124
Dunbar-Ortiz, Roxanne – 6, 20

Ennser-Kananen, Johanna – 4, 101
Eugenics – 36, 37, 42, 159,

Fanon, Franz – 85, 86, 114, 124
Flores, Nelson – 2, 4, 49, 53, 72, 78, 100
Florida International University – 100, 101
Floyd, George – ix, 80, 81, 118, 132
Freire, Paolo – 103, 119, 152

Galton, Francis – 36, 37, 39
Grit – 39, 157

Harris, Cheryl I. – 2, 21, 22

Imperialism – 21, 85, 87, 95, 158,
Interest Convergence – 4, 24
IQ – 43, 44,
Ives, Lindsey – 64, 65, 67, 82

Kendi, Ibram X. – 42, 79, 115
Kubota, Ryuko – 72

Leonardo, Zeus – 41, 42
Loewen, James – 22, 123

Maghbouleh, Neda – 16
Matias, Cheryl – 3, 67, 79
Mechanic, Michael – 155
Metzl, Jonathan – 24, 25
Minstrelsy – 27, 28, 29, 30
Morrison, Toni – 32, 102

Native speakers – 64, 65, 66, 67, 70, 74, 80, 82, 85, 112, 127, 149,
Neurodivergence – vii, x, 38, 41, 42, 117, 164
Nielsen, Kim E. – 2, 8, 34, 35, 38

Painter, Nell – 3, 6, 14, 15, 16, 19,
Pathologization – ix, 10, 37, 40, 57, 84, 86, 97, 98, 101, 108, 138, 143, 148, 153, 155, 156, 158, 160, 161, 163
Phillipson, Robert – 85, 86
Picower, Bree – 121
Policing – 1, 5, 17, 18, 19, 118, 119, 133, 144
Precarity – 70, 71, 72, 74, 75
Prescriptivism – 129, 130, 153

Racialized Organizations/Industry – 65, 115, 116, 117, 123
Raciolinguistic Ideologies – 49, 50, 51, 52, 100, 102, 108, 114, 138, 146, 148, 149, 165,
Ramjattan, Vijay A. – 65, 70, 102, 103, 153, 169
Ray, Victor – 65, 116
Research Questions – 117
Robinson, Cedric – 7
Roediger, David – 16
Rosa, Jonathan – 2, 4, 49, 50, 53, 72, 78, 100
Ruecker, Todd – 64, 65, 67, 82

Schalge, Susan – 113, 114
Settler Colonialism – viii, ix, x, 6, 7, 15, 21, 22, 23, 25, 38, 39, 40, 44, 55, 89

Soga, Kay – 113, 114
South Korea – vii, 29, 30, 32, 63, 64, 65, 66, 67, 68, 71, 73, 75, 76, 95, 96, 106, 127, 150, 159
Standardization – 7, 8, 45, 50, 92, 96, 97, 128, 146, 147, 148
Stillar, Scott – 153
Sundown Towns – 22, 122, 123

TESOL International Association – 81, 82, 139, 140, 141, 143, 161
Testing – 46, 78, 96, 128, 131, 143, 150, 151
Translanguaging – 7, 50, 53, 72, 78, 114
Tuck, Eve – 115

Ullucci, Kerri – 121
Unstandardized English – 9, 10, 47, 57, 74, 94, 115, 139, 156, 157, 160

Vitale, Alex – 17
Vocal Fries, The – 115

White Perceiving Subject/Listener – 2, 49, 51, 58, 75, 100, 103, 150

Yang, K. Wayne – 115

CPSIA information can be obtained
at www.ICGtesting.com
Printed in the USA
JSHW031451230922
30945JS00003B/18